Essential English Vocabulary 1400

語彙力向上研究会

ASAHI PRESS

Essential English Vocabulary 1400

Copyright © 2019 by Asahi Press

All rights reserved. No part of this publication may be reproduced in any form without prior written permission from the authors and the publisher.

Printed in Japan.

Photographs by Geographic British Isles and iStockphoto
Illustration by Yasuco Sudaka (p. vii, 10, 110)

Published by Asahi Press
3-3-5 Nishi Kanda, Chiyoda-ku, Tokyo 101-0065 Japan
Phone (03)-3239-0271 / Fax (03)-3239-0479
E-mail: text-e@asahipress.com
URL: http://text.asahipress.com/english/

この本の使い方

英語の力をつけるには、「文法知識」と「単語（語彙）知識」が必要です。これらなくしては英文読解も英作文も思うようにはできません。誰もが経験することですが、語彙学習は機械的な暗記作業中心になりがちで、覚えたつもりでもすぐに記憶から抜け落ちていってしまいます。この方法では語彙情報が記憶装置に引っかかってくれないのです。本書はこの点を重要視し、記憶に残りやすいように内容や構成を工夫し、効率的に語彙を増やすことを目的に作られた演習書です。本書のポイントは以下の五点です。

（1） 使用頻度が高く、また近年その重要度が高まっているTOEIC受験でもおさえておくべき語彙を1,400語厳選しました。これらを難易度別に大きく三段階に分け、セクションA（基礎レベル）は30ユニット600語、セクションB（中級レベル）は30ユニット600語、セクションC（上級レベル）は10ユニット200語としました。各ユニットは20語とし、一回で覚えられる程度の分量となっています。

（2） 各ユニット左のページは語彙の意味だけにとどまらず、言葉の生い立ち、間違いやすい用法などを挙げることにより、読み物的に語彙知識を得、記憶に残りやすいようにしました。

（3） セクションA、Bでは、右のページにそのユニットで覚えた語彙を確認する練習問題を二種類載せています。語彙の定着には暗記だけでなく演習が絶対に必要なのでかならずやってみましょう。また練習問題の中にはそのユニットで取り上げられた単語の「派生語」、たとえばexpect「期待する（動詞）」→ expectation「期待（名詞）」のように異なる品詞もふんだんに織りまぜてあるので、知らず知らずのうちに品詞と語彙の関係がわかるようになるでしょう。

（4） セクションCは各ユニットの語彙のセレクションをテーマ別とし、また右ページは長文読解としました。長文にはそのユニットで習った語彙のみならず前のユニットの語彙もふんだんに使われています。チャレンジ問題として、また総合的な語彙チェックとして活用してください。

（5） 語彙は口に出して覚えると定着度がさらに高まります。各見出し語に添えてある発音記号を参照して正しい発音ができるようにしましょう。なお本書の発音は標準的米国発音に準拠しています。

他の単語学習書と大きく異なるのは、上の（2）でも述べたように各ユニットの左ページです。ここでは言葉の冒頭につく接頭辞、後ろにつく接尾辞を重視することにより他の品詞への派生形を知らず知らずのうちに理解できるよう構成されています。また言葉を単独の語として覚えるだけでなく、二語またはそれ以上の言葉からなる句表現も身につけることができるように工夫されています。派生形、句表現といった語彙知識は、TOEICでも重視されているものであり、セクションCの長文読解とともに活用することにより、TOEICの語彙対策および力だめしとしても適した演習書となっています。

語彙学習は受動的な取り組みであってはいけません。それぞれの言葉の背景を知り、その語

がどんな文脈で使われるかを理解しながら読んだり書いたりする能動的な学習によってはじめて語彙は頭に定着するのです。

本書を授業で使用する場合も、個人で使用する場合も、ユニットを一区切りとしてある程度の頻度・スピードでメリハリをつけて学んでいきましょう。そして大切なことは、一回読んで終わりにするのではなく何度も読み返して、語彙が定着しているかを確認することです。特にセクションCの長文は読みかえすことにより読解する自信もつき、語彙力も確実に向上させることができるので、ぜひ試してみてください。

本書が皆さんの語彙力向上の一助となり、ひいては読む・書く・聴く・話すという四技能すべてにおいて成果を発揮していただければ著者として望外の幸せです。

最後になりますが、本書の上梓にあたり朝日出版社編集部の日比野忠氏、朝日英一郎氏、小川洋一郎氏、伊藤宏実氏には企画の段階から大変お世話になりましたことをこの場を借りて厚くお礼申し上げます。

2018年 秋

語彙力向上研究会
森 節子, 田邉 義隆, 森山 智浩
Paul Joyce, Torrin Shimono

目　次

この本の使い方 i

凡例 iv

接頭辞一覧 v

Units
    Section A 2
    Section B 64
    Section C 126

Index 148

凡　例

【名】	名詞	
	例：event【名】出来事，事件，結果	
【動】	動詞	
	例：hide【動】〜を隠す；隠れる	
【形】	形容詞	
	例：main【形】主要な	
【副】	副詞	
	例：perhaps【副】ひょっとして	
【助動】	助動詞	
	例：dare【助動】[How dare 〜 ? で] あつかましくも	
【前】	前置詞	
	例：through【前】〜を通して	
[米]	主に米国で使用される意味、語または表現	
	例：【米】visit with 〜「〜に訪問して雑談する」	
[英]	主に英国で使用される意味、語または表現	
	例：baggage「手荷物」≒【英】luggage	
《連語》	二語以上からなる連語表現、熟語表現	
	例：limit《連語》be limited to 〜 〜に限定される	
名尾	語を名詞化する接尾辞	
	例：proper「固有の」-ty 名尾 property「財産」	
形尾	語を形容詞化する接尾辞	
	例：include「含む」-sive 形尾 inclusive「包括的な」	
動尾	語を動詞化する接尾辞	
	例：simple「単純な」-ify 動尾 simplify「単純化する」	
副尾	語を副詞化する接尾辞	
	例：factual「事実の」-ly 副尾 factually「事実の面で」	
→	意味変化：元の意味から転じた意味	
	例：bright【形】（光を出して；反射して）輝いている → 明るい	
▶	語彙解説：その単語の生い立ちや関連情報など	
	例：join【動】〜をつなぐ▶「2つ以上のものをじかに接合する」	
⟷	反義表現：反対の意味を持つ単語または表現	
	例：include「〜を含む」⟷ exclude「〜を排除する」	
≒	類義表現：意味の似た単語または表現	
	例：modern【形】現代の，現代的な（≒ up-to-date）	

接頭辞一覧

▼「間」系
 (1) inter-（enter-）:「2者間に挟まれた領域／位置」の意
   e.g. **inter**national 二国間の；国際的な　▶national 国の

▼「前方；交換；目的物獲得」系
 (1) pro-, pre-, fore-:「前方」の意
   [※ pro- は物理的，pre- は抽象的事象を表すことが多い]
   e.g. **pro**ceed 前進する → 進行する　▶-ceed 移動する
   e.g. **pre**caution 用心；警戒，予防策　▶caution 注意
   e.g. **fore**head 額（ひたい）－ [位置の投影] →（物の）前部；前面　▶head 頭
   e.g. **pro**noun 代名詞　▶noun 名詞。ここでの pro- は「交換」。
   e.g. **pro**-abortion 中絶賛成の　▶abortion 中絶。ここでの pro- は「中絶意見の獲得→賛成」。

▼「到達点／方向」系
 (1) ad-（a-, ac-, af-, ag-, al-, an-, ap-, ar-, as-, at-）:「到達点／方向」の意
   [※ c, k, q の前では ac-, f の前では af-, g の前では ag-, l の前では al-, n の前では an-, p の前では ap-, r の前では ar-, s の前では as-, t の前では at-]
   e.g. **ad**here [adhere to ～] ～に固執する　▶-here くっつく
   e.g. **ac**cess 接近　▶-cess 移動
 (2) ob-（of-）:「到達点／方向」の意
   e.g. **ob**scure 薄暗くてよく見えない → ぼんやりして曖昧（あいまい）な　▶-scure 覆う

▼「同伴」系
 (1) com-（co-, col-, con-, cor-）:「同伴 －［必要なものが揃う］→ 強意」の意
   [※母音および h の前では co-, l の前では col-, r の前では cor-, その他の場合は con-]
   e.g. **com**fort 慰（なぐさ）め　▶-fort 力強い状態
   e.g. **co**here [cohere to ～] ～に密着する　▶-here くっつく
 (2) syn-（syl-, sym-, sys-）:「同伴 －［必要なものが揃う］→ 強意」の意
   [※ l の前で syl-, m, p, b の前で sym-, s, t の前では sys-]
   e.g. **syn**onym 類義語　▶-onym 名前
   e.g. **syl**lable 音節　▶-lable つかむ。「つかんで並び合わせたもの」のイメージ。

▼「反対；対抗」系
 (1) anti-（ant-, anth-）:「対抗」の意
   [※母音および h の前で ant-。ante- と同源。anti-（ant-, anth-）の意味変化は「前方→目の前のものと対峙する→対抗；反対」]
   e.g. **anti**pathy 反感　▶-pathy（苦しみの）感情

(2) contra-（contro-, counter-）:「対抗」の意
　　　e.g. **contra**st 対照的な　▶-st 立つ－[目の前に立つ]→存在する；目立つ
(3) dis-:「対抗」の意
　　　e.g. **dis**honest 不正直な　▶honest 正直な
(4) re-:「元の場所へ」の意
　　　e.g. **re**turn 戻る　▶turn 回転する；向きを変える

▼「円」系
(1) circu-（circum-）:「円 → 円の一部；孤」の意
　　　e.g. **circu**late 循環する　▶-ate 動尾
(2) peri-:「円→円の一部；孤」の意
　　　e.g. **peri**pheral 周辺的な　▶-pher（荷物を）運ぶ→中心地から移動する・-al 形尾

▼「近接」系
(1) para-:「真横；より近い」の意
　　　e.g. **para**llel 平行（の）；類似（の）▶-llel お互いの
(2) by-:「漠然とした近さ→主となるものの近く（＝副）」の意
　　　e.g. **by**way / **by**road / **by**path わき道　▶way 道のり／road 県間を結ぶ道／path 小道
　　　e.g. **by**-product 副産物　▶product 産物；製品

▼「貫通」系
(1) dia-:「貫通」の意
　　　e.g. **dia**meter 直径　▶-meter 物差し
(2) per-:「貫通 → 一貫してやり通す；完了」
　　　e.g. **per**fect 完全な　▶-fect 作る

▼「越えて；超えて」系
(1) trans-:「交差 → 横切って」の意
　　　e.g. **trans**port 〜を輸送する　▶-port（港から港へ）運ぶ
(2) super-（supra-, sur-）:「越えて；超」の意
　　　e.g. **super**natural 超自然的な　▶natural 自然の；自然的な
(3) hyper-:「越えて；超」の意
　　　e.g. **hyper**market [英]（巨大な駐車場付きの）スーパー・マーケット　▶market 市場
(4) over-:「半円の移動軌跡 －[渡って]→ 越えて」の意
　　　e.g. **over**come 〜を克服する　▶come 正常な状態に移行する
(5) ultra-:「ある範囲を越えて；超」の意
　　　e.g. **ultra**modern 超現代的な　▶modern 現代の；現代的な

▼「下」系
　（1）sub-（suc-, cuf-, sug-, sum-, sup-, sus-）：「下」の意
　　　[※ c の前では suc-, f の前では suf-, g の前では sug-, m の前では sum-, p の前では sup-, t の前では sus-]
　　　　　e.g. **sub**way 地下鉄　▶way 道のり
　　　　　e.g. **sup**press ～を抑圧する　▶press 圧する
　（2）hypo-：「下」の意
　　　　　e.g. **hypo**thesis 仮説　▶thesis 命題；主題

▼「以前」系
　（1）ante-（anti-）：「前；前もって」の意
　　　　　e.g. **anti**cipate ～を予期する　▶-cipate つかむ；取る→捉える
　（2）ex-：（「地位・官職・身分」などを表す合成語を作り）「以前の；前…」の意
　　　　　e.g. **ex**-president 前大統領，前会長，前社長　▶president 大統領，会長，社長

▼「うしろ／あと」系
　（1）retro-：「（過去から未来に流れる時間軸で）後ろ → 過去」の意
　　　◎イメージ図：

　　　　　e.g. **retro**spect 回顧する　▶-spect 目を向ける；見る
　（2）post-：「（未来から過去に過ぎ去る経過で）後ろ → 未来」の意
　　　◎イメージ図：

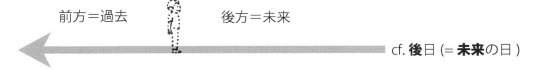

　　　　　e.g. **post**pone ～を延期する　▶-pone 置く

▼「分離」系
　（1）de-（di-, dif-）：「分離→（重力で）下降 -［程度が下降］→ 悪化」の意
　　　　　e.g. **de**fy 反抗する　▶-fy 信じる
　（2）a-, ab-, abs-：「分離」の意
　　　　　e.g. **a**vert 視線をそらす；惨事を回避する　▶-vert 回転する；向きを変える
　（3）apo-：「分離」の意
　　　　　e.g. **apo**logy お詫び　▶-logy 語；言葉。「その場を離れる（apo-）ための言葉（-logy）」。

（4）se-：「分離」の意
  e.g. **se**duce ～を誘惑する　▶-duce 導く

（5）ex-（ef-, e-, ec-, es-）：「分離」の意
  [※ f の前では ef-, その他の子音の前では e-, c または s の前ではしばしば ec-]
  e.g. **ex**pel ～を追い出す　▶-pel 推進する
  e.g. **e**lect 選挙する　▶-lect 選ぶ

（6）extra-（extro-, exo-）：「分離」の意
  e.g. **extra**ordinary 異常な；非凡な　▶ordinary 普通の；平凡な

▼「空間」系

（1）en-（em-）：「空間内部における位置／運動」の意
  [※ b の前では im-]
  e.g. **en**close ～を囲む　▶close 閉じる
  e.g. **em**brace ～を抱擁（ほうよう）する　▶-brace 腕

（2）in-（il-, im-, ir-）：「空間内部への移動」の意
  [※ b, m, p の前では im-, l の前では il-, r の前では ir-]
  e.g. **in**come 収入　▶come（話し手／聞き手の存在場所に）移動する
  e.g. **im**port ～を輸入する　▶-port 運ぶ

（3）intro-（intra-, endo-）：「空間内部への移動」の意
  e.g. **intro**duce ～を紹介する　▶-duce 導く

▼「欠如」系

（1）in-（ig-, il-, im-, ir-）：「欠如」の意
  [※ n の前では ig-, l の前では il-, r の前では ir-, p, b, m の前で im-]
  e.g. **in**accurate 不正確な　▶accurate 正確な
  e.g. **il**legal 不法の　▶legal 合法的な

（2）non-（an-）：「欠如」の意
  e.g. **non**sense 無意味　▶sense 意味
  e.g. **an**archy 無政府（状態）　▶-archy 支配→政治

Section A

Unit 1

- **class** [klǽs]
  - 【名】部類；種類 − [分けられたもの] → クラス → クラスの学生, 授業
  - 【形】classic（古代ローマの種類の）→ 古典の → 第一流の, 典型的な ▶-ic 形尾
  - 【形】classical（古代ローマの種類の）→ 古典の → 古典文学の；古典語の
  - ▶-ical 形尾。「クラシック音楽」は classical music。×classic music
  - 【動】classify ～を分類する ▶-ify 動尾 【名】classification 分類 ▶-fication 名尾

- **event** [ɪvént]
  - 【名】出来事, 事件, 結果 ▶ e- = ex- 外へ・-vent 存在する。「出現 → 生じたもの」。
  - 【形】eventual 結果的な ▶-al 形尾 【副】eventually 結果的に ▶-ly 副尾
  - 【形】eventful 出来事の多い；波乱(はらん)に富む ▶-ful 形尾(満ちている)

- **glass** [glǽs]
  - 【名】ガラス → (ガラス製の)コップ；グラス [glasses] メガネ

- **hospital** [hɑ́:spɪtl]
  - 【名】病院 ▶原義は「客を歓待するところ」。host と同源。host の項参照。
  - 《連語》be in (the) hospital 入院している
  - ⟷ be out of (the) hospital 退院している ▶ the がつくのは [米] 用法。
  - 【名】hospitality 歓待；もてなし ▶-ity 名尾

- **machine** [məʃí:n]
  - 【名】機械 [machinery] 機械類 ▶-ry 複数個の集まり。例：poet(詩) → poetry

- **scene** [sí:n]
  - 【名】景色 [scenery] (自然全体の)風景 ▶-ry 複数個の集まり

- **war** [wɔ́ːr]
  - 【名】戦争 ▶ battle は局所的な戦い。「第二次世界大戦」は World War II。

- **admit** [ədmít]
  - 【動】[admit ～ ing] ～したことをしぶしぶ認める ▶-mit 通過 → 許可
  - ▶動詞の目的語が to 不定詞(to do)の場合はその動詞の時点よりも「未来」のイメージ（例：hope to do）, 動名詞(～ ing)の場合は「それ以外(主に過去)」のイメージ。
  - 【名】admission 許可 ▶-sion 名尾。admission fee は「入会金；入場料」。

- **cry** [kráɪ]
  - 【動】大声で叫ぶ；泣く − [泣きつく] → 陳情(ちんじょう)する
  - ▶ weep は「涙を流して泣く」ことに焦点。

- **exist** [ɪgzíst]
  - 【動】存在する ▶ ex- 外へ・-ist = -sist 立つ
  - 【形】existent 存在している ▶-ent 形尾 【名】existence 存在 ▶-ence 名尾
  - 《連語》come into existence/being 生まれる ⟷ go out of existence 滅亡する

- **happen** [hǽpən]
  - 【動】(偶然に)起こる；生じる
  - 【名】happening (偶然の)出来事 ▶-ing 名尾(～すること)

- **hide** [háɪd]
  - 【動】～を隠す；隠れる ▶「かくれんぼ」は hide and seek。

- **last** [lǽst]
  - 【動】続く；継続する 【形】最後の
  - ▶ late(遅れて)の最上級。「時間」の意では late < later(より遅い) < latest(最も遅い → 最近の)。「順序」の意では late < latter(後半の) < last(最後の)。

- **reach** [rí:tʃ]
  - 【動】～に手が届く − [目的(地)に達する] → ～に到着する 【名】(届く)範囲
  - 《連語》within one's reach 手の届く範囲に ⟷ beyond one's reach

- **sell** [sél]
  - 【動】～を売る
  - [well など主語の性質から生じる程度の副詞と共に] ～が売れる

- **turn** [tə́ːrn]
  - 【動】～を回転させる；～の向きを変える 【名】回転 − [回し合い] → 順番
  - ▶ turn は「回転」のイメージ。ただし, 「円の一部の軌跡」でも可(例：turn the corner)。

- **alone** [əlóʊn]
  - 【副】一人で → ～だけで ▶ all + one, つまり「全体で1つ」のイメージ。

- **main** [méɪn]
  - 【形】主要な
  - 《連語》in the main 大部分は；概して (≒ in general / on the whole)

- **several** [sévərəl]
  - 【形】いくつかの ▶ some は several よりも少ない数を指す。

- **indeed** [ɪndí:d]
  - 【副】実際に；実際は − [実際そうだ] → 確かに ▶ in- 上に・-deed 事実

EXERCISE A

各文の下線部分に入る適切な語を左ページの見出し語から選びましょう。

1. I clean my clothes using a washing _____ .
2. Windows are made of _____ .
3. Do you plan to travel _____ or with friends?
4. Jane was the _____ person to arrive. Everyone else was there.
5. The two countries are at _____ with each other.
6. When I broke my leg, I had to stay in the _____ for two weeks.
7. It took _____ years to save the money.
8. When the boy cut his finger, he started to _____ .
9. Go down the road, then _____ left at the corner.
10. A lot of students were late for _____ today.

EXERCISE B

左の語の定義として正しいものを右のコラムより選び、（ ）にアルファベットを書き入れましょう。

Part 1

1. （ ） main   a. a group of students
2. （ ） admit   b. make move around
3. （ ） last   c. coming at the end
4. （ ） hospital   d. agree that something is true
5. （ ） turn   e. keep something where no one can find it
6. （ ） cry   f. get money for something
7. （ ） hide   g. most important
8. （ ） reach   h. arrive somewhere
9. （ ） class   i. have tears coming from one's eyes when sad
10. （ ） sell   j. a place where people go when they are sick

Part 2

1. （ ） glasses   a. something that happens
2. （ ） scene   b. fighting between two or more countries
3. （ ） machine   c. continue to be or live
4. （ ） war   d. a view or picture of a place
5. （ ） alone   e. without any question; in reality
6. （ ） exist   f. more than two, but not many
7. （ ） event   g. something that does a specific job, such as a car or computer
8. （ ） happen   h. take place without being planned
9. （ ） indeed   i. without anyone
10. （ ） several   j. things that help one see better

Unit 2

- **amount** [əmáunt] 【名】量；総計；総額 ▶ a- = ad- 方向・mount 山に登る → 頂上に達する
  ▶ a large amount of money で「巨額の金」(≒ a large sum of money)。
- **art** [άːt] 【名】芸術；美術 ▶ artist (< art + -ist (専門家)) は「芸術家」。
- **chance** [tʃǽns] 【名】(天から降りかかるモノ) → 偶然；機会 − [時機の予測] → 見込み
  《連語》by chance 偶然に (≒ accidentally)
  ⟷ on purpose 意図的に (≒ intentionally)
- **group** [grúːp] 【名】集団；群れ
- **land** [lǽnd] 【名】(海に対する) 陸 → (耕作地の) 土地 ▶ 空に対する陸は earth, ground。
  【動】〜を上陸させる；着陸させる, 着陸する ▶ belly-landing は「胴体着陸」。
- **material** [mətíəriəl] 【名】(生み出されたもの；物質) → 原料；材料 ▶ mammal (哺乳類) と同源。
  【形】物質の ▶ -al 形尾
- **seat** [síːt] 【名】座席 【動】〜を座らせる ▶ 自動詞は sit (座る)。sit, seat, set と同源。
- **pain** [péɪn] 【名】苦痛 − [苦痛を伴う努力] → [pains] 苦労；骨折り ▶ 長い鈍痛は ache。
  《連語》take pains 苦労する；骨を折る ▶ 【形】painstaking で「骨の折れる」。
  【形】painful 痛い ▶ -ful 形尾 (満ちている)
- **winter** [wíntɚ] 【名】冬 ▶「人生の末期；晩年」は比喩的に the winter of life という。
- **control** [kəntróʊl] 【動】〜を制御する 【名】制御
  《連語》be in control of 〜 〜を制御する ⟷ be out of control of
  【名】controller 制御する人 → (航空) 管制官 ▶ -er 名尾 (〜する人)
- **demand** [dɪmǽnd] 【動】〜を要求する 【名】要求 − [市場での商品購買の要求] → 需要
  ⟷ supply 【動】〜を供給する 【名】供給 − [生活への供給物] → [supplies] 備蓄
  《連語》supply and demand 需要と供給
  supply 人 with 物 人に物を供給する (≒ supply 物 to / for 人)
- **fill** [fíl] 【動】〜を満たす
  《連語》be filled with 〜 〜で満たされている (≒ be full of)
- **intend** [ɪnténd] 【動】[intend to do] 〜することを意図する；〜するつもりである
  【名】intention 意図 ▶ -tion 名尾 【形】intentional 意図的な ▶ -al 形尾
  【副】intentionally 意図的に (≒ on purpose) ▶ -ly 副尾。chance の項参照。
- **leave** [líːv] 【動】〜を去る → [leave for 〜] 〜へ出発する − [後に残す]
  → 〜を置いて立ち去る → [leave O C] O を C のままにする
- **respect** [rɪspékt] 【動】〜を尊敬する (≒ look up to) ⟷ despise 〜を軽蔑する (≒ look down on)
  【名】(改めて見る) − [それほど価値がある] → 尊敬
  − [注意深く見るところ] → 点 ▶ re- 元の場所へ → 改めて・-spect 見る
  【形】respectable 立派な ▶ -able 形尾 (可能)
  respectful 尊敬の念に溢れている ▶ -ful 形尾 (満ちている)
  respective それぞれの ▶ -ive 形尾 (〜の性質を持った)
- **spread** [spréd] 【動】〜を広げる；広がる 【名】広がり；普及 ▶ spray (スプレー) と同源。
- **steal** [stíːl] 【動】[steal 物 from 人] 人から物をこっそり盗む
  【名】stealer 空き巣 ▶ -er 名尾 (〜する人)。robber は「強盗」。rob の項参照。
- **clean** [klíːn] 【形】透明な → 澄んだ；きれいな (⟷ dirty) 【動】〜をきれいにする
- **excellent** [éksələnt] 【形】優れた ▶ -ent 形尾
  【名】excellence 優秀さ ▶ -ence 名尾 【動】excel 〜に勝る
- **gentle** [dʒéntl] 【形】(生まれがよい) → 穏やかな → 優しい；(思いやりがあって) 親切な

EXERCISE A

各文の下線部分に入る適切な語を左ページの見出し語から選びましょう。

1. There's a high _____ of winning.
2. It's going to be a long, cold _____ .
3. The ship will reach _____ today.
4. The man in the hospital bed is in terrible _____ .
5. When the police caught the man, he was going to _____ some money from the bank.
6. The clothes are _____ . My mother washed them yesterday.
7. That's a large _____ of money.
8. Excuse me, would you mind if I sat in this _____ ?
9. What kind of _____ is the dress made of? Is it cotton?
10. I'm looking forward to visiting some _____ galleries in town.

EXERCISE B

左の語の定義として正しいものを右のコラムより選び、（ ）にアルファベットを書き入れましょう。

Part 1

1. ( ) amount   a. how much there is of something
2. ( ) land   b. feel that someone or something is good or important
3. ( ) steal   c. take something that belongs to someone else
4. ( ) excellent   d. an area of ground
5. ( ) artist   e. very good
6. ( ) demand   f. something that is used for sitting
7. ( ) seat   g. someone who is good at painting or drawing
8. ( ) intention   h. coldest season of the year
9. ( ) respect   i. ask for something
10. ( ) winter   j. something that one plans to do

Part 2

1. ( ) pain   a. have power over something
2. ( ) group   b. put something into a container
3. ( ) fill   c. something used for a specific purpose
4. ( ) chance   d. having a kind or quiet nature
5. ( ) leave   e. a number of people who are in the same place
6. ( ) clean   f. luck
7. ( ) material   g. a bad feeling in the body when one is sick
8. ( ) control   h. become larger; move into more places
9. ( ) gentle   i. go away from some place
10. ( ) spread   j. wash

Unit 3

- ☐ **average** [ǽvrɪdʒ] 【名】平均 【形】平均的な
  《連語》on average 平均して
- ☐ **circle** [sə́ːkəl] 【名】円 – [ひとまとまりになっているもの] → サークル
  【形】circular 円形の, 循環的な ▶-ar 形尾
- ☐ **company** [kʌ́mpəni] 【名】(パンを共に食べる人) → 仲間；一緒にいること ┐
  └[同じことをする集まり] → 会社 ▶com- = con- 共に・-pan パン (＝bread)
  《連語》in company with 〜 〜と一緒になって；〜と連れ立って
- ☐ **doubt** [dáʊt] 【名】疑い 【動】〜を疑う ▶double と同源。「2つのいずれを選ぶか迷う」。
- ☐ **farm** [fάːrm] 【名】農場；農園 ▶田園(fields)と住居・納屋を含む広大な地域を指す。
  【名】farmer 農夫 ▶-er 名尾 (〜する人)
- ☐ **hope** [hóʊp] 【名】希望 【動】[hope to do] 〜することを希望する [hope for〜] 〜を望む
- ☐ **law** [lɔ́ː] 【名】法律 ▶lie (横たわる)と同源。「人々を勝手に活動させないモノ」。
  【名】lawyer 弁護士 ▶-er 名尾 (〜する人)。lawyer's fees で「弁護料」。
- ☐ **month** [mʌ́nθ] 【名】月 ▶October は本来「8番目の月」。1月・2月が後世に作られ「10月」となる。
- ☐ **pound** [páʊnd] 【名】ポンド (＝重量の単位, 英国の通貨単位 (＝£))
  ▶ponder (〜をよく考える)の元になった語。「心の中で物事の重さを量る」イメージ。
- ☐ **result** [rɪzʌ́lt] 【名】結果 ▶re- 元の場所へ・-sult 跳ねる。「原因から跳ね返ってくるモノ」。
  【動】[result in 〜] 〜に終わる [result from 〜] 〜から結果として生ずる
- ☐ **advance** [ədvǽns] 【動】前進する, 〜を進める 【名】前進
  《連語》in advance 前もって
  【形】advanced (他よりも進んだ) → 上級の ▶-ed 形尾 (〜された)
- ☐ **bring** [brɪ́ŋ] 【動】〜を持ってくる ←→ take 〜を持って行く
- ☐ **destroy** [dɪstrɔ́ɪ] 【動】〜を破壊する
  【形】destructive 破壊的な ▶-tive 形尾 (〜された)
  【名】destruction 破壊 ▶-tion 名尾
- ☐ **exchange** [ɪkstʃéɪndʒ] 【動】[exchange A for B] AとBとを交換する ▶for は「交換」のイメージ。
  【名】交換 ▶an exchange student で「交換留学生」。
- ☐ **feed** [fíːd] 【動】〜に食事を与える；えさをやる
  【名】food 食べ物 ▶「牛肉」が ox meat でなく beef なのは 1066 年の仏国の英国征服による。beef は仏語由来。仏が食べる側, 英が飼育する側。pork, chicken も同様。
- ☐ **influence** [ínfluəns] 【動】〜に影響を与える 【名】影響
  ▶influenza (インフルエンザ)と同源。疫病は星からの影響と考えられていた。
  【形】influential 影響力のある ▶-tial 形尾
- ☐ **struggle** [strʌ́gl] 【動】[struggle with 〜] 〜と奮闘する
  [struggle for 〜] 〜を得るために奮闘する ▶for は「交換 → 目的物獲得」。
  【名】奮闘；苦闘 ▶struggle for existence で「生存競争」。
- ☐ **fine** [fáɪn] 【形】(最後のもの) → (完成して)見事な；素晴らしい ┐
  └(健康面で素晴らしく)元気な → (天候上素晴らしく)快晴な
  ▶fine は「細かい」の意も持つ。fine sand は「細かい砂」の意。
  【名】罰金 ▶fine は finish と同源。「争いごとを終わらせるもの」のイメージ。
- ☐ **private** [práɪvət] 【形】個人の；私的な – [公ではないという意から] → 私立の, 非公開の
- ☐ **serious** [síriəs] 【形】重大な；深刻な – [厳しいさまであることから] → 真剣な, 生真面目な
  ▶serious disease で「深刻な病気」。×heavy disease

EXERCISE A

各文の下線部分に入る適切な語を左ページの見出し語から選びましょう。

1. I play tennis once a _____ .
2. If you drive too fast, you break the _____ .
3. On _____ , the staff work for 40 hours per week.
4. It was a _____ to pass the university entrance test.
5. Yes, I'm _____ , thanks. And how are you?
6. There is still some _____ about whether the wedding will happen or not.
7. Did you hear the soccer _____ ?
8. The teacher never smiles. He's so _____ .
9. Could you _____ me my glasses? I have left them on the table over there.
10. Let's _____ phone numbers. I will call you as soon as I can.

EXERCISE B

左の語の定義として正しいものを右のコラムより選び、( )にアルファベットを書き入れましょう。

Part 1

1. ( ) farm   a. amount or level that is typical of a group of people or things
2. ( ) private   b. try very hard to do something
3. ( ) law   c. having the power to change someone or something
4. ( ) result   d. being only for one person or group
5. ( ) struggle   e. a group of people who work together to make money
6. ( ) exchange   f. something that is caused by something else
7. ( ) bring   g. land used for growing vegetables or raising animals
8. ( ) company   h. the system of rules made by the government
9. ( ) average   i. give something and receive something in return
10. ( ) influential   j. come with something or someone

Part 2

1. ( ) month   a. a feeling of not knowing something
2. ( ) hope   b. make something end or no longer exist
3. ( ) fine   c. one of the twelve parts of the year
4. ( ) doubt   d. move forward
5. ( ) advance   e. a perfectly round shape
6. ( ) circle   f. being important
7. ( ) ponder   g. a feeling of wanting something to happen
8. ( ) destroy   h. good
9. ( ) feed   i. give food to someone or something
10. ( ) serious   j. think about carefully

Unit 4

- ☐ **business** [bíznəs] 【名】(自分の経営している)事業；商売 → 本分；務め
  ▶ job は「賃金を取ってする仕事」, labor は「(疲労・不快感を伴う)賃金労働」, task は「課された仕事；作業」, toil は「苦しくてつらい仕事」, profession は「専門的職業」, career は「生涯を通した仕事」。None of your business. は「余計なことをするな」。

- ☐ **life** [láɪf] 【名】生命 − [生命を持って活動] → 生活；一生 − [人間の一生] → 人生
  ▶ life expectancy は「余命」。live a daily life は「日々の生活をおくる」。

- ☐ **language** [lǽŋɡwɪdʒ] 【名】言語
  ▶ second language acquisition は「第二言語習得」。

- ☐ **ring** [ríŋ] 【名】輪, 指輪 ▶ 以下の名詞・動詞用法の意とは別語源。
  【名】(鐘・ベル・電話などが)鳴る音
  【動】鳴る；〜を鳴らす ▶ 英用法。米用法は call。

- ☐ **spring** [sprɪ́ŋ] 【名】春, 泉, バネ 【動】急に跳ねる；とび上がる, [spring up] 急に生じる
  ▶ すべて「真上にとび出す」イメージ。「春」は「芽が地面からとび出す」季節を指す。

- ☐ **town** [táʊn] 【名】町
  ▶ village よりも大きく city よりも小さい。downtown は「町の中心部；繁華街」。

- ☐ **voice** [vɔ́ɪs] 【名】声 【動】〜を言葉に表す ▶ voice opinions で「意見を述べる」。

- ☐ **accept** [əksépt] 【動】〜を喜んで受け入れる ▶ receive は単に「受け取る」。
  【名】acceptance 受け入れること ▶ -ance 名尾

- ☐ **expect** [ɪkspékt] 【動】〜を予期する；期待する ▶ ex- 外へ・-pect 視線を向ける→先を見る
  【名】expectation 予想；期待 ▶ -ation 名尾

- ☐ **hang** [hǽŋ] 【動】〜を吊るす；吊る ▶ 活用は hang < hung < hung が正式。
  《連語》hang around ぶらぶら歩く ▶ 提灯などが吊り下がって揺れ動く様に由来。
  　　　　hang on / hang up (the telephone) 電話を切る
  ▶ 昔は電話機が壁の上方に設置。「受話器を電話機に接触(on)するように吊るす(hang)」/「上方に(up)吊るす(hang)」イメージ。

- ☐ **offer** [ɔ́:fɚ] 【動】〜を差し出す → 〜を提供する − [意見を差し出す] → 〜を申し出る
  【名】提供, 申し出

- ☐ **shake** [ʃéɪk] 【動】〜を振る；揺さぶる
  《連語》shake one's head (否定・落胆などで)頭を横に振る
  　　　　shake hands (with 〜) (〜と)握手をする ▶ 複数形 hands に注意。

- ☐ **taste** [téɪst] 【動】〜を味わう；〜の味がする 【名】味, 好み

- ☐ **understand** [ʌndɚsténd] 【動】〜を理解する ▶ stand under に由来。相手の発言を捉えて(catch)しっかり見る(see)には, ボールを捕るかのように真下に立つ必要がある。

- ☐ **equal** [í:kwəl] 【形】等しい, [be equal to 〜] 〜に等しい → 〜に対応できる ▶ -al 形尾
  【名】equality 同等；平等 ▶ -ity 名尾

- ☐ **famous** [féɪməs] 【形】有名な ▶ -ous 形尾
  【名】fame 名声

- ☐ **local** [lóʊkəl] 【形】地方の；ある特定の地域に限られた ▶ -al 形尾

- ☐ **already** [ɑ:lrédi] 【副】(肯定文で)すでに, (疑問文, 否定文で)もう

- ☐ **instead** [ɪnstéd] 【副】(通例文頭, 文尾で)その代わりに, [instead of 〜] 〜の代わりに

- ☐ **perhaps** [pɚhǽps] 【副】ひょっとして
  ▶ 確信度は, 50%程度：perhaps, maybe, possibly, 50%〜90%：likely, probably, 90%以上：necessarily, definitely, certainly, undoubtedly。

EXERCISE A

各文の下線部分に入る適切な語を左ページの見出し語から選びましょう。

1. I'll _____ the picture on this wall over here.
2. One meter is _____ to 100 centimeters.
3. English is his first _____ , but he can speak Spanish, too.
4. My _____ is not doing very well. The economy is poor at the moment.
5. Sugar has a sweet _____ .
6. He's a very _____ movie star.
7. He never wears his wedding _____ .
8. I think that the band's singer has a great _____ . I love listening to their music.
9. In Britain, when people meet for the first time, they often _____ hands.
10. Which _____ do you live in?

EXERCISE B

左の語の定義として正しいものを右のコラムより選び、( )にアルファベットを書き入れましょう。

Part 1

1. ( ) expect   a. in place of
2. ( ) understand   b. know the meaning of something
3. ( ) business   c. known by many people
4. ( ) instead   d. think that something will certainly happen
5. ( ) hang   e. move back and forth or up and down quickly
6. ( ) spring   f. put a jacket in the closet, for example
7. ( ) famous   g. system of words that humans use for communication
8. ( ) language   h. the activity of selling and buying goods or giving services
9. ( ) voice   i. the season that comes after winter
10. ( ) shake   j. the sound produced through the mouth

Part 2

1. ( ) town   a. a place where people live that is smaller than a city
2. ( ) accept   b. the period of time from birth to death
3. ( ) perhaps   c. the same in number, amount or quality
4. ( ) taste   d. something that one likes
5. ( ) ring   e. give someone the chance to take something
6. ( ) local   f. being from a small area, especially outside of a city
7. ( ) equal   g. maybe
8. ( ) already   h. before this time; before now
9. ( ) life   i. a piece of jewelry worn on the finger
10. ( ) offer   j. take something that is offered

Unit 5

- ☐ **address** [(名) ǽdrɛs, (動) ədrɛ́s]　【名】(speech より形式ばった)演説 ─ [言葉を向ける先] → 住所；(手紙・E-mail の)あて先　【動】〜に演説する，〜にあて名を書く

- ☐ **character** [kǽrɪktɚ]　【名】(刻印) [(劇場用の仮面に刻印されたことから)顔立ち；人相] → 登場人物 →(人相は人の性質を映し出すことから)特徴 ─ [印刷物に刻まれたもの] → 文字
  【形】characteristic 特徴的な ▶-ic 形尾 [be characteristic of 〜] 〜に特有だ

- ☐ **exercise** [éksɚsaɪz]　【名/動】(束縛から出る；体を動かす) → 運動(する) → 練習(する)
  ▶ ex- 外へ・-ercise 束縛する

- ☐ **ground** [gráʊnd]　【名】(空に対する)地面(≒earth) ─ [活動する場所] → 練習場

- ☐ **honor** [ɑ́:nɚ]　【名】(尊敬；敬意) → 名誉 [in honor of 〜] 〜に敬意を表して
  【形】honorable 尊敬すべき ▶-able 形尾(可能)

- ☐ **opportunity** [ɑ:pɚtúːnəti]　【名】好機 ▶-ity 名尾。原義は「港の方向に船を運ぶ追い風」。
  【形】opportune 好機の ▶ op- = ad- 方向・-port 港

- ☐ **step** [stép]　【名】一歩；歩み → 足取り；歩調 [steps] 階段　【動】歩を進める
  《連語》step by step 一歩ずつ；少しずつ　watch one's step 足元に気をつける

- ☐ **agree** [əgríː]　【動】[agree with 人／to 案] 人／案に同意する ⟷ disagree 同意しない
  【名】agreement 同意 ▶-ment 名尾 ⟷ disagreement 反対；不一致

- ☐ **begin** [bɪgɪ́n]　【動】〜を始める；始まる ⟷ end 〜を終える；終わる　【名】beginning 始まり
  ▶ start ⟷ finish。end は「終えて何もなくなる」, finish は「仕上がる」イメージ。

- ☐ **die** [dáɪ]　【動】[die of 直接的死因] 〜で死ぬ [die from 間接的死因] 〜で死ぬ
  ▶ of は out of に由来。from の背後には [from-to] が存在。出発点から到達点に至るには「一定の経路」が必要。この経路介入の余地を逆手にとって「間接性」が生まれた。

  例) He died **of** cancer.　例) He died [of lung cancer] **from** excessive smoking.

- ☐ **fix** [fíks]　【動】〜をしっかり固定する ─ [部品を適所に据える] → 〜を修理する
  ─ [食材を適所に据える] →(加熱しないで)料理を作る

- ☐ **hear** [híɚ]　【動】〜が自然に聞こえてくる，〜を注意して聞く
  ▶ listen to 〜は「〜に耳を傾ける；聞き耳を立てる」。

- ☐ **prevent** [prɪvént]　【動】[prevent 人 from 〜 ing] 人が〜することを妨げる
  ▶「止めさせる」系統の表現(stop / hinder 人 from 〜 ing)には from が用いられる。

- ☐ **stand** [stǽnd]　【動】立つ；立っている ─ [姿勢を崩さないように踏ん張る] → 〜を我慢する

- ☐ **favorite** [féɪvrət]　【形】最もお気に入りの　【名】お気に入りの人／物 ▶-ite 名尾(〜の人)
  【名】favor 好意 ▶ May I ask a favor of you? は「お願いがあるのですが。」の意。

- ☐ **possible** [pɑ́:səbl]　【形】可能な ⟷ impossible 不可能な ▶ poss- 力がある・-ible = -able 形尾(可能)

- ☐ **necessary** [nésəseri]　【形】必要な
  【副】necessarily 必ず ▶-ly 副尾。not necessarily で「必ずしも〜というわけではない」。

- ☐ **usual** [júːʒuəl]　【形】いつもの
  【副】usually いつものように；たいてい(≒ as usual) ▶ always の項参照。

- ☐ **likely** [láɪkli]　【形】ありそうな；起こりそうな [be likely to do] 〜しそうである

- ☐ **early** [ɚ́ːli]　【副】(予定・定刻などより)早く

EXERCISE A

各文の下線部分に入る適切な語を左ページの見出し語から選びましょう。

1. The weather report said that it was _____ to rain today.
2. Please _____ still. When I have finished talking to you, you can go.
3. There are many colors that I like. However, red is my _____ .
4. Could you tell me your email _____ ?
5. This sun block should _____ you from getting sunburn.
6. Business people often have to leave their homes _____ in the morning.
7. The music is very quiet, but I can still _____ it.
8. The main _____ from the movie is very popular with children.
9. Let's _____ the class by looking at page 5 of the textbook.
10. Please watch your _____ when you walk across the field.

EXERCISE B

左の語の定義として正しいものを右のコラムより選び、( )にアルファベットを書き入れましょう。

Part 1

1. ( ) exercise   a. the respect that people have for someone
2. ( ) step   b. a formal speech given to a group of people
3. ( ) favorite   c. the most liked
4. ( ) necessary   d. before the time that is expected
5. ( ) beginning   e. must be had or needed
6. ( ) honor   f. move in a specific direction by lifting and lowering one's feet
7. ( ) prevent   g. make better
8. ( ) fix   h. stop something from happening
9. ( ) address   i. an activity used to get a stronger or healthier body
10. ( ) early   j. the start of something

Part 2

1. ( ) ground   a. able to be done
2. ( ) possible   b. unique feature
3. ( ) hear   c. have the same opinion
4. ( ) stand   d. have one's body in an upright position supported by one's feet
5. ( ) agree   e. stop living
6. ( ) likely   f. a chance to do something or situation in which something can be done
7. ( ) opportunity   g. normal
8. ( ) usual   h. land
9. ( ) die   i. seeming to be true
10. ( ) characteristic   j. be aware of sounds through the ear

Unit 6

- **bank** [bǽŋk] 【名】銀行, 土手
  ▶原義は「一段高い所」。昔の高利貸しは一段高い所に番頭が座っていた。
- **college** [káːlɪdʒ] 【名】単科大学 ▶ university は「総合大学」, [英]junior college は「短大」。
- **edge** [édʒ] 【名】(鋭い)縁→端；はずれ ▶ verge は「土地の端」, rim は「円形の物の縁」。
  《連語》be on the edge of ～ (～の瀬戸際にいる) → 今にも～しそうである
- **factory** [fǽktəri] 【名】工場 ▶ fact- 作る・-ory 名尾(場所)
- **limit** [límət] 【名】(最小・最大の)限度；制限 【動】～を限定する；～を制限する
  《連語》be limited to ～ ～に限定される
- **party** [páːti] 【名】(部分の集合；個々の集合)→ パーティー, 一団, 政党
  [参与者] → 当事者 ▶ a third party で「第三者」。
- **sail** [séɪl] 【名】帆 - [昔は帆船で航行したことから] → 航海 【動】航海する
  【名】sailor 船員；水兵 ▶ -or = -er 名尾(～する人)
- **test** [tést] 【名】検査 - [学力検査] → 試験 【動】～を試す；検査する, ～を試験する
- **act** [ǽkt] 【動】～を行う；行動する；活動する - [人前で行う] → 振舞う；演じる
  → [活動して影響を及ぼす] → [act on ～] (薬などが)～に作用する
  【名】行動, (劇の)幕
  【形】actual 実際の ▶ -al 形尾 【副】actually ところが実際は ▶ -ly 副尾
  【形】active 活動的な, 積極的な ▶ -ive 形尾
  【名】action 行動, 演技, 作用 ▶ -ion 名尾
- **build** [bíld] 【動】～を建てる, ～を組み立てる ▶活用は build < built < built。
  【名】building 建築；建物 ▶ -ing 名尾(～すること)
- **choose** [tʃúːz] 【動】～を(2つの中から)選ぶ ▶ select は「3つ以上の中から吟味して選ぶ」。
  【名】choice 選択 ▶ have no choice to do で「～せざるを得ない」。
- **describe** [dɪskráɪb] 【動】～を描写する
  【名】description 描写 ▶ -tion 名尾。beyond description で「言葉では表せない程」。
- **include** [ɪnklúːd] 【動】～を含む ▶ in- 中に・-clude 閉じる ⟷ exclude ～を排除する ▶ ex- 外へ
  【形】inclusive 包括的な ▶ -sive 形尾 ⟷ exclusive 排他的な
- **suffer** [sʌ́fər] 【動】[suffer from ～] ～を被(こうむ)る；～に苦しむ ▶ suf- = sub- 下に・-fer 運ぶ
  ▶キリストの受難に由来する語。自身がはりつけになって死ぬべき十字架を背負い, 現世の苦悩を一身に背負ってゴルゴダの丘に登って行く。まさにこの「ものを支えて(sub-)運ぶ(-fer)→ 苦しみを背負う」イメージ。
- **busy** [bízi] 【形】忙しい → 仕事に従事している
  → 騒がしい；にぎやかな - [声が通じない] → (電話が)話し中で
- **foreign** [fɔ́rən] 【形】外国の, 異質の
  【名】foreigner よそ者；外国人
  ▶ -er 名尾(人) ▶ 「外国人」は a person from another country が妥当。
- **straight** [stréɪt] 【形】まっすぐな → 実直な - [考え方が曲がっていない] → 正しい
- **moreover** [mɔrόʊvər] 【副】その上
  ▶重要な情報を付け加えるときに用いられる。
- **quite** [kwáɪt] 【副】まったく
  《連語》quite a few 可算名詞 / quite a little 不加算名詞　たくさんの～
- **beneath** [bɪníːθ] 【前】～のすぐ下に, 重なったものの下に
  ▶ be- そばに・-neath 下に。under は「真下」しかも「一定の距離」がある場合, underneath は「覆われている」か「見えない状態」で下にある場合。

EXERCISE A

各文の下線部分に入る適切な語を左ページの見出し語から選びましょう。

1. The student successfully graduated from _____ .
2. Even though it will be a lot of hard work, the family wants to _____ their own home.
3. My family and I live on the _____ of town.
4. There is a large _____ near my house that makes cars.
5. Could you _____ in detail what you have lost?
6. Each week, I go to the _____ to get some money.
7. The police know who stole the painting. _____ , they think they know where he lives.
8. I _____ from bad headaches.
9. Let's sit in the shade _____ that tree.
10. Please draw a _____ line from one side of the paper to the other side.

EXERCISE B

左の語の定義として正しいものを右のコラムより選び、（　）にアルファベットを書き入れましょう。

Part 1

1. (　) suffer
2. (　) bank
3. (　) party
4. (　) edge
5. (　) build
6. (　) test
7. (　) describe
8. (　) limit
9. (　) foreign
10. (　) moreover

a. give details about what something is like
b. again; in addition
c. being outside or being from outside a country
d. have pain
e. a set of questions to check someone's knowledge
f. a line where an object begins or ends
g. an event with entertainment, food and drinks
h. make something such as a house by using bricks, wood and other material
i. a point beyond which it is not possible to go
j. a business where people keep money

Part 2

1. (　) quite
2. (　) beneath
3. (　) busy
4. (　) sailor
5. (　) include
6. (　) college
7. (　) factory
8. (　) straight
9. (　) actually
10. (　) choose

a. take what you want from a group of things
b. someone who works on a boat
c. a building where products are made
d. very
e. have as part of a group
f. a school that comes after high school
g. directly under
h. not having curves
i. really; in truth
j. be actively doing something

Unit 7

- **base** [béɪs]
  - 【名】土台；基礎 − [軍の活動の土台となる場所] → 基地
  - 【形】basic 基礎的な ▶-ic 形尾 【副】basically 基本的には ▶-ly 副尾
  - 【名】basis 基礎 − [考えや言動の基盤；よりどころ] → 根拠
  - ▶複数形は bases。「論文」を表す [単] thesis ⟷ [複] theses と同様。
- **council** [káʊnsəl] 【名】(公の)会議 ▶ coun- 共に・-cil 呼ぶ
- **enemy** [énəmi] 【名】敵 ▶「好敵手；競争相手」は rival。rival の項参照。
- **health** [hélθ]
  - 【名】健康 ▶ be in bad health (具合が悪い)のように,「健康状態」も表される。
  - 【形】healthy 健康的な ▶-y 形尾
- **moment** [móʊmənt]
  - 【名】(天秤を動かすはずみ(momentum)となる最小重量) → [最小の時間量] → 瞬間 − [物事を動かすはずみとなる瞬間] → 重大性
  - 【形】momentary 瞬間的な ▶-ary 形尾 【形】momentous 重大な ▶-ous 形尾
- **opinion** [əpínjən] 【名】意見 ▶ option(選択)と同源。public opinion で「世論」。
- **add** [ǽd]
  - 【動】[add (A) to B] (A を)B に加える
  - ⟷ subtract (A) from B (A を)B から引く ▶ sub- 下に → 減らす・-tract 引く
  - 【名】addition 追加, 足し算 ▶-tion 名尾 ⟷ subtraction 引くこと, 引き算
  - 《連語》in addition その上　in addition to 〜 〜に加えて
- **change** [tʃéɪndʒ]
  - 【動】〜を変える；変わる, 〜を取り替える 【名】変化；変更, 両替；お釣り
  - 《連語》change trains 電車を乗り換える ▶複数形に注意。
- **increase** [(動)ɪnkríːs] [(名)ínkriːs]
  - 【動】増加する, [increase in 〜] 〜が増加する 【名】増加
  - ▶ in- 上に → 積み重なる(=on)・-crease 伸びる ⟷ decrease 減少する, 減少 ▶ de- 下
  - 《連語》on the increase 次第に増加して ⟷ on the decrease 次第に減少して
- **paint** [péɪnt]
  - 【動】絵の具で描く；ペンキを塗る 【名】絵の具；ペンキ
  - ▶ paint a picture は「絵の具で絵を描く」, draw a picture は「線画で絵を描く」の意。
- **propose** [prəpóʊz]
  - 【動】〜を提案する ▶ pro- 前に・-pose 置く。suggest は「〜を暗に示す」。
  - 【名】proposition 提案 ▶-tion 名尾。proposal(提案)より明確な条件を示す。
- **sort** [sɔ́ːrt]
  - 【動】〜を区分する；分類する ▶以下の「なんとなく」は「一種の〜」のイメージ。
  - 【名】[a sort of 〜] 一種の〜 (≒ a kind of)
  - [sort of 〜] なんとなく〜 (≒ kind of)
- **write** [ráɪt]
  - 【動】〜を書く, 手紙を書く ▶下記 writing の2つの意については defeat の項参照。
  - 【名】writing 書くこと, 書かれたもの [writings] 諸作品 ▶-ing 名尾(〜すること)
- **current** [kə́ːrənt]
  - 【形】(流れている) → (時の流れから)現在の → (貨幣の流れから)流通している ▶ cur- 走る − [直線の連続性] → 流れる・-ent 形尾
  - 【名】currency 通貨 (≒ current money) ▶-ency 名尾
- **few** [fjúː]
  - 【形】[a few 可算名詞] 少し〜がある [few 可算名詞] ほとんど〜ない
  - ▶ a little 〜(少し〜ある), little 〜(ほとんどない)は不加算名詞と共に使用。
  - 《連語》not / only a few 〜 ほとんど〜ない (≒ few)
  - 　　　quite a few 〜 たくさんの〜 (≒ many)
- **glad** [glǽd] 【形】嬉しい ⟷ sad 悲しい [be glad to do] 〜して嬉しい
- **regular** [régjələr] 【形】規則正しい；定期的な → 通常の ▶ regul- 定規・-ar 形尾(〜のような)
- **almost** [ɔ́ːlmoʊst] 【副】ほとんど；もう少しで ▶ al- 全部(=all)・-most 大部分
- **everywhere** [évriweər]
  - 【副】いたるところで；どこにも
  - ▶ every あらゆる・-where 場所
- **yet** [jét] 【副】まだ〜ない, (疑問文で)もう 【接】しかし ▶「対比」を強めるイメージ。

EXERCISE A

各文の下線部分に入る適切な語を左ページの見出し語から選びましょう。

1. I haven't done my homework _____ .
2. The man will give his _____ to anyone who will listen.
3. I am very _____ to meet you, too.
4. Let's _____ the room yellow!
5. The woman is in great _____ .
6. I am going to _____ a letter to my pen pal in Costa Rica.
7. _____ everyone in my family likes ice cream.
8. I live near an army _____ .
9. He's a _____ visitor to the museum.
10. The lion is the zebra's main _____ .

EXERCISE B

左の語の定義として正しいものを右のコラムより選び、( )にアルファベットを書き入れましょう。

Part 1

1. ( ) paint　　　　　a. someone who hates another
2. ( ) currency　　　b. very important
3. ( ) almost　　　　c. put or separate something into order
4. ( ) glad　　　　　d. a colored liquid spread on something
5. ( ) sort　　　　　e. until now; so far
6. ( ) basis　　　　　f. a reason for doing something
7. ( ) enemy　　　　g. feeling happiness
8. ( ) yet　　　　　　h. become different
9. ( ) change　　　　i. money that a country uses
10. ( ) momentous　　j. only a little less than; nearly

Part 2

1. ( ) regular　　　　a. in all places
2. ( ) propose　　　　b. a belief or way of thinking about something
3. ( ) addition　　　　c. become larger in size or amount
4. ( ) few　　　　　　d. the act of joining something with something else
5. ( ) council　　　　e. make marks on paper with a pen or pencil
6. ( ) everywhere　　f. give something for people to think about
7. ( ) write　　　　　g. the condition of being well and without sickness
8. ( ) increase　　　　h. not many
9. ( ) opinion　　　　i. a group of people chosen to decide something
10. ( ) healthy　　　　j. happening over and over at the same time

Unit 8

- **advantage** [ədvǽntɪdʒ]　【名】有利なこと；有利な点 ▶「メリット」に相当。英語の merit は「長所」の意。
  ⇔ disadvantage 不利なこと；不利な点 ▶ dis- 否定
  《連語》take advantage of ～ ～につけこむ；～を利用する
- **chief** [tʃíːf]　【名】(組織・団体の)長(おさ) 【形】主な；主要な
- **evening** [íːvnɪŋ]　【名】夕方；晩
- **fact** [fǽkt]　【名】事実；実際に起こった事柄 [in (actual) fact] ところが実際は
  【形】factual 事実の ▶ -al 形尾　【副】factually 事実の面で ▶ -ly 副尾
- **number** [nʌ́mbɚ]　【名】数；数字 【動】～を数える ▶ [a number of 複数名詞] で「多数の～」。
  [the number of ～] で「～の数」。後者は単数名詞扱い。
  【形】numerous 極めて多数の ▶ -ous 形尾
  【形】innumerable 無数の (≒ numberless) ▶ in- 否定・-able (可能)
- **motor** [móʊtɚ]　【名】原動機；発動機 − [その利用物] → 自動車, モーターボート, オートバイ
- **shoulder** [ʃóʊldɚ]　【名】肩
- **bear** [béɚ]　【動】運ぶ ┬ [産道を通して胎児の身を運ぶ] → ～を産む
  ├ [荷物を背負って運ぶ；重荷を背負う] → ～を耐える；我慢する
  └ [運ぶために手で持つ] → ～を(抽象的に)持っている
  《連語》bear / keep ～ in mind (将来役立ちそうなので)～を覚えておく
  bear fruits (植物が)実をつける → (努力の成果が)実を結ぶ
- **catch** [kǽtʃ]　【動】(動くものを)捕まえる ┬ (流感性の病気に)かかる
  ├ [昔の汽車は最後尾の車両後方につかむ所があった] → 乗り物に間に合う
  └ [しっかりと見る (see) ために捉える] → ～を理解する
- **gather** [gǽðɚ]　【動】～を集める；集まる ▶ together, gregarious (群居する) と同源。
- **pay** [péɪ]　【動】～を支払う → [商品と支払い額がつりあう] → (苦労などが)見合う
  《連語》pay attention to ～ ～に注意を払う
  【名】支払い, 給料
  ▶ salary は「年俸などの固定給」, wage は「肉体労働に対する賃金」。
- **reduce** [rɪdúːs]　【動】～を減少させる ▶ re- 元の場所へ → 後ろへ・-duce 引く
  【名】reduction 減少 ▶ -tion 名尾
- **settle** [sétl]　【動】～を置く − [落着；定着] → ～を落ち着かせる ▶ sit, seat, set と同源。
  《連語》settle down 落ち着く, 定住する
  settle down to do 腰を据えて～し始める
- **vote** [vóʊt]　【動】～に投票する 【名】投票 [the vote] 投票権 (≒ voting right)
- **ancient** [éɪnʃənt]　【形】古代の ▶ an- 先に；以前に。ancestor (祖先) と同源。
- **common** [kɑ́ːmən]　【形】共通の − [どこにでもある] → ありふれた ▶「常識」は common sense。
  《連語》have ～ in common ～を共有している
- **dark** [dɑ́ɚk]　【形】闇の；暗い → 色が濃い ⇔ light 明るい (≒ bright) 【名】暗闇；夕闇
- **quiet** [kwáɪət]　【形】静かな ⇔ noisy 騒がしい
- **forward** [fɔ́ɚwɚd]　【副】前方へ ▶ for- = front 前・-ward 方向
  《連語》look forward to ～ ～を楽しみにしている
  ▶「前向きに物事に目を向ける」イメージ。この to は前置詞。× to do
- **hardly** [hɑ́ɚdli]　【副】ほとんど～ない (≒ scarcely)
  《連語》hardly any ～ ほとんど～ない；まず～ない

EXERCISE A

各文の下線部分に入る適切な語を左ページの見出し語から選びましょう。

1. _____ anyone came to the meeting.
2. The man carried the bag on his right _____ .
3. Please turn on the light. It's very _____ .
4. The guests took full _____ of the pool at the hotel.
5. He's the _____ of police.
6. He will arrive home this _____ .
7. I want to play chess with you, but please _____ in mind that I have only played once before.
8. An angry crowd quickly began to _____ around the police station.
9. The president will not get my _____ in the election. We need a new leader.
10. I am going to throw you the ball. Please _____ it!

EXERCISE B

左の語の定義として正しいものを右のコラムより選び、( )にアルファベットを書き入れましょう。

Part 1

1. ( ) catch   a. end; reach an agreement
2. ( ) pay   b. having little or no light
3. ( ) ancient   c. use one's hands to stop and hold something
4. ( ) advantage   d. something that puts someone or something in a better position
5. ( ) numerous   e. the part of the body where the arm is connected
6. ( ) dark   f. very old
7. ( ) settle   g. the last part of the day before night
8. ( ) shoulder   h. toward the front
9. ( ) forward   i. existing in large numbers
10. ( ) evening   j. give money for goods or services

Part 2

1. ( ) quiet   a. a machine that produces power
2. ( ) hardly   b. make a choice for or against someone or something
3. ( ) motor   c. bring together into a group
4. ( ) gather   d. almost not
5. ( ) fact   e. shared by two or more people
6. ( ) reduce   f. making very little noise
7. ( ) vote   g. highest in rank
8. ( ) common   h. make smaller in size or amount
9. ( ) bear   i. accept a bad situation
10. ( ) chief   j. something that truly exists or happens

Unit 9

- **answer** [ǽnsɚ]
  - 【名】答え – [問い・手紙などに答える] → 返事
  - 【動】〜に答える，〜に返事する
- **corner** [kɔ́ɚnɚ]
  - 【名】角(かど)；(部屋などの)すみ
  - ▶ Spring is just around the corner.(春がもう目の前に来ている)
- **danger** [déɪndʒɚ]
  - 【名】危険 ▶ be in danger で「危険な状態にある」。risk は「自ら覚悟して犯す危険」。
  - 【形】dangerous 危険な ▶ -ous 形尾
- **hall** [hɔ́:l]
  - 【名】(屋根のある所)→ 会館，[hallway の省略形] 玄関(の広間)；廊下
- **village** [vílɪdʒ]
  - 【名】村 ▶ villa 田舎の邸宅・-age 名尾(集合)
- **window** [wíndoʊ]
  - 【名】窓 ▶ wind 風・-ow 目 – [形状の類似] → 穴
- **world** [wɚ́ld]
  - 【名】世界, 世の中
  - 《連語》(why, where など)疑問詞＋in the world/on earth 〜？ 一体全体〜？
- **become** [bɪkʌ́m]
  - 【動】[become 名詞／形容詞] 〜になる ▶ 語源は come to be。
  - ▶ ×become to do とは言わない。正しくは come to do(〜するようになる)。
- **determine** [dɪtɚ́:mən]
  - 【動】〜を決心する；決意する
  - 【形】[be determined to do] 〜することを固く決意する ▶ -ed 形尾(〜された)
  - 【名】determination 決心；決意 ▶ -ation 名尾
- **feel** [fí:l]
  - 【動】[feel 形容詞] 〜のように感じる ▶ 本来は「肌；触覚で感じる」の意。
  - [feel 名詞] 〜を感じる　[feel O C] O を C だと感じる
  - 《連語》feel like 〜 ing 〜したい気がする　feel one's way 手探りしながら進む
  - 【名】feeling 触覚；感覚, 感情 ▶ -ing 名尾(〜すること)
- **own** [óʊn]
  - 【動】〜を所有する【形】自身の【名】自身のもの
  - 《連語》on one's own 独力で　of one's own 〜 ing 自分自身で〜した
  - 【名】owner 所有者 ▶ -er 名尾(〜する人)
- **refuse** [rɪfjú:z]
  - 【動】〜を(きっぱり)断る
  - ▶ 原義は「捨てる」。他の「拒否する」動詞は reject(＜ re- 元の場所へ・-ject 投げる →投げ返す)，turn down(裏向きにする → 却下する)，decline(＜ de- 分離・-cline 傾く →受け流す；遠慮する)。拒否の強さは reject ＞ refuse ＞ turn down ＞ decline。
- **spend** [spénd]
  - 【動】(金・労力を)費やす – [時は金なり] →(時を)費やす
  - ▶ spend A on ／[米] for B で「A を B に費やす」。
- **think** [θíŋk]
  - 【動】〜を思考する；〜を思う [think O [to be] C] O を C だと思う
  - 【名】thought 思考
- **cheap** [tʃí:p]
  - 【形】安い；安っぽい【副】安っぽく ▶「商売, 割引値」が原義。salary(給料)や income(収入, 所得)に対しては使わない。これらには low や small を用いる。
- **heavy** [hévi]
  - 【形】重い, (雨量や交通量などが)激しい
  - ▶「(中身の)量が多い」イメージ。heavy work(つぎ込むエネルギー量が多い仕事 → つらい仕事)，heavy cold(症状の量が多い風邪 → ひどい風邪)も同様。
- **narrow** [nǽroʊ]
  - 【形】(幅が)狭い ▶「狭い家」は ×narrow house ではなく，small house。
- **normal** [nɔ́ɚməl]
  - 【形】標準の, 正常な ▶ norm 標準・-al 形尾 ⟷ abnormal 異常な ▶ ab- 分離
- **always** [ɔ́:lweɪz]
  - 【副】いつも [not always] [部分否定] いつも〜とは限らない
  - ▶ 頻度は 100％：always ＞ 80％：usually, generally ＞ 60％：often, frequently ＞ 50％：sometimes ＞ 20％：occasionally ＞ 10％：seldom, rarely ＞ 0％：never
- **therefore** [ðéɚfɔɚ]
  - 【副】それゆえ
  - ▶ there- それ(＝that)・-fore 〜のために(＝for)

EXERCISE A

各文の下線部分に入る適切な語を左ページの見出し語から選びましょう。

1. The woman left the _____ open to get some fresh air into the house.
2. Don't _____ all your money! You need to buy things next week, too.
3. The fireman said that his life was in _____ .
4. I live in a small _____ . It has an elementary school and a church.
5. I can't lift this _____ suitcase. I will have to take some things out of it.
6. When he was young, the man traveled around the _____ .
7. A number of famous musicians have played in this historical concert _____ .
8. What's the _____ to the question?
9. I had to _____ his kind offer even though I didn't want to.
10. No, the river is not wide. It's _____ .

EXERCISE B

左の語の定義として正しいものを右のコラムより選び、( )にアルファベットを書き入れましょう。

Part 1

1. ( ) answer   a. touch something with your fingers to see what it is like
2. ( ) cheap   b. officially decide something based on facts
3. ( ) always   c. possibly causing death
4. ( ) determine   d. long and not wide
5. ( ) become   e. an opening in a wall with a piece of glass in it
6. ( ) refuse   f. begin to be
7. ( ) narrow   g. at all times
8. ( ) dangerous   h. a reaction to a question, letter or telephone call
9. ( ) feel   i. not costing a lot of money
10. ( ) window   j. say that you will not accept something

Part 2

1. ( ) hall   a. a building or large room
2. ( ) village   b. for that reason; because of that
3. ( ) corner   c. use money to pay for something
4. ( ) heavy   d. the Earth and everything on it
5. ( ) therefore   e. the place where two sides meet
6. ( ) think   f. having great weight
7. ( ) owner   g. a group of houses in the country
8. ( ) spend   h. have in one's mind
9. ( ) world   i. usual
10. ( ) normal   j. a person who has something

Unit 10

- **capital** [kǽpətl] 【名/形】(頭)→(羊の頭数を財産の量と考えたことから)資本
  - (頭が身体の先頭に位置していることから)柱頭, 頭文字の；大文字の
  - (頭が大事な部位であることから)主要な → 首都, 死に値する
  - ▶ capital の cap- は「頭」。captain(頭領)も同様。capital punishment は「死刑」。

- **detail** [díːtèɪl] 【名】詳細；細部【形】詳細な；細部の ▶ de- 分離・-tail 切る；細かく切断する
  - 《連語》in detail 詳細に

- **expense** [ɪkspéns] 【名】支出；必要な経費
  - ▶ ex- 外へ・-pense = -pend 吊るす → 天秤で量り分ける → 支払う
  - 【形】expensive 高価な ▶ -sive 形尾 【名】expenditure 出費 ▶ -ure 名尾

- **oil** [ɔ́ɪl] 【名】油, 石油 ▶ 種類を言うとき以外は無冠詞で用いる。複数形にもしない。
  - 【形】oily 油っこい ▶ -y 形尾。料理時は調理用油で油っこい場合。fatty(脂っこい)は具材の脂肪分で脂っこい場合。

- **secretary** [sékrətɛri] 【名】秘書 ▶ secret 秘密・-ary 名尾(〜に関する人)

- **sound** [sáʊnd] 【名】音 【動】[sound 形容詞] 〜のように聞こえる
  - 【形】健全な ▶ strong と同源。「(身体が強い)→ 身体が健全な → 精神が健全な」。

- **valley** [væli] 【名】(山と山の間で川が流れているような)低地；谷(間)

- **believe** [bəlíːv] 【動】〜を信じている, 〜を信用している
  - ▶ believe in her は「人格的に彼女を信用している」, believe her は「彼女の言葉を信じている」。
  - 【名】belief 信じること；信用 ▶ 複数形は beliefs。

- **escape** [ɪskéɪp] 【動】[escape (from / out of) 〜] 〜から逃れる【名】逃亡

- **notice** [nóʊtəs] 【動】〜に気がつく【名】注目 → 事前の通告 ▶ not- 知る(=know)・-ice 名尾
  - 《連語》notice board 掲示板

- **permit** [(動) pɚmít] [(名) pɚ́mɪt] 【動】〜を(公に)許可する [permit 人 to do] 人が〜することを許可する
  - ▶「許可/強制」系統の動詞は to 不定詞をとる。(例：allow/compel・force 人 to do)
  - 【名】許可証【名】permission 許可 ▶ -sion 名尾

- **remember** [rɪmémbɚ] 【動】〜を覚えている [remember to do] (未来のことを)忘れないでいる
  - [remember 〜 ing] 〜したことを覚えている
  - ▶ to 不定詞は動詞の時点よりも「未来」, 動名詞は「それ以外(主に過去)」のイメージ。

- **stay** [stéɪ] 【動】留まる → 滞在する ▶ stand と同源。「立っている → じっとしている」。

- **whistle** [wísl] 【動】口笛を吹く；(口)笛で合図する → 鳥がピーピーさえずる

- **certain** [sɚ́tn] 【形】確実な；確かな [名詞句の前で](話し手だけが知っている)或(あ)る
  - 《連語》be certain of 〜 〜を確信する (≒ be sure of 〜) ▶ 主語の確信
  - be certain to do きっと〜する (≒ be sure to do) ▶ 話し手の確信
  - 【副】certainly 確かに ▶ -ly 副尾
  - 【動】certify 〜を証明する ▶ cert- 確かに・-ify 動尾 【名】certificate 証明書

- **low** [lóʊ] 【形】低い ⟷ high 高い ▶ high は頂頭部分, tall は地面から頭頂部分まで焦点化。high は幅のある高さ, tall はひょろっとした高さ。

- **sweet** [swíːt] 【形】(砂糖などで)甘い ▶ sugar(砂糖)の形容詞形 sugary は「態度が甘ったるい」。

- **together** [təɡéðɚ] 【副】いっしょに ▶ ga- / ge- は「集合」のイメージを持つ。詳しくは gather の項参照。

- **nowhere** [nóʊwɛɚ] 【副】どこにも〜ない ▶ no 否定・where 場所

- **through** [θrúː] 【前】〜を通して ▶ 「貫通」のイメージ。「やり通す → 完了」の意味用法も持つ。
  - 《連語》look through 〜 〜に目を通す
  - go through 〜 〜を経験する, 〜を終える

EXERCISE A

各文の下線部分に入る適切な語を左ページの見出し語から選びましょう。

1. Do you _____ in Santa?
2. The couple don't live _____ anymore. They live in separate apartments.
3. The price of cooking _____ is increasing.
4. That bridge is so _____ that many trucks cannot go under it.
5. London is the _____ city of Britain.
6. The man couldn't _____ from the police. He was caught very quickly.
7. We'll _____ another night at the hotel.
8. We live in a beautiful _____ , which has a lovely river flowing through it.
9. Sugar tastes _____ .
10. Do you still _____ when my birthday is? I think you have forgotten.

EXERCISE B

左の語の定義として正しいものを右のコラムより選び、( )にアルファベットを書き入れましょう。

Part 1

1. ( ) nowhere   a. a city in which the main offices of government of a country are
2. ( ) secretary   b. the amount of money spent
3. ( ) expense   c. not in any place
4. ( ) valley   d. not having any doubt about something
5. ( ) capital   e. let something happen
6. ( ) permit   f. get away from a place where one is being held
7. ( ) remember   g. full of sugar; not bitter
8. ( ) sweet   h. become aware of something again after some time
9. ( ) escape   i. an area of low land between mountains
10. ( ) certain   j. a person who does office work

Part 2

1. ( ) stay   a. a black liquid used for making fuel
2. ( ) together   b. make musical notes by blowing air through one's lips
3. ( ) oil   c. become aware of something
4. ( ) detail   d. think that something is true
5. ( ) through   e. into one side and out the other side
6. ( ) sound   f. with each other
7. ( ) notice   g. a fact or information about something
8. ( ) believe   h. something that is heard
9. ( ) whistle   i. continue to be in the same place
10. ( ) low   j. less than the usual amount or number

Unit 11

- **association** [əsòusiéɪʃən]
  - 【名】連想, 交際, 連合；提携 ▶-tion 名尾
  - 【動】[associate A with B] AとBを結びつけて考える；AでBを連想する
    [associate with 〜] 〜と交際する，〜と連合する；〜と提携する
  - ▶ as-＝ad- 方向・soci- 結ぶ・-ate 動尾。すべて「結びつける」イメージ。
- **battle** [bætl] 【名】(局地的な)戦争, (二者間の)戦闘 ▶ war の項参照。
- **figure** [fígjɚ] 【名/動】姿；形
  - ─[容姿] → 人
  - ─[物体の量を形にしたもの] → 数字
  - ─[形となって見えてくる] → 〜を理解する
  - 《連語》figure out 完全に理解する ▶ out 外に出して → はっきりと
- **note** [nóut]
  - 【名】覚書 【動】〜を書き留める ▶ 語源は「知る(know)」。notebook の note に相当。
  - 【形】notable(人々に知られ得る)→ 注目すべき ▶-able 形尾(可能)
  - ▶ noble は「(人々に知られ得るほど生まれがよい)→ 高貴な」。
  - 【形】notorious(悪い事でよく知られている)→ 悪名高い ▶-ori 性質・-ous 形尾
- **remark** [rɪmáɚk]
  - 【名】所見；感想 【動】〜と(ぽつんと)述べる
  - ▶「再び(re-)印(mark)をつける → そこに注目する → 見た結果を述べる」イメージ。
  - 【形】remarkable 注目すべき ▶-able 形尾(可能)
- **stream** [stríːm] 【名】小川, 流れ ▶ brook(小川)より大きく, river より小さい川を指す。
- **trouble** [trʌ́bl]
  - 【名】心配ごと；困難
  - 《連語》be in trouble(with 〜)(〜で)困難な状態にある
- **uncle** [ʌ́ŋkəl] 【名】おじ ⟷ aunt おば
- **cause** [kɔ́ːz]
  - 【動】〜を引き起こす ▶ because は by the cause of(〜の原因によって)が一語化。
  - 【名】原因 ⟷ effect(原因の直接的な)結果, result(最終的な)結果
  - 《連語》cause and effect 因果関係
- **fail** [féɪl]
  - 【動】[fail in 〜] 〜に失敗する [fail to do] 〜し損なう
  - 《連語》never fail to do(決して〜し損なわない)→ 必ず〜する
  - 【名】failure 失敗 ▶-ure 名尾
- **march** [máɚtʃ] 【動】(兵士などが)行進する →(物事が)進行する
- **observe** [əbzɚ́v]
  - 【動】〜を観察する →(観察して)〜に気づく−[見守る] → 〜を固く守る
  - 【名】observation 観察 ▶-ation 名尾 【名】observatory 天文台 ▶-ory 名尾(場所)
  - 【名】observance 遵守 ▶-ance 名尾
- **print** [prínt] 【動】〜を印刷する 【名】印刷 [the prints](新聞・雑誌などの)出版物
- **seize** [síːz] 【動】〜を(いきなり)つかむ → 奪い取る−[物事を捉えて見る]
  - └ 〜を把握する
- **wave** [wéɪv] 【動】(手・旗などを)振る 【名】波
- **clear** [klíɚ]
  - 【形】透明な, 晴れた, 明らかな ▶「遮蔽(しゃへい)物がない」イメージ。
  - 【動】[clear A of B] AからBを除く ▶ of は「分離」の意味用法。
- **late** [léɪt] 【形】遅い ▶「時間的な遅い」：late ＜ later(より遅い) ＜ latest(最も遅い → 最近の),
  「順序的に遅い」：late ＜ latter(後半の) ＜ last(最後の)
- **popular** [pɑ́ːpjələɚ] 【形】人気のある；大衆的な, 一般民衆の ▶ popul- 人々・-ar 形尾(〜に関連した)
  - 【名】popularity 人気 ▶-ity 名尾 【名】population 人口 ▶-ation 名尾
- **further** [fɚ́ːðɚ] 【副】遠くに；さらに 【形】遠い；さらなる
  - ▶ farther は距離, further は程度・範囲。
- **otherwise** [ʌ́ðɚwaɪz]
  - 【副】別のやり方で, さもなければ
  - ▶ other 他の・-wise 〜のように

EXERCISE A

各文の下線部分に入る適切な語を左ページの見出し語から選びましょう。

1. The children _____ to their parents from the bus every day.
2. My _____ and aunt live in a beautiful house in the country.
3. Could you _____ an extra copy for me? I need one more copy for my class.
4. All the students seem to like him, so I think he is a very _____ teacher.
5. The army will _____ for 20 kilometers today.
6. I haven't studied much, so I think I will _____ the test!
7. There was some _____ between a couple of the students in the class.
8. Please don't call me _____ at night.
9. Could I _____ your class? I want to get some good ideas to use with my students.
10. I wrote a _____ for my husband and put it onto the kitchen table.

EXERCISE B

左の語の定義として正しいものを右のコラムより選び、（　）にアルファベットを書き入れましょう。

Part 1

1. ( ) wave   a. after the usual or expected time
2. ( ) print   b. make something happen or exist
3. ( ) stream   c. at a greater distance
4. ( ) march   d. move one's hand back and forth to greet someone
5. ( ) late   e. a group of people with the same interest or job
6. ( ) association   f. a small river
7. ( ) remark   g. the shape of a person or animal
8. ( ) figure   h. walk with regular steps as a group
9. ( ) cause   i. use a machine to make books or magazines
10. ( ) further   j. something that someone says or writes

Part 2

1. ( ) fail   a. the brother of one's father or mother
2. ( ) uncle   b. unusual or interesting
3. ( ) popular   c. take something quickly
4. ( ) notable   d. a fight or war
5. ( ) seize   e. in a different way or manner
6. ( ) trouble   f. easily understood or seen
7. ( ) otherwise   g. problem or difficulty
8. ( ) observe   h. not win; not pass
9. ( ) battle   i. watch something carefully
10. ( ) clear   j. liked or enjoyed by many people

Unit 12

- **account** [əkáʊnt] 【名】計算 → 利益 → [accounts] 勘定書 ▶ ac- = ad- 方向・count 数える [計算的思考] → 考慮 ▶ accountant で「(勘定する人)→会計士」。
  《連語》take ～ into account ～を考慮に入れる(≒ take ～ into consideration)

- **case** [kéɪs] 【名】箱；容器 − [限られた空間] → 場合 − [個々の場合] → 事例 − [法律] → 訴訟 《連語》in case S V もし S が V なら

- **difference** [dífərəns] 【名】異なり；違い ▶ -ence 名尾
  【形】different 異なった；種々の ▶ -ent 形尾
  【動】[differ from ～] ～と異なる

- **fellow** [félou] 【名】(通例形容詞を伴って)～な奴 ▶ 親しみ, 軽蔑の気持ちを込めて使われる。

- **level** [lévəl] 【名】水平 → (水平面の)高さ → 階(≒ story) − [高さの区切り] → レベル

- **nation** [néɪʃən] 【名】国家；国 − [その住人] → 国民 ▶ na- 生まれ・-tion 名尾。nature と同源。

- **population** [pɑ̀ːpjəléɪʃən] 【名】人口 ▶ -ation 名尾。人口の「多い／少ない」は large/small で表す。
  【形】popular 人気のある；大衆的な, 一般民衆の
  ▶ popul- 人々(= people)・-ar 形尾(～に関する)

- **rank** [ræŋk] 【名】列；並び → (チェス盤の)横すじ；横列 → 階級

- **science** [sáɪəns] 【名】科学 ▶ sci- 知る・-ence 名尾。conscious(意識がある)の sci- と同源。
  【形】scientific 科学の ▶ -ic 形尾 【名】scientist 科学者 ▶ -ist 名尾(専門家)

- **afford** [əfɔ́ːrd] 【動】[cannot afford to do] ～する余裕がない
  【形】affordable ～する余裕がある；何とか買えそうな ▶ -able 形尾(可能)

- **belong** [bɪlɔ́ːŋ] 【動】[belong to ～] ～に属している；～の持ち物である
  【名】belongings 持ち物 ▶ -ing 名尾(集合)

- **guard** [gɑ́ːrd] 【動】～を見張る；監視する → ～を(危害から)保護する → (秘密を)守る
  【名】監視, 保護 → 監視人, 護衛者；守衛「ガードマン」is security guard。

- **mention** [ménʃən] 【動】～に言及する(≒ refer to) 【名】言及(≒ reference)
  《連語》[英] Don't mention it. どういたしまして。(≒ [米] You are welcome.)
  not to mention ～ ～は言うまでもなく

- **provide** [prəváɪd] 【動】[provide 人 with 物](必要なものを講じて)人に物を供給する
  (≒ provide 物 for 人) ▶ pro- 前もって・-vide 見る。vision の vis- と同源。
  【形】provident 将来に備える ▶ -ent 形尾 【名】providence 先見の明 ▶ -ence 名尾
  【名】provision (必需品の)供給 [provisions] 食料 ▶ -sion 名尾

- **recognize** [rékəgnaɪz] 【動】(以前の経験を振り返って誤りなく実体を)認識する, ～を承認する
  ▶ re- 元の場所へ → 返って・-cog 知る・-ize 動尾
  【形】recognizable 認識できる, 承認できる ▶ -able(可能)
  【名】recognition 認識, 承認 ▶ -tion 名尾

- **share** [ʃéər] 【動】[share (A) with B] (A を) B と共有する；分け合う

- **complete** [kəmplíːt] 【形】完全な 【動】～を完全なものにする；完成させる ▶ com- 共に・-plete 満たす
  【名】complement 完全にするもの − [補って完全文にする] → 補語 ▶ -ment 名尾

- **human** [hjúːmən] 【形】人間の 【名】人間 ▶ hum- 大地。泥からアダムが創造された聖書の記載による。
  【形】humane 人間らしい；人情味のある ▶ 発音は「ヒューメイン」。

- **enough** [ɪnʌ́f] 【副】必要なだけ 【形】必要なだけの；必要に足る
  《連語》形容詞 + enough to do ～するに足るほどの…である

- **pretty** [príti] 【副】かなり 【形】(ずる賢い) − [利口で巧みな；好ましい] → 可愛らしい − [とてもよい；程度が高い] → かなりの

EXERCISE A

各文の下線部分に入る適切な語を左ページの見出し語から選びましょう。

1. I prefer math class to _____ class.
2. My cousin looked so different. I could hardly _____ him!
3. Do you _____ to the hiking group?
4. It was the lawyer's most difficult _____ .
5. Have you eaten _____ ? There is some more left.
6. The country's _____ is falling, even though the people are living longer and longer.
7. The weather is _____ bad today.
8. Let's _____ our food with the birds. They are looking very hungry.
9. I can't _____ to buy this watch. It's too expensive.
10. There was a large _____ of opinion among the group.

EXERCISE B

左の語の定義として正しいものを右のコラムより選び、（　）にアルファベットを書き入れましょう。

Part 1

1. (　) provide   a. a position in a society or group
2. (　) account   b. being cheap enough for most people to buy or pay for
3. (　) fellow   c. have or use with others
4. (　) share   d. a member of a group of people who have the same interests
5. (　) rank   e. not of the same kind
6. (　) guard   f. give someone something that they need
7. (　) different   g. watch someone so that they do not escape
8. (　) nation   h. an area of land controlled by its own government
9. (　) affordable   i. in the amount needed
10. (　) enough   j. a record of money received or spent

Part 2

1. (　) complete   a. knowledge about or study of the natural world
2. (　) population   b. a person
3. (　) level   c. know and remember
4. (　) science   d. a specific height
5. (　) case   e. the number of people living in an area
6. (　) recognize   f. a situation that is an example of something
7. (　) belong   g. be accepted as part of a group
8. (　) pretty   h. finish making or doing something
9. (　) human   i. speak about something with few details
10. (　) mention   j. not too much but not too little; to some degree

Unit 13

- **beauty** [bjúːti]
  - 【名】美しさ；美 ▶ -y 名尾（抽象名詞を作る役割）
  - 【形】beautiful 美しい ▶ -ful 形尾
- **coast** [kóʊst]
  - 【名】海岸；沿岸
  - 【形】coastal 海岸の；沿岸の ▶ -al 形尾
- **desire** [dɪzáɪɚ]
  - 【名】欲求【動】〜を強く望む ▶ de- 分離・-sire 星。幸運の守護星への祈願に由来。
  - 【形】desirable 望ましい ▶ -able 形尾（可能）
- **experience** [ɪkspíriəns]
  - 【名】経験【動】〜を経験する
  - ▶ undergo（経験する）はマイナスイメージの経験。
- **fashion** [fǽʃən]
  - 【名】流行；一時的な風習
  - 【形】fashionable 流行の ▶ -able 形尾（可能）
- **inch** [íntʃ]
  - 【名】インチ
  - ▶ 長さの単位。1 feet（＝ 3 分の 1 yard；30.48 cm）の 12 分の 1；2.54 cm。
- **order** [óɚdɚ]
  - 【名／動】列 –[順序だった状態] → 整頓 –[順序の維持] → 秩序 –[秩序を求める指示] → 〜を命令（する）→ 〜を注文（して取り寄せる）
- **race** [réɪs]
  - 【名】競争, 人種 ▶ それぞれは別語源。
- **steel** [stíːl]
  - 【名】鋼鉄；はがね
- **worth** [wɚ́θ]
  - 【名】（金額相当量の）価値 →（精神的・道徳的な）価値
  - 【前】[be worth doing] 〜する価値がある
  - 《連語》be worth while doing ／ to do
    - 〜するのに時間／労力をかける価値がある
  - 【形】worthy 価値のある [be worthy of 〜] 〜するに値する ▶ -y 形尾
  - 【形】worthwhile（時間／労力をかける）価値がある ▶ while 時間
- **produce**
  - 【動】〜を生産する；生み出す【名】農産物；生産高 ▶ pro- 前・-duce 引き出す
  - [（動）prədúːs]
  - [（名）próʊduːs]
  - 【形】productive 生産力のある ▶ -tive 形尾
  - 【名】product 産物【名】production 生産 ▶ -tion 名尾
- **break** [bréɪk]
  - 【動】〜を壊す, 〜を破る, 〜を割る
  - ▶「力を加えて不連続にする」イメージ。break an electronic wire「電線が切れる」。
  - 《連語》break one's ／ a promise 約束を破る ⟷ keep one's ／ a promise
    - break out（発疹などが）吹き出す,（戦争などが）勃発する
  - ▶「溜まっていたエネルギーが外に出て（out）表面を破る（break）」イメージ。
    - break the ice 沈黙を破る ▶ 原義は「覆っていた氷を破って川が流れ出す」。
- **carry** [kǽri]
  - 【動】〜を持って運ぶ, 〜を輸送する
  - 《連語》carry out 〜を運び出す –[計画が形となって現れ出る] →〜を実行する
- **contain** [kəntéɪn]
  - 【動】〜を含む ▶ con- 共に・-tain 保つ
  - 【名】container 容器 ▶ -er 名尾（〜するもの）
- **gain** [géɪn]
  - 【動】〜を得る –[時を稼ぐ] → 時計が進む【名】利益
- **listen** [lísn]
  - 【動】[listen to 〜] 〜に耳を傾ける ▶ hear との違いについては hear の項参照。
- **possess** [pəzés]
  - 【動】（才能, 富；財産を）持つ [be possessed of 〜] 〜を所有する
  - 【名】possession 所有；所有物 ▶ -sion 名尾
- **try** [tráɪ]
  - 【動】[try to do] 〜しようと試みる [try 〜 ing] 試しに〜してみる
  - 《連語》try on 〜を（服などを）試しに着てみる ▶ on は身体との「接触」のイメージ。
- **familiar** [fəmíljɚ]
  - 【形】よく知られた ▶ family 家族・-ar 形尾（〜のような）⟷ unfamiliar
  - 《連語》be familiar with 〜 〜と親しい　be familiar to 〜 〜によく知られている
- **strange** [stréɪndʒ]
  - 【形】見慣れない；見知らぬ → 奇妙な ▶ extra-（外の；外部の）と同源。

EXERCISE A

各文の下線部分に入る適切な語を左ページの見出し語から選びましょう。

1. Would you like to _____ to my new music?
2. The bridge is made of _____ .
3. Joe is an _____ taller than Jim.
4. I would like to get some work _____ while I am a university student.
5. We all enjoyed the swimming _____ . I finished first!
6. Japanese and American companies _____ a lot of the world's cars.
7. I love the natural _____ of the mountains. They look great.
8. We traveled along the _____ .
9. Please _____ the chocolate into two pieces.
10. She's an Italian _____ designer.

EXERCISE B

左の語の定義として正しいものを右のコラムより選び、( )にアルファベットを書き入れましょう。

Part 1

1. ( ) beautiful   a. cause to separate into parts
2. ( ) race   b. want or wish for something
3. ( ) fashion   c. good enough; important enough
4. ( ) listen   d. a popular way of dressing
5. ( ) break   e. often seen or heard
6. ( ) worthwhile   f. being physically pleasing
7. ( ) familiar   g. get; increase
8. ( ) possess   h. a contest between people or animals
9. ( ) desire   i. pay attention in order to hear what someone is saying
10. ( ) gain   j. have; own

Part 2

1. ( ) try   a. different from what is usual or normal
2. ( ) steel   b. a unit that is 1/12 of a foot
3. ( ) experience   c. keep within something
4. ( ) carry   d. the steps in which things are put together
5. ( ) strange   e. move while holding something
6. ( ) coast   f. make an effort to do something
7. ( ) contain   g. the land along the sea or ocean
8. ( ) order   h. something made to be used or sold
9. ( ) product   i. a strong hard metal
10. ( ) inch   j. the skill or knowledge one gets by doing something

Unit 14

- **bridge** [bríd3] 【名】橋 ▶ build bridges で「橋渡しを作る → 調停する」。
- **crowd** [kráʊd] 【名】群衆, 観衆；聴衆 【動】〜に群がる
  【形】crowded 混雑した ▶ -ed 形尾（〜された；〜した）
- **example** [ɪgzǽmpl] 【名】例 ▶ instance（例）は実証例, example は代表例；典型例。
  《連語》for example 例えば（≒ for instance）
- **field** [fíːld] 【名】(広々とした)野原, 畑, 牧草地 −［一面の広がり］→（研究などの）分野
- **garden** [gάɚdn] 【名】(花, 木, 野菜などが植えてある)庭；庭園
- **market** [mάɚkət] 【名】市場, 市場取引 −［個別に特定］→ 食料品店
  【形】marketing 市場活動 ▶ -ing 名尾（〜すること）
- **operation** [ɑ:pəréɪʃən] 【名】作動, 手術, 作戦 ▶ -tion 名尾
  【動】operate 作動する →（効果的に）作用する；影響を与える
  → 〜を操作する；運転する, 作戦行動をとる −［メスを操作する］→ 手術をする
  【名】operator 電話交換手 ▶ -or = -er 名尾（〜する人）
- **secret** [síːkrət] 【名】秘密；秘訣（ひけつ）【形】秘密の
  【形】secretary ▶ -ary 名尾（〜に関する人）
- **system** [sístəm] 【名】制度, 組織, 体系 ▶ sy- = syn- 共に・-stem 配置する。「結合させる」イメージ。
  【形】systematic 組織的な, 体系的な ▶ -ic 形尾
- **allow** [əláʊ] 【動】〜を(個人的に)許す ［allow 人 to do］人に〜させておく
  ▶「許可／強制」系統の動詞は to 不定詞をとる。(例：permit/compel・force 人 to do)
  【名】allowance(許可されたもの；割当て量)→ 手当て；小遣い ▶ -ance 名尾
- **declare** [dɪkléɚ] 【動】〜を宣言する → 〜を申告する ▶ de- 分離・-clare 明らかにする（= clear）
  【名】declaration 宣言, 申告 ▶ -ation 名尾
- **forget** [fɚgét] 【動】〜を忘れる ［forget to do］〜することを忘れる
  ［forget 〜ing］〜したことを忘れる ▶ remember の項参照。
  【形】forgetful 忘れやすい ▶ -ful 形尾(満ちている)
- **pass** [pǽs] 【動】通り過ぎる, (時が)経つ, 合格する, 〜を手渡す ▶「通過する」イメージ。
  【名】passage 通過；通路, 経過, (文・楽曲の)一節 ▶ -age 名尾(行為, 状態)
- **regard** [rɪgάɚd] 【動／名】[regard A as B] A を B として見なす −［見るところ］→ 観点
  ▶ re- 再び・-gard 見守る。以下 regardless の less は形尾で「〜がない」イメージ。
  《連語》in this regard この点 with regard to 〜 〜について
  【形】[regardless of 〜]（〜を注視しない → 関係なく）→ 〜にもかかわらず
- **serve** [sɚ́ːv] 【動】〜に仕える → 〜に食事を出す
  → [serve 人 with 〜] 人に必要物を供給する
- **travel** [trǽvəl] 【動】旅行する →（〜へ）行く →（光・音・知らせなどが）伝わる
  ▶ travail(骨折り)と同源で原義は「苦労して旅する」。trip は「短い旅行」, tour は「周遊」。
  journey は「目的地までにかかる旅の時間と道のり」に重点。
- **close** [(形) klóʊs] [(動) klóʊz] 【形／動】[close to 〜] 〜にごく近い −［二者間の接近］→ 〜を閉ざす；閉じる
- **final** [fáɪnl] 【形】最後の, 決定的な, 決勝の ▶ finish(〜を終える；終わる)と同源。
- **high** [háɪ] 【形】(空間的な位置が上方にあって)高い →（価格・地位・含有率が)高い
  ▶ tall との違いについては low の項参照。
- **native** [néɪtɪv] 【形】出生地の, その土地に生まれた
  ▶ nature(自然)と同源。「生まれながら」のイメージ。native speakers は「母語話者」。

EXERCISE A

各文の下線部分に入る適切な語を左ページの見出し語から選びましょう。

1. John is a _____ English speaker.
2. There's a large _____ of people outside.
3. I can't buy it. The price is too _____ .
4. The government built a _____ across the river.
5. Many people _____ by car during the holiday season.
6. Don't tell anyone. It's a _____ .
7. The country's transportation _____ is very old.
8. The time will _____ quickly.
9. I bought the food at the fish _____ .
10. The restaurant will _____ dinner soon. Please come back quickly.

EXERCISE B

左の語の定義として正しいものを右のコラムより選び、（ ）にアルファベットを書き入れましょう。

Part 1

1. ( ) example   a. an area around a house where plants grow
2. ( ) high   b. something used for going over a river or another road
3. ( ) declare   c. a way of doing something that follows a set of rules
4. ( ) garden   d. say or state in a public way
5. ( ) serve   e. a specific thing used to understand general statement
6. ( ) operate   f. work; be in action
7. ( ) system   g. give someone a meal in a restaurant
8. ( ) close   h. near in space; not far away
9. ( ) pass   i. greater than usual in amount or number
10. ( ) bridge   j. move past someone or something

Part 2

1. ( ) native   a. happening or coming at the end
2. ( ) marketing   b. permit; take something as acceptable
3. ( ) field   c. an open area of land without trees or building
4. ( ) final   d. a piece of information that is hidden from other people
5. ( ) travel   e. go on a trip
6. ( ) crowd   f. not being able to remember things easily
7. ( ) secret   g. describing the place where one was born
8. ( ) forgetful   h. a large group of people in one place
9. ( ) allow   i. the activities used to sell a company's products to people
10. ( ) regard   j. think of someone or something in a certain way

Unit 15

- ☐ **branch** [bræntʃ] 【名】枝, 支流, (鉄道の)支線, 支部 ⟷ trunk 胴体, 幹, 本流, 本線
  ▶ branch の語源は「手足」。「胴体に付着する手足の姿・形」のイメージ。「支部」の branch の対義語は headquarters/head office (本部)。head は「頭＝指示を出す所」。

- ☐ **clock** [klá:k] 【名】置き時計; 掛け時計
  ▶ 原義は「ベル(bell)」。鐘の音で時間を判断した風習による。

- ☐ **earth** [ə́ːθ] 【名】大地; 地面 → [the earth] 地球 ▶ globe は「(球体を強調した)地球」。
  《連語》(why, where など)疑問詞 + on earth/in the world ～? 一体全体～?

- ☐ **history** [hístəri] 【名】歴史 ▶ hi- の音が弱くて消失した形が story。story の項参照。

- ☐ **manner** [mǽnɚ] 【名】(手の) → 方法 − [情況に応じた方法] → 態度 [manners] 作法
  ▶ manual と同源。複数形で意味が変わるもの: air(空気) − airs(気取り), authority(権力) − authorities(当局), force(力) − forces(軍隊), sand(砂) − sands(砂漠), arm(腕) − arms(武器), custom(慣習) − customs(関税; 税関), 等。

- ☐ **quarter** [kwɔ́ɚtɚ] 【名】4分の1 ▶ a quarter of an hour は「15分」, a quarter of a century は「25年」。

- ☐ **scale** [skéɪl] 【名】目盛り; 物差し − [計られた大きさ] → 規模
  ▶ scale(天秤), scale(うろこ)は別語源。on a large scale で「大規模に」。

- ☐ **thought** [θɔ́ːt] 【名】考えること; 思考 → 考え ▶ idea よりも理性的。動詞形は think の項参照。

- ☐ **compare** [kəmpéɚ] 【動】[compare (A) with B] (Aと)Bとを比較する
  [compare (A) to B] (Aを)Bにたとえる ▶ com- 共に・-pare 並べる (= pair)
  【形】comparative 比較的 ▶ -tive 形尾 【形】comparable 類似の ▶ -able 形尾(可能)
  【名】comparison 比較, 類似 ▶ in comparison with ～で「～と比較すると」。

- ☐ **decide** [dɪsáɪd] 【動】[decide to do] ～することを決心する; 決意する ▶ de- 分離・-cide 切る
  【名】decision 決心; 決意 ▶ -sion 名尾

- ☐ **employ** [ɪmplɔ́ɪ] 【動】～を雇い入れる
  ▶ em- = in- 中・-ploy 布。「布で覆う → 空間内に入れる」イメージ。
  ⟷ fire ～を解雇する ▶「火をつけて発射する → 空間外へ放出する」イメージ。
  【名】employer 雇用主
  ▶ -er 名尾(～する人) ⟷ employee 従業員 ▶ -ee 名尾(～される人)

- ☐ **mean** [míːn] 【動】～を意味する [mean to do] ～するつもりである
  【形】意地悪な 【名】[means] 手段, 資産 ▶【動】,【形】,【名】は各々別語源。
  《連語》by means of ～ ～によって   by all means 是非とも
  　　　by no means 決して～ない

- ☐ **measure** [méʒɚ] 【動】～を測る 【名】尺度; 寸法 [take measures] 対策をとる

- ☐ **raise** [réɪz] 【動】～を起こす →(軽いものを必要な位置まで)上げる ▶ 自動詞形は rise。

- ☐ **throw** [θróʊ] 【動】～を投げる
  《連語》throw up ～を吐く ▶「食物が胃から喉へ上がって口から投げ出す」。

- ☐ **watch** [wɑ́ːtʃ] 【動】(動いているものを)見続ける → ～を見張る 【名】腕時計; 懐中時計
  ▶ look は「動かないものに視線を向ける」。

- ☐ **difficult** [dífɪkəlt] 【形】難しい ▶ have difficulty (in) doing で「～するのが困難である」。
  【名】difficulty 困難 ▶ -y 名尾

- ☐ **modern** [mɑ́ːdɚn] 【形】現代の, 現代的な (≒ up-to-date)

- ☐ **ordinary** [ɔ́ɚdəneri] 【形】通常の → ありふれた; 平凡な
  ▶ ordin- 規則正しい順序 (= order)・-ary 形尾

- ☐ **political** [pəlítɪkəl] 【形】政治の, 政治学の ▶ polit- 政治・-ical 形尾。政治家は statesman。
  【名】politics 政治学 ▶ -ics 学問 【名】politician 政治屋 ▶ -ian 名尾(専門家)

EXERCISE A

各文の下線部分に入る適切な語を左ページの見出し語から選びましょう。

1. The two companies _____ over 400 people altogether.
2. Please hang the _____ on the wall.
3. It's very _____ to say what will happen in the future.
4. We all live on the _____ .
5. I belong to a _____ party.
6. Japan has a very long _____ .
7. We have to _____ when we have the next meeting.
8. _____ the ball to your friend.
9. She has a very professional _____ . I think she will be a great business woman.
10. Please let me _____ a horror movie tonight!

EXERCISE B

左の語の定義として正しいものを右のコラムより選び、（　）にアルファベットを書き入れましょう。

Part 1

1. ( ) ordinary   a. not easy; needing much skill and effort
2. ( ) difficult   b. someone who pays people to work for them
3. ( ) measure   c. a device for weighing things
4. ( ) throw   d. the way something is done or happens
5. ( ) scale   e. find out the size, length or amount of something
6. ( ) earth   f. land; the planet humans live on
7. ( ) manner   g. a local office of a shop or company
8. ( ) branch   h. cause to move out of your hand quickly to a far away place
9. ( ) employer   i. normal; usual
10. ( ) watch   j. look at something or someone for an amount of time

Part 2

1. ( ) quarter   a. relating to government
2. ( ) political   b. a device that shows what time it is
3. ( ) thought   c. not kind
4. ( ) compare   d. an idea, plan or opinion
5. ( ) decision   e. one of four equal parts
6. ( ) modern   f. the study of past events
7. ( ) mean   g. relating to the present time
8. ( ) raise   h. lift or move to a higher position
9. ( ) clock   i. look at two things to determine what is similar or different about them
10. ( ) history   j. a choice that someone makes about something

Unit 16

- ☐ **bill** [bíl] 【名】請求書；勘定, 紙幣 ⟷ receipt レシート
  ▶ 語源は「押印した文書」。食堂などの勘定書は [米] check。
- ☐ **blood** [blʌ́d] 【名】血液 ▶「血管」は blood vessel。
  【動】bleed 出血する
- ☐ **degree** [dɪgríː] 【名】(階段) → 程度；(温度などの) 度 → 等級；階級 – [最終段階] → 学位
  ▶ de- 下 ・-gree 一歩 (grade)。by degrees で「次第に」。この by は「差」の意味用法。
- ☐ **peace** [píːs] 【名】平和 → 平穏；平静
  【形】peaceful 平和な；穏やかな ▶ -ful 形尾 (満ちている)
- ☐ **season** [síːzn] 【名】季節 【動】～に風味を添える；～を味付けする ▶ 原義は「種をまく (季節)」。
  【名】seasoning 調味料 ▶ -ing 名尾 (～すること；～するもの)
- ☐ **substance** [sʌ́bstəns] 【名】(物事の根底に存在するモノ) → 本質；実体 – [外観に対する実体]
  → 内容 – [他のものと区別される内容構成物] → 物質
  ▶ sub- 下 → 根底 ・-st 立つ (= stand) – [目の前に立つ] → 存在する ・-ance 名尾
  【形】substantial 本質的な；重要な – [中身の量が焦点化] → かなりの ▶ -ial 形尾
- ☐ **type** [táɪp] 【名】型；種類 – [活版印刷の文字の型] → 活字 【動】(タイプで文字を) 打つ
  【形】typical 典型的な ▶ -ical 形尾
- ☐ **command** [kəmǽnd] 【動/名】～を命ずる；命令 – [支配して自由に扱う]
  – [人・隊を自由に扱う] → ～を意のままに指揮する
  – [言葉を自由に扱う] → 言葉を自由に使いこなす；使いこなす能力
  – [景色を自由に扱う] → ～を見渡す；見渡し
  ▶ con- 完全に ・-mand 委ねる。「別の人に委ねる → それほど自由に扱える」イメージ。
  mandate (委託する, 命令する) と同源。command a fine view は「見晴らしがよい」。
- ☐ **connect** [kənékt] 【動】[connect A to B] A を B につなげる ▶ con- 共に ・-nect 結ぶ
  [connect A with B] A と B とを関係づける
  【名】connection 接続, 関係；コネ ▶ -tion 名尾
- ☐ **enjoy** [ɪndʒɔ́ɪ] 【動】～を楽しむ – [喜んで受け入れ, 自分のものにする] → ～を享受する
  《連語》enjoy oneself 愉快に過ごす
- ☐ **lift** [líft] 【動】(重いものを) 持ち上げる；～を上げる ▶ raise の項参照。【名】リフト
- ☐ **prepare** [prɪpéɚ] 【動】[prepare for～] ～に備える；準備する ▶ pre- 前もって ・-pare 揃える
  【形】preparatory 予備の；準備の ▶ -ory 形尾。preparatory school で「予備校」。
  【名】preparation 準備 ▶ -ation 名尾。in preparation for ～で「～に備えて」。
- ☐ **rush** [rʌ́ʃ] 【動】急いでいく；突進する → 殺到する 【名】突進, 殺到
- ☐ **separate**
  [(動) sépərèɪt] 【動】～を引き離す；分ける
  [(形) sépərət] 【形】[separate from ～] ～と離れた；別個の
  【名】separation 分離；隔たり ▶ -ation 名尾
- ☐ **visit** [vízɪt] 【動】～を訪問する；見舞う (≒ pay a visit to) 【名】訪問；見舞い ▶ vis- 見る
- ☐ **warm** [wɔ́ɚm] 【形】暖かい → 温かい 【動】～をあたためる ▶ 肌の暖かみが心の温かみに変化。
- ☐ **actual** [ǽktʃəwəl] 【形】実際の ▶ act (行動；活動) ・-al 形尾 (性質) ▶ 詳しくは act の項参照。
- ☐ **bright** [bráɪt] 【形】(光を出して；反射して) 輝いている → 明るい；鮮明な
  → 輝かしい；有望な ▶ brilliant の方が明るさは強い。
- ☐ **poor** [púɚ] 【形】貧しい – [才能に乏しい] → 下手な；不得意な ▶ poverty の項参照。
- ☐ **simple** [símpl] 【形】単純な；簡単な → 簡素な → (飾り気がなく) 無邪気な
  【動】simplify ～を単純化する；簡単にする ▶ -ify 動尾

EXERCISE A

各文の下線部分に入る適切な語を左ページの見出し語から選びましょう。

1. This month's gas _____ is so high!
2. I _____ reading books. It's what I like to do most in my free time.
3. Can you _____ to the Internet with your new computer yet?
4. Summer is my favorite _____ .
5. Because of the deep cut, the man lost a lot of _____ .
6. Everyone wants _____ on earth!
7. Don't _____ ! Please do it more slowly. There is plenty of time.
8. I try to pay a _____ to the city's history museum once a year.
9. It's cold today, but the sun is very _____ . I'll need to put my sunglasses on.
10. No, he's not rich. He's very _____ .

EXERCISE B

左の語の定義として正しいものを右のコラムより選び、（ ）にアルファベットを書き入れましょう。

Part 1

1. ( ) peace   a. large in amount, size or number
2. ( ) actual   b. a state in which there is no war or fighting
3. ( ) visit   c. move to a higher position
4. ( ) poor   d. join together
5. ( ) lift   e. real; existing in fact
6. ( ) rush   f. tell someone to do something
7. ( ) bill   g. a document stating how much money must be paid
8. ( ) command   h. go somewhere and spend time there
9. ( ) connect   i. hurry
10. ( ) substantial   j. having little money

Part 2

1. ( ) simple   a. something added to make food taste better
2. ( ) warm   b. make ready
3. ( ) type   c. not joined or connected
4. ( ) separate   d. a certain kind of group of things or people
5. ( ) enjoy   e. the red liquid that flows through the human body
6. ( ) bright   f. take pleasure in something
7. ( ) blood   g. producing a lot of light
8. ( ) seasoning   h. neither hot nor cool or cold
9. ( ) degree   i. amount or level that can be measured
10. ( ) prepare   j. not hard to understand or do

Unit 17

- **breadth** [brétθ]
  - 【名】幅；横幅 ▶-th 名尾(抽象名詞) ⟷ length 長さ；縦, depth 深さ；奥行き
  - 【形】broad(通常よりも)広い；広々とした ▶ wide は「幅が広い」。
- **faith** [féɪθ]
  - 【名】信頼
  - 【形】faithful 信頼のある；忠実な ▶-ful 形尾
- **heaven** [hévən]
  - 【名】天国(のような所) ⟷ hell 地獄(のような所) [the heavens] 天；空
- **minute**
  - [(名)mínət]
  - [(形)maɪnjúːt]
  - 【名】分, 瞬間 【形】詳細な
  - ▶ minor(小さい方の)と同源で「より小さいもの」。hour(時間)を「より小さく」したものが minute, その「二番目」に小さいものが second(秒)。【形】は発音注意。
- **power** [páwɚ]
  - 【名】力；能力
  - ▶「力」の総称。「体力, 知力, 精神力, 権力；勢力」いずれにも使用可。
  - 【形】powerful 強い；強力な, 強大な：勢力のある ▶-ful 形尾(満ちている)
- **sight** [sáɪt]
  - 【名】見ること, 視力；視界, 光景；眺め [the sights] 名所 ▶ see の名詞形。
  - 《連語》come into sight / view 視界に入る ⟷ go out of sight / view
- **society** [səsáɪəti]
  - 【名】社会 ▶ socie- 続く → つながり；仲間・-ty 名尾。community は「地域社会」。
  - 【形】sociable 社交的な ▶-able 形尾(可能)
- **water** [wɑ́ːtɚ]
  - 【名】水 【動】(花などに)水をやる
- **week** [wíːk]
  - 【名】週 ▶ 米では日曜日から土曜日, 英では月曜日から日曜日までを1週と考える。
  - 【副】weekdays 平日に ⟷ weekends 週末に
- **appear** [əpíɚ]
  - 【動】姿を現す [appear to 状態動詞 / (to be) C](外見が)～のように見える
  - ▶ ap-＝ad- 方向・-pear 現れる。⟷ disappear 姿を消す ▶ dis- 逆
  - 【形】apparent(目に見える所から判断して)明らかな, 外見だけの ▶-ent 形尾
  - 【名】appearance 外見 ▶-ance 名尾
- **blow** [blóʊ]
  - 【動】(風が)吹く ┬ ～を吹き動かす → ～を吹き飛ばす
  - └ (風の代わりに)息を吹きかける →(息で)楽器を演奏する
  - 《連語》blow up ～を爆破する　blow off ～を吹き飛ばす
- **continue**
  - [kəntínju]
  - 【動】～を持続する；続ける
  - ▶ con- 共に → 連ねて・-tinue＝-tin/-tain 張る → 広げる
  - 【形】continuous(中断なく)続いている ▶-ous 形尾
  - 【形】continual(中断を挟みながらも)続いている ▶-al 形尾
- **dare** [déɚ]
  - 【動】[dare to do] あえて／思い切って～する
  - ▶ dare は「勇気のある」イメージ。
  - 【助動】[How dare ～?] あつかましくも／よくも～できるね？
- **involve** [ɪnvɑ́ːlv]
  - 【動】～を巻き込む [be involved in ～] ～に関係する ▶ in- 中・-volve 回転する
- **receive** [rɪsíːv]
  - 【動】～を受け取る ▶ re- 元の場所へ・-ceive つかむ。accept の項参照。
  - 【名】receipt レシート
- **shine** [ʃáɪn]
  - 【動】輝く‒[輝かせる] → ～を磨く
  - ▶「輝く」では shine＜shone＜shone。「～を磨く」では shine＜shined＜shined。
- **unite** [jʊnáɪt]
  - 【動】～を団結させる ▶ uni- 1つの；一体の
  - ▶ the United Nations で「国際連合」, the United States of America で「アメリカ合衆国」。
  - 【名】unity 統一, 統一性；統一体 ▶-ity 名尾
  - 【動】unify ～を一つにする；結合させる ▶-fy 動尾
- **due** [d(j)úː]
  - 【形】当然支払われるべき [due to ～] ～のために ▶「返済義務」のイメージ。
- **perfect** [pɚ́fɪkt]
  - 【形】完全な；まったくの ▶ per- 貫通‒[やり通す] → 完全に・-fect 作る(＝make)
- **sharp** [ʃɑ́ɚp]
  - 【形】鋭い → 鋭敏な；頭の鋭い ⟷ dull 切れ味の鈍い → 頭が鈍い

EXERCISE A

各文の下線部分に入る適切な語を左ページの見出し語から選びましょう。

1. Would you like a glass of _____ ?
2. A _____ lasts 60 seconds.
3. Let's _____ walking until we reach the top of the hill.
4. I'd like to go to _____ . However, I think I'm more likely to go to hell.
5. A pin is very _____ .
6. A lot of schools were closed _____ to the bad weather.
7. Could we meet next _____ ?
8. You should _____ your shoes before you go to an interview.
9. Don't _____ out the candle yet.
10. I haven't got much _____ in this medicine. It doesn't seem to work well.

EXERCISE B

左の語の定義として正しいものを右のコラムより選び、( )にアルファベットを書き入れましょう。

Part 1

1. ( ) blow   a. get or be given something
2. ( ) unite   b. any day except Saturday and Sunday
3. ( ) sociable   c. create moving air with your mouth
4. ( ) perfect   d. having no mistakes
5. ( ) weekday   e. liking to be with people
6. ( ) heaven   f. not be too afraid to do something
7. ( ) dare   g. the place where God lives
8. ( ) powerful   h. showing true and continuing support for someone
9. ( ) receive   i. having the ability to control things or people
10. ( ) faithful   j. join together to do something

Part 2

1. ( ) minute   a. have a bright appearance
2. ( ) sharp   b. sudden and quick; able to cut
3. ( ) due   c. the space from one side to the other of something
4. ( ) sight   d. the act of seeing something
5. ( ) shine   e. do something without stopping
6. ( ) involve   f. the clear liquid that falls from the clouds
7. ( ) water   g. very small
8. ( ) apparent   h. easy to see or understand
9. ( ) breadth   i. have or include as a part of something
10. ( ) continue   j. needed or expected to pay for something

Unit 18

- **country** [kʌ́ntri] 【名】(広々として未開発の)土地 → 地域；いなか → (地理的な意味での)国
- **center** [séntɚ] 【名/動】中央；中心 ┌ [最も重要な位置] → (話題などの)中心
  └ [中心に集める] → 集中する
  【形】central 中央の；中心の ▶ -al 形尾
- **experiment** [ɪkspérəmənt] 【名】実験 ▶ ex- 強意・-peri 試みる (= try)・-ment 名尾(行為)
  【形】experimental 実験的な ▶ -al 形尾
- **occasion** [əkéɪʒən] 【名】機会；好機 ▶ oc- = ad- 方向・-ca 倒れる・-sion 名尾。「好機到来」のイメージ。
  《連語》on occasion 時々 ▶ 忘れかけた頃、たまに起きる場合。頻度は (every) now and then, sometimes > on occasion > seldom, rarely。
  【形】occasional 時々の ▶ -al 形尾 【副】occasionally 時々 ▶ -ly 副尾
- **program** [próʊgræm] 【名】プログラム；予定(表), 番組
  ▶ pro- 前に → 公に・-gram 書いたもの
- **shadow** [ʃǽdoʊ] 【名】(人・物など輪郭が明確な)影 ▶ shade は「(輪郭が不明瞭な)日陰；物陰」。
- **silence** [sáɪləns] 【名】無言；沈黙 → 静けさ ▶ -ence 名尾
  【形】silent 無言の；沈黙した, 静かな ▶ -ent 形尾。quiet は「無音の → 静かな」。
- **accord** [əkɔ́ɚd] 【動】[accord with 〜] 〜とぴったり一致する ▶ ac- = ad- 方向・-cord 心
  【名】accordance 一致 ▶ -ance 名尾
  《連語》in accordance with 〜 〜と一致して；〜に従って
  【形】[according to 〜] 〜に従って；〜によれば
  【副】accordingly 従って ▶ -ly 副尾
- **appoint** [əpɔ́ɪnt] 【動】〜を約束して決める [appoint 人 (to be / as) C] 人を〜に任命する
  ▶ ap- = ad- 方向・point 指差す
  【名】appointment 約束；アポ, 任命 ▶ -ment 名尾
- **deliver** [dɪlívɚ] 【動】〜を配達する, 〜を引き渡す ▶ de- 分離・-liver 自由にする → 手放す
  《連語》deliver a speech / a lecture 講演をする　deliver a verdict 評決を下す
  【名】delivery 配達, 引渡し, 話し(ぶり) ▶ -y 名尾
- **join** [dʒɔ́ɪn] 【動】〜をつなぐ, 〜に参加する；〜と一緒になる
  ▶「2つ以上のものをじかに接合する」イメージ。
  【名】joint 関節, 接合 ▶ join の過去分詞から生まれた語。
- **grow** [gróʊ] 【動】成長する, [grow C] 〜の状態になる ▶ 他動詞形は bring up (〜を育てる)。
  【名】growth 成長 ▶ -th 名尾(抽象名詞)
- **occupy** [á:kjəpaɪ] 【動】〜を占める ▶ oc- = ad- 方向・-cupy つかむ。「つかんで手に入れる → 占有する」。
  【名】occupation 占有 → [荘園制度：占有地で働く] → 職業 ▶ -ation 名尾
- **roll** [róʊl] 【動】転がる, 〜を巻く 【名】巻物 → 目録；名簿 ▶ 対象物そのものが「回転する」。
  【動】enroll 〜を名簿に載せる → 〜を入隊させる；入会させる ▶ en- 中 (= in)
- **stretch** [strétʃ] 【動】(手足を)伸ばす → (手を)差し伸べる → 〜を張る 【名】広がり；伸張
- **double** [dʌ́bl] 【形】二倍の 【動】〜を二倍にする ▶ doubt(どちらを選ぶか迷う)と同源。
- **entire** [ɪntáɪɚ] 【形】無傷の → 完全な → まるごと全部の ▶ en- 否定・-tire 触れる
- **fair** [féɚ] 【形】皮膚が白い, 金髪の, 晴れた, 清らかな, 公平な ― [程度の焦点化] ┐
  └ かなりの ▶ 原義は「麗(うるわ)しい」。「澄んでいて綺麗 → 透明」のイメージ。
- **hard** [hɑ́ɚd] 【形/副】(密度が濃い) → かたい ― [内容が濃い] → 困難な, 激しい ┐
  └ [つぎ込むエネルギーが濃い] → 熱心な, 熱心に
- **ready** [rédi] 【形】用意ができて；準備ができて ▶「夕食ができた」は Dinner is ready.
  《連語》get ready for 〜 / get ready to do 〜の／〜する準備をする

EXERCISE A

各文の下線部分に入る適切な語を左ページの見出し語から選びましょう。

1. Before you get into the swimming pool, please _____ your muscles first.
2. Will you _____ the health club? It's not too expensive, you know.
3. Could you _____ the letter for me?
4. The scientist did the _____ alone.
5. Are you watching the TV _____ tonight about Osaka Castle?
6. Are you _____ to begin?
7. I _____ vegetables in my garden.
8. I enjoy living in the _____ of town. I think that it's very convenient.
9. Drugs are not just a problem in our country. They are a problem for the _____ world.
10. After you leave university, do you want to live in the _____ or the city?

EXERCISE B

左の語の定義として正しいものを右のコラムより選び、（ ）にアルファベットを書き入れましょう。

Part 1

1. ( ) experiment   a. make longer and wider by pulling
2. ( ) entire   b. difficult; very firm
3. ( ) hard   c. an agreement to meet with someone at a specific time
4. ( ) country   d. be in a place
5. ( ) program   e. a plan for how things are to be done for a specific purpose
6. ( ) join   f. land that is away from the city or towns
7. ( ) silence   g. not having sound or noise
8. ( ) appointment   h. full; complete
9. ( ) occupy   i. bring or put two or more things together
10. ( ) stretch   j. a scientific test

Part 2

1. ( ) grow   a. an area of darkness created when an object blocks the light
2. ( ) deliver   b. average or acceptable
3. ( ) fair   c. a special event or time
4. ( ) shadow   d. a formal agreement
5. ( ) roll   e. the middle point
6. ( ) accord   f. become larger
7. ( ) center   g. move across the ground by turning over and over
8. ( ) ready   h. made of two parts that are exactly alike
9. ( ) double   i. prepared to do something
10. ( ) occasion   j. take something to a person

Unit 19

- **army** [ɑ́ːmi] 【名】軍隊, 陸軍 ▶ arms(武器)より派生。-y は名尾。
- **condition** [kəndíʃən] 【名】(健康)状態 [conditions] 状況；事情 − [事柄成立の前提事情] → 条件
  《連語》on condition that S V S が V するという条件で (≒ only if S V)
- **disease** [dɪzíːz] 【名】病気；疾病(しっぺい)
  ▶ dis- 否定・-ease 安楽。sickness に対して病名が明確な病気。
- **god** [gɑ́ːd] 【名】神；造物主 ▶ goddess は「女神」。形容詞的には divine(神の)が用いられる。
- **iron** [áɪən] 【名】鉄 →(鉄のように)硬く強いもの − [材料 − 製品] → アイロン
- **money** [mʌ́ni] 【名】金；金銭 ▶ 女神 Jūno Monēta を祭る神殿でローマ最初の貨幣が作られた。
- **page** [péɪdʒ] 【名】頁(ページ) [略して] p. ▶ 複数ページに渡る省略記号は [pp.〜]。
- **rule** [rúːl] 【名/動】(定規；物差し)→ 規則 − [日常の決まりに基づく行い]┐
  └→(個々の)習慣 − [他者に規則を課す] → 〜を支配する；統治する
  《連語》make it a rule to do / make a rule of 〜 ing 〜することにしている
- **story** [stɔ́ːri] 【名】話；物語 −[昔の建物は各階に異なる物語が描かれていたことから] → 階
  ▶ 詳しくは history の項参照。two-story house で「二階建ての家」。
- **arise** [əráɪz] 【動】(問題などが)生じる [米] 起き上がる；立ち上がる (≒ rise)
  ▶ a- 強意・rise 起きる → 生じる。「風立ちぬ」のように「目の前に立つ = 存在する」の意。
- **discover** [dɪskʌ́vɚ] 【動】〜を発見する ▶ dis- 分離・cover 覆(おお)い
  【名】discovery 発見 ▶ -y 名尾。
- **owe** [óʊ] 【動】[owe 人 〜] 人に〜を借りている → 〜は人のお陰である ┐
  └ [借りた恩に応える] → 人に〜すべきである
  [owe 〜 to 人] 〜を人に借りている → 〜は人のお陰である
  ▶ IOU は「借用書」で I owe you.(あなたに借りている)に由来。
  《連語》owing to 〜 (〜に借りている → 〜に原因を負う) → 〜のために
- **organize** [ɔ́ɚgənaɪz] 【動】〜を組織する ▶ organ 組織・-ize 動尾。organ の項参照。
  【名】organization 組織化；機構 ▶ -ation 名尾
- **protect** [prətékt] 【動】〜を保護する；守る ▶ pro- 前・-tect 覆(おお)う
  【名】protection 保護 ▶ -tion 名尾
- **scream** [skríːm] 【動】金切り声で叫ぶ；叫び声をあげる 【名】叫び；悲鳴
  ▶ shout は「大声で叫ぶ」、cry は「泣いて叫ぶ」。
- **suppose** [səpóʊz] 【動】〜であると思う；想定する [Suppose (that) S V] もし〜としたら
  ▶ sup- 下・-pose 置く。「問題を仮定の下に置く」。「思う」の意では think よりも弱い。
  【名】supposition 想定, 仮定 ▶ -tion 名尾
- **many** [méni] 【形】多くの ▶ 可算名詞に使用。
- **scarce** [skéɚs] 【形】乏しい；不十分な ▶ s- 〜から・-carce 果物をもぎ取る。「残りが少なくなる」。
  【副】scarcely ほとんど〜ない (≒ hardly) ▶ hardly の項参照。
- **various** [vériəs] 【形】様々な [a various (kinds) of 〜 s] 様々な〜 (≒ a variety of 〜 s)
  【動】vary 変わる；様々である 【形】variable 変わりやすい ▶ -able 形尾(可能)
  【形】variant 異なった ▶ -ant 形尾(性質) 【形】varied 様々な ▶ -ed 形尾(〜された)
  【名】variety 多様性 ▶ -ty 名尾(性質；状態) 【名】variation 差異 ▶ -ation 名尾
- **vain** [véɪn] 【形】無駄な 【名】[in vain] 無駄に ▶ vacant(中身のない)と同源。

EXERCISE A

各文の下線部分に入る適切な語を左ページの見出し語から選びましょう。

1. In some parts of Africa, food is _____ .
2. I've spent all my _____ . I have to go to the bank to get some more.
3. I _____ him a lot of money.
4. Christian people believe in _____ .
5. This metal pole is made of _____ .
6. Let's _____ a party for your birthday! We can ask all of your friends to come.
7. It's important to _____ young children from danger.
8. Please open your textbooks to _____ 121.
9. I'm a soldier in the _____ .
10. Please continue telling me the _____ . I want to hear what happens at the end.

EXERCISE B

左の語の定義として正しいものを右のコラムより選び、（ ）にアルファベットを書き入れましょう。

Part 1

1. ( ) many   a. a way of living or existing
2. ( ) army   b. a common, heavy metal
3. ( ) page   c. a large group of men and women involved in a war
4. ( ) iron   d. a number of different things
5. ( ) suppose   e. believe something to be true
6. ( ) variety   f. keep danger away from someone or something
7. ( ) condition   g. one floor level of a building
8. ( ) story   h. large number of people or things
9. ( ) protect   i. become aware of something for the first time
10. ( ) discover   j. one side of piece of paper in a book

Part 2

1. ( ) rule   a. something used to pay for things
2. ( ) scarce   b. say something very loudly
3. ( ) god   c. a being that has great power
4. ( ) vain   d. a statement that says what one may or may not do
5. ( ) arise   e. need to give back
6. ( ) scream   f. begin to happen or exist
7. ( ) organize   g. not many; very small in amount or number
8. ( ) disease   h. illness; sickness
9. ( ) owe   i. having no success
10. ( ) money   j. plan an event

Unit 20

- **animation** [ænəméɪʃən] 【名】動画 ▶ animate (〜に生命を吹き込む → 〜を元気づける) の名詞形。anim- は「生命のある」のイメージ。animal (動物) と同源。
- **church** [tʃə́ːtʃ] 【名】教会 ▶ 原義は「キリストの家」。クリスチャンにとって教会は home に相当。《連語》be at church お祈り中で ▶ be at (the) table (食事中で)。
- **handle** [hǽndl] 【名】取っ手 ▶ 自動車のハンドルは (steering) wheel, 自転車のそれは handlebar。
  【動】〜に手を触れる →(問題などを) 取り扱う ▶ hand 手・-le 小さいもの
- **future** [fjúːtʃɚ] 【名】未来；将来 ⟷ past 過去, 過去の [futures] 先物取引；先物契約
- **neighbor** [néɪbɚ] 【名】隣の人；近所の人 ▶ one's next-door neighbor で「隣の人」。
  ▶ neigh は古語で「近い」。neigh < near (より近い) < next (最も近い) が昔の活用。
  【名】neighborhood 近所 [the neighborhood] 近所の人々 ▶ -hood 集団
- **reason** [ríːzn] 【名】理由, 理性, 推理, 道理 【動】推論する
  【名】reasoning 推論 ▶ -ing 名尾 (〜すること)
  【形】reasonable 道理をわきまえた；妥当な →(値段が) 手頃な ▶ -able 形尾
- **university** [juːnəvɚ́səti] 【名】(総合)大学 ▶ -ity 名尾。単科大学は college, 短大は [英] junior college。
  【名】universe 宇宙, 全世界 ▶ uni- 1つ・-verse 回転 (= turn) → ぐるりと見る
  【形】universal 普遍的な ▶ -al 形尾。university とは時代に流されない「普遍的な (universal)」知識を身につける場所。
- **adopt** [ədɑ́ːpt] 【動】〜を採用する − [親子関係で] → 〜を養子にする ▶ ad- 方向・-opt 選ぶ
  【名】adoption 採用, 養子縁組 ▶ -tion 名尾
- **develop** [dɪvéləp] 【動】〜を発達する；発展する, 〜を開発する
  ▶ de- 分離 → 開ける・-velop 包む。「包みを開く − [中身が見える] → 目立つようにする」イメージ。Cancer developed. (癌が目立つようになった → 発癌(がん)した)。
  【名】development 発達；発展, 開発 ▶ -ment 名尾
- **kill** [kíl] 【動】〜を殺す [be killed in 〜](事故などで)死ぬ
  ▶ 「暗殺する」は assassinate, 「虐殺する」は slaughter。「大虐殺」は genocide。
- **lay** [léɪ] 【動】〜を横たえる；横にする − [鳥の行為に限定] →(卵を)産む
  ▶ 活用は lay < laid < laid。現在分詞形は laying。自動詞は lie (横たわる)。活用は lie < lay < lain。現在分詞形は lying。なお, lie は「嘘をつく (≒ tell a lie)」の意も持つ。
- **press** [prés] 【動】〜を押しつける；圧する → アイロンをかける
  【名】押しつけること → アイロンをかけること, 印刷；出版
  【名】pressure 押すこと；押されること；圧力 → 精神的圧迫 ▶ -ure 名尾
- **send** [sénd] 【動】〜を送る → 〜を派遣する ▶ 「派遣社員」は temporary staff / worker。
- **touch** [tʌ́tʃ] 【動】〜に触れる；触る 【名】触れること；触ること ▶ 「触覚」は sense of touch。
- **slip** [slíp] 【動】つるっと滑る →(滑るように)行き過ぎる；いつの間にか過ぎ去る
  【名】滑ること − [滑るように着られるもの] →(下着の)スリップ
- **evil** [íːvəl] 【形】(道徳上)悪い；邪悪な ▶ 「悪霊」は evil spirit。
- **deep** [díːp] 【形】深い ⟷ shallow 浅い [数字 + meters deep] 〜メートルの深さ
  【動】deepen 〜を(一層)深くする →(知識・印象などを)深める ▶ -en 動尾
  【名】depth 深さ；奥行き ▶ -th 名尾 (抽象名詞)。breadth の項参照。
- **former** [fɔ́ːmɚ] 【形】前の [the former] 前者の ⟷ [the latter] 後者の ▶ late の項参照。
- **less** [lés] 【副】より少なく [劣等比較級で] より〜でなく 【形】より少ない
  ▶ little とは本来, 別語源であるが, 現代では little (少ない) < less < least (最も少ない)。
  《連語》not less than 少なくとも 〜 (≒ at least) ⟷ not more than 多くても 〜
  no less than 〜 〜もの (≒ as many [much] as) ⟷ no more than 〜しか
- **rather** [rǽðɚ] 【副】むしろ, かなり ▶ 程度の対照を強調。

EXERCISE A

各文の下線部分に入る適切な語を左ページの見出し語から選びましょう。

1. I'm going to _____ an email to my best friend tonight.
2. George W. Bush is a _____ U.S. president. He was president from 2001 to 2009.
3. What is the main _____ for leaving your job?
4. Slow down! If you drive too fast, you might _____ someone.
5. Please hold the suitcase by the _____ .
6. The water is really _____ in the middle of the river.
7. The devil is _____ .
8. The doctor advised me to smoke fewer cigarettes and drink _____ beer.
9. Many British people go to their local _____ on a Sunday morning.
10. After graduating from high school, Jim decided to study music at _____ .

EXERCISE B

左の語の定義として正しいものを右のコラムより選び、（ ）にアルファベットを書き入れましょう。

Part 1

1. (　) handle　　　　　　a. cause to grow or become more advanced
2. (　) slip　　　　　　　b. a part of something designed to be held in the hand
3. (　) universal　　　　 c. not so much
4. (　) deep　　　　　　 d. lose one's balance
5. (　) develop　　　　　e. a living thing that is not a human or a plant
6. (　) neighborhood　　 f. done or experienced by everyone
7. (　) send　　　　　　 g. cause something to go
8. (　) less　　　　　　　h. place something in a flat position
9. (　) lay　　　　　　　 i. far downward from the top
10. (　) animal　　　　　 j. a section of a town or city

Part 2

1. (　) evil　　　　　　　a. legally take the child of other parents as one's own
2. (　) former　　　　　 b. put one's hand or finger on something
3. (　) touch　　　　　　c. to some degree or extent
4. (　) rather　　　　　　d. fair; not too expensive
5. (　) church　　　　　 e. a building used for religious services
6. (　) reasonable　　　 f. push with controlled power at one place
7. (　) kill　　　　　　　g. a period of time after the present
8. (　) future　　　　　　h. cause the death of someone or something
9. (　) press　　　　　　i. existing in the past
10. (　) adopt　　　　　　j. very bad

Unit 21

- **affair** [əféɚ] 【名】(世間を騒がせる)出来事, 日々の業務 ▶ love affair で「情事」。
- **creature** [kríːtʃɚ] 【名】(神によって創造されたもの) → 生き物 ▶ -ure 名尾
  - 【動】create 〜を創造する 【形】creative 創造力のある ▶ -ative 形尾
  - 【名】creation 創造 ▶ -ation 名尾
- **effort** [éfɚt] 【名】努力 ▶ e- = ex- 外へ・-fort 強い力
  - 《連語》make an effort to do 〜しようと努力をする
- **interest** [íntərəst] 【名】興味；関心 → (関与することによる)利害関係；利益 → 利子
  - 【形】[be interested in 〜] 〜に興味がある ▶ -ed 形尾(〜された)
  - 【形】interesting 興味を引き起こす；面白い ▶ -ing 形尾(〜している)
- **job** [dʒáːb] 【名】(賃金が発生する)仕事；職 ▶ business の項参照。
  - ▶ job hunting は「就職活動」, job interview は「就職の面接試験」。
- **object** [áːbdʒɪkt] 【名/動】客体；物体 ┬ [主体の行為を投げかける客体] → 目的；対象
  - ├ [文中で主体の行為を投げかける客体] → 目的語 ▶ ob- = ad- 方向・-ject 投げる
  - └ [〜に対して客体と捉える；主体とは異なる] → [object to 〜] 〜に反対する
  - 【形】objective 客観的な ▶ -ive 形尾 【名】objection 反対 ▶ -tion 名尾
- **thread** [θréd] 【名】糸；縫い糸 【動】〜に糸を通す ▶「糸を通した針」は needle and thread。
- **quality** [kwáːləti] 【名】質 [形容詞的に] 良質の ⟷ quantity 量
- **stone** [stóʊn] 【名】石, 石材 ▶ A rolling stone gathers no moss.(転がる石は苔も生さず)。この moss は, 移動好きの米国人は良いモノ, 移動嫌いの英国人は悪いモノと捉える。
- **apply** [əpláɪ] 【動】[apply for 〜] 〜に申し込む [apply (A) to 〜] 〜に(Aを)適用する
  - 【名】application 志願, 適用 ▶ -ation 名尾
  - 【名】applicant 志願者；応募者 ▶ -ant 名尾(〜する人)
- **spoil** [spɔ́ɪl] 【動】〜を甘やかす − [厳しく扱わなかった結果] → 〜を台無しにする
  - ▶ Spare the rod, spoil the child.(ムチを惜しめば子供を台無しにする)
- **express** [ɪksprés] 【動】〜を表現する, 〜を速達で送る 【名】急行 ▶ ex- 外へ → 出す・press 押す
- **finish** [fínɪʃ] 【動】〜を終える；終わる ▶ end は「無くなる」, finish は「仕上がる」イメージ。
- **learn** [lɚ́ːn] 【動】〜を学んで身につける；習得する
  - 【名】learning 学ぶこと；学習 ▶ -ing 名尾(〜すること)
- **promise** [práːməs] 【動】〜を約束する 【名】約束
  - 《連語》keep one's / a promise 約束を守る(≒ keep one's / a word)
  - ⟷ break one's / a promise 約束を破る(≒ break one's / a word)
  - 【形】promising(将来が約束されていて)有望な ▶ -ing 形尾(〜している)
- **suggest** [sədʒést] 【動】〜を暗に示す
  - 《連語》suggest to 人 that S (should) V 人に that 以下を提案する
  - ▶ sug- 下・-gest 運ぶ。「言葉の下に真意を隠して運ぶ」イメージ。suggest は「暗に示す」。暗に示したものが相手に「到達(to)」して初めて「提案する」ことになる。
  - 【名】suggestion 暗に示すこと；示唆(しさ) ▶ -tion 名尾
- **wish** [wíʃ] 【動】(可能とは思わないが)〜を願う ▶ hope は「可能と信じて望む；希望する」。
- **general** [dʒén(ə)rəl] 【形】全体的な；(専門的でなく)一般的な ▶ gener- 全体・-al 形尾(〜に関する)
  - 【副】generally 一般的に ▶ -ly 副尾。generally speaking で「一般的に言えば」。
- **practical** [prǽktɪkəl] 【形】実際的な；実用的な ▶ -al 形尾 ⟷ impractical 非現実的な；非実用的な
  - 【名】practice 実際；実用 − [繰り返し実用] → (意識して行う)習慣
  - 《連語》in practice 実際上は
- **special** [spéʃəl] 【形】特別の ▶ speci- 視線を向ける・-al 形尾。especial(特別な；顕著な)と同源。
  - 【動】[specialize in 〜] 〜を専攻する ▶ -ize 動尾

EXERCISE A

各文の下線部分に入る適切な語を左ページの見出し語から選びましょう。

1. I won't have time to _____ writing this essay tonight. I'll continue writing it tomorrow.
2. I have a part-time _____ as a waiter.
3. This diamond is very high _____ . How much did you pay for it?
4. _____ me that you will call me tonight!
5. You are always late! Make an _____ to come on time.
6. This building is made of _____ . It is hundreds of years old.
7. I _____ I could fly! I would love to fly with the birds in the sky.
8. I want to _____ to speak Chinese. Perhaps I will start taking classes next year.
9. If you have an _____ in movies, you should join the cinema club.
10. I'm going to _____ for a job at the factory. I heard that the salary is good.

EXERCISE B

左の語の定義として正しいものを右のコラムより選び、( )にアルファベットを書き入れましょう。

Part 1

1. ( ) thread   a. damage something
2. ( ) wish   b. the energy used to do something
3. ( ) practice   c. stop doing something because it is completed
4. ( ) finish   d. want to be true or happen
5. ( ) job   e. work someone regularly does to make money
6. ( ) affair   f. something hard from the ground used for building
7. ( ) stone   g. a social event or activity
8. ( ) promise   h. a long, thin piece of fiber
9. ( ) spoil   i. do an activity over and over to get better at it
10. ( ) effort   j. tell someone that one will do something

Part 2

1. ( ) interest   a. the act of making or producing something
2. ( ) application   b. relating to most people or things in a group
3. ( ) creation   c. gain knowledge or skills by studying
4. ( ) quality   d. talk or write about one's thoughts or feelings
5. ( ) objective   e. a goal or purpose
6. ( ) learn   f. a written request for something
7. ( ) express   g. mention something as a possible thing to be done
8. ( ) suggest   h. how good or bad something is
9. ( ) special   i. a feeling of wanting to learn more about something
10. ( ) general   j. different from what is normal or usual

Unit 22

- **reward** [rɪwɔ́ɚd] 【名】報酬；礼金【動】〜に報いる ▶re- 元の場所へ → 後ろ・-ward 見守る
  【形】rewarding 有益な；価値のある ▶-ing 形尾
- **board** [bɔ́ɚd] 【名】板 − [台にして食事をする] → 食卓 − [机を囲んだ話し合い] → 委員会
  【動】〜に乗り込む ▶a- 接触（＝on）・board 板／床
  《連語》on board（乗り物に）乗って（≒aboard）
- **deal** [díːl] 【名】量 [a great / good deal of 〜] 大量の〜 ▶「分配されたもの」のイメージ。
  【名】（商品分配）→ 商取引
  【動】〜を分配する −[トランプで] → カードを配る
  《連語》deal with 〜（事柄を）扱う；対処する deal in 〜（商品を）扱う
- **gate** [ɡéɪt] 【名】門；出入り口 − [空港に限定] →（飛行機の）搭乗口
- **heat** [híːt] 【名】熱, 熱さ；暑さ【動】熱する；暖める [the heat] 興奮；激しさ
- **length** [léŋθ] 【名】長さ；縦；丈 ▶-th 名尾（抽象名詞）。breadth の項参照。
  《連語》at length 長々と；詳細に − [長いプロセスを経て] → とうとう（≒at last）
- **stain** [stéɪn] 【名】しみ【動】〜にしみをつける ▶distain（変色させる）と同源。
  【形／名】stainless しみのない, ステンレス製の食器類 ▶-less 形尾（〜がない）
- **river** [rívɚ] 【名】川 ▶川の名称は, [米] で [the + 名称 + River], [英] で [the + (River) + 名称]。
- **attack** [ətǽk] 【動】〜を攻撃する →（病気が）〜を襲う【名】攻撃, 病気の発作
- **consider** [kənsídɚ]【動】（良い方向に）〜を考慮する
  ▶con- 強意・-sider 星。原義は「占いで星を観察する」。
  【形】considerate 思慮深い；思いやりのある ▶-ate 形尾（〜がある）
  【形】considerable（考えられ得る → 無視できない）→ かなりの
  ▶-able 形尾（可能）
  【名】consideration 考慮 ▶-ation 名尾
  《連語》take 〜 into consideration 〜を考慮する（≒take 〜 into account）
- **enter** [éntɚ] 【動】〜に入る → 〜の一員になる
  【名】entrance 入り口, 入会, 入場 ▶-ance 名尾【名】entry 記入 → 加入 ▶-y 名尾
- **lack** [lǽk] 【動】〜を欠いている【名】欠乏（≒want）[be lacking in〜] 〜に欠いている
- **miss** [mís] 【動】的を当て損なう；狙ったものが外れる, [miss 〜 ing] 〜し損なう
  → 〜の機会を逃す；〜に乗り遅れる ←→ catch（乗り物に）間に合う
  → 〜を見損なう；聞き損なう → 〜を理解し損なう
  → [会い損なう；〜の不在に気づく] → 〜がいなくて寂しく思う
  【形】missing 行方不明の ▶-ing 形尾（〜している）
- **prove** [prúːv] 【動】[prove C] 〜であると（疑いの余地なく）判明する
  【名／形】proof（確実な）証明 →（立証）検査
  → [proof against〜]（検査済みで火・水に）耐えられる
- **shave** [ʃéɪv] 【動】[shave oneself] ひげを剃（そ）る ▶この oneself は「自身の肉体」を指す。
- **support** [səpɔ́ɚt] 【動】〜を支える → 〜を支持する；援助する → 家族を養う【名】支え, 援助
- **warn** [wɔ́ɚn] 【動】〜を警告する ▶原義は「触れないように覆い隠す」。名詞は warning（警告）。
- **waste** [wéɪst] 【動】（金・体力；能力・時間を）浪費する【名】浪費, 廃棄物
  【形】wasteful 浪費している；無駄な, もったいない ▶-ful 形尾（満ちている）
- **flexible** [fléksəbl] 【形】柔軟性のある → 融通のきく ▶flex- 曲げる・-ible ＝-able 形尾（可能）
- **rough** [rʌ́f] 【形】ざらざらした；きめの粗い → 粗野な；粗暴な → 概略の

EXERCISE A

各文の下線部分に入る適切な語を左ページの見出し語から選びましょう。

1. The _____ flows past my house.
2. The old man's hands are not smooth. They are very _____ .
3. When you leave the flower garden, don't forget to close the _____ .
4. I'm going to _____ a chess tournament. I hope that I can win it.
5. My husband spends 30 minutes to _____ and take a shower before he goes to work.
6. Don't _____ your time with this! You have better things to do.
7. The five-year-old boy swam the _____ of the swimming pool by himself.
8. I will _____ my friend about the storm. He'll need to bring a raincoat.
9. In 2001, there was a terrorist _____ on New York City.
10. I've got an oil _____ on my T-shirt.

EXERCISE B

左の語の定義として正しいものを右のコラムより選び、( )にアルファベットを書き入れましょう。

Part 1

1. ( ) attack   a. cut the hair off very close to the skin
2. ( ) shave   b. fail to catch, reach or hit
3. ( ) heat   c. try to cause pain or destroy someone or something
4. ( ) stain   d. tell someone about possible danger
5. ( ) miss   e. use more of something than is necessary
6. ( ) deal   f. a door that is used for going into something
7. ( ) reward   g. a dirty mark made on a piece of clothing
8. ( ) waste   h. the energy that causes things to become warmer
9. ( ) entrance   i. an agreement in business on conditions for buying something
10. ( ) warn   j. money given or received for something that has been done

Part 2

1. ( ) length   a. agree with something or someone
2. ( ) support   b. capable of being bent
3. ( ) rough   c. a large flow of water
4. ( ) flexible   d. the measurement of something from one end to the other
5. ( ) prove   e. show the truth of something
6. ( ) board   f. think about something carefully
7. ( ) river   g. a place in a fence that can be opened and closed like a door
8. ( ) gate   h. a long, thin piece of wood
9. ( ) consider   i. not being even
10. ( ) lack   j. not have something

Unit 23

- ☐ **content** [kάntɛnt] 【名】中身 → 内容 ▶ con- 共に・-tent 保つ。「容器と共に保たれたもの」のイメージ。
  【形】contented(心という容器の中身が満たされた) → 満足した ▶ -ed 形尾
- ☐ **custom** [kʌ́stəm] 【名】慣習 [customs] 関税；税関 ▶ 個人的な習慣は habit。manner の項参照。
  【名】customer 顧客；常連 ▶ -er 名尾(〜する人)。「習慣づいた人」。
- ☐ **distance** [dístəns] 【名】距離 ▶ dis- 分離・-stance 立っていること
  《連語》at a distance ある距離を置いて　in the distance 遠方に
  【形】distant 距離のある；遠い - [心的距離] → よそよそしい ▶ -stant 立っている
- ☐ **fortune** [fɔ́ərtʃən] 【名】幸運 → 運；運命 (≒ luck, lot) → (幸運によって得られた) 富；財産
  ⟷ misfortune 不運 ▶ mis- 悪い・fortune 運
  【形】fortunate 幸運な ▶ -ate 形尾 ⟷ unfortunate 不運な
- ☐ **idea** [aɪdíə] 【名】考え；観念 ▶ a person of ideas で「着想に富んだ人」。
  【形】ideal(考えられる最も素晴らしい状態) → 理想の ▶ -al 形尾
- ☐ **metal** [métl] 【名】金属；合金 [形容詞的に] 金属性の
- ☐ **picture** [píktʃɚ] 【名】絵；絵画 - [文明の発達] → 写真, 映像 ▶ 原義は「描かれたもの」。
  《連語》get the picture 事態を理解する ▶ この picture は日本語の「実像」に相当。
- ☐ **plant** [plǽnt] 【名】植物；草木 【動】〜を植える
- ☐ **arrive** [əráɪv] 【動】[arrive at 〜] 〜に到着する　[arrive in 〜] 〜の中に到着する
  ▶ arrive at the station であれば「駅の中か駅の周辺か」どちらに到着したかわからない。
  【名】arrival 到着 ▶ -al 名尾
- ☐ **attempt** [ətémpt] 【動】〜を試みる ▶ at-=ad- 方向・-tempt 試みる。「殺人未遂」は attempted murder。
  【名】(失敗に終わることが多い) 試み
- ☐ **claim** [kléɪm] 【動】〜を(当然の権利だと／自分のモノだと)主張する 【名】要求；権利
- ☐ **lead** [líːd] 【動】〜を導く → 〜を先導する；率いる → 相手に勝る；リードする
  [lead to 〜] (〜に導く) → 〜に至る；通ずる 【名】先導；率先, 優位
  【名】leader 先導者；リーダー ▶ -er 名尾(〜する人)
- ☐ **keep** [kíːp] 【動】〜を持ち続ける → 〜を維持する；保つ
  《連語》keep a dog 犬を飼う ▶ keep a diary で「日記をつけている」。
  keep 人 from doing 人に〜させない (≒ stop / hinder 人 from 〜 ing)
- ☐ **show** [ʃóʊ] 【動】〜を見せる → 〜を(見せて)教える 【名】展示会；ショー
  《連語》show up(約束どおり)現れる
  ▶ この up は「上方 → 出現」のイメージ。turn up は「予想外に現れる」。
- ☐ **strike** [stráɪk] 【動】〜を打つ - [心を打つ] → (恐怖・驚きを)心に起こす
  【名】打つこと - [策を打つ] → ストライキ ▶ striking で「心を打つような」。
- ☐ **tear** [téɚ] 【動】[tear up 〜 / tear 〜 up] 〜を細かく引き裂く；裂く 【名】涙 [tíɚ]
  ▶ 動詞と名詞は別語源。この up は「上方 → 出現 → 引き裂いて狭間の空間が出現」。
- ☐ **wonder** [wʌ́ndɚ] 【動】〜を不思議に思う 【名】不思議なもの／こと ▶ wander は「さまよう」。
  【形】wonderful 不思議な → (驚くほど)素晴らしい ▶ -ful 形尾(満ちている)
- ☐ **another** [ənʌ́ðɚ] 【形】もう一つ／一人の → 別の ▶ [an + other] に由来。
- ☐ **direct** [dərékt] 【形】まっすぐな - [第三者を迂回しない] → 直接の
  ▶ di-=dis- 分離・-rect まっすぐ ⟷ indirect まっすぐでない, 間接の ▶ in- 否定
  【動】〜に向ける → 〜に道を教える → 〜を導く；指示する
  【名】direction 方向 - [ある目的へ方向づけること] → 指示 ▶ -tion 名尾
  【名】director 指示する人 → 重役 ▶ -er 名尾(〜する人)
- ☐ **public** [pʌ́blɪk] 【形】公の；公共の；公衆の → 公立の ▶ publish(公にする → 出版する)と同源。

EXERCISE A

各文の下線部分に入る適切な語を左ページの見出し語から選びましょう。

1. The artist painted a beautiful _____ .
2. Would you like _____ cup of tea?
3. Let's water the _____ . It looks like it needs a drink.
4. I _____ why the movie star came to this small town.
5. Does anyone have a good _____ for Jane's birthday party?
6. Please _____ me your homework.
7. There is a _____ train from Tokyo to Osaka. You do not have to change trains.
8. I need to call my mother from a _____ phone. I forgot to bring my cell phone.
9. The plane will _____ from London at 8 o'clock.
10. Coins are made of _____ .

EXERCISE B

左の語の定義として正しいものを右のコラムより選び、（　）にアルファベットを書き入れましょう。

Part 1

1. (　) distant
2. (　) ideal
3. (　) picture
4. (　) claim
5. (　) arrive
6. (　) strike
7. (　) direction
8. (　) keep
9. (　) content
10. (　) wonder

a. to feel surprise or amazement; have interest in learning or knowing something
b. continue having or holding something
c. hit in a powerful way
d. a painting or drawing of someone or something
e. existing far away
f. reach a place after traveling
g. exactly right for a certain purpose
h. say that something is true when others may say it is not true
i. the path in which something is moving
j. the things that are in something

Part 2

1. (　) show
2. (　) another
3. (　) metal
4. (　) plant
5. (　) fortune
6. (　) tear
7. (　) lead
8. (　) attempt
9. (　) customer
10. (　) public

a. guide someone to a specific place
b. cause or allow something to be seen
c. a living thing that usually has leaves and flowers
d. a very large amount of money
e. one more; in addition
f. a substance that has a shiny appearance
g. someone who buys goods from a business
h. relating to all or most people
i. try to do something
j. separate into parts by pulling or cutting it

Unit 24

- **bar** [bάɚ] 【名】棒；横木－[陪審員／バーテンとの区切りとなる横木] → 法廷, 酒場
- **care** [kéɚ] 【名】（心配）→（細心の）注意 → 世話；管理 【動】～を心配する；気にする
  《連語》take care of ～ ～に気を配る, ～を世話する
  care for ～（～を気にする（≒ care about））→ ～を世話する, ～を好む
  【形】careful 注意深い；用心深い ▶ -ful 形尾（満ちている）
- **district** [dístrɪkt] 【名】地区；地方 ▶ region より狭い。「関西地方」は the Kansai district。
- **effect** [ɪfékt] 【名】[effect on ～] ～に関する結果／効果／影響 ▶「作り出されたもの」。
  【形】effective 効果的な；有効な ▶ -ive 形尾
- **habit** [hǽbət] 【名】（個人的な）習慣 ▶ custom は社会的な慣習。
  【形】habitual 習慣的な；いつもの ▶ -al 形尾
- **letter** [létɚ] 【名】文字－[文字の集まり] → 手紙 ▶ 派生語については literature の項参照。
- **member** [mémbɚ] 【名】（手足）－[組織の手足] → 一員 ▶ membership は「会員の身分」。
- **project** [prάːdʒekt] 【名／動】（前に広げる）→ 計画－[予定] → ～を見積もる
  [スクリーンに広げる] → ～を投影する ▶ pro- 前・-ject 投げる → 広げる
  【名】projector 映写機；プロジェクター ▶ -or ≒ -er 名尾（～するもの）
- **rate** [réɪt] 【名】割合；比率,（時間給・駐車料金など）時間ごとに増えていく料金
  ▶ 料金：（1）物品：price 値（price tag 値札）, cost 代価（running cost 維持費）（2）サービス：fee 専門家／専門的場所への料金（lawyer's fee 弁護料 admission fee 入会金）（3）交通：fare 運賃（bus fare バスの運賃）, toll 通行料（bridge toll 橋の通行料）
- **shape** [ʃéɪp] 【名】形；具体化－[観察して判るもの] → 状態；調子 ▶ in shape で「健康で」。
- **burn** [bɚ́ːn] 【動】[burn up]（燃え上がって）全焼する／させる
  [burn down (to the ground)]（焼け崩れて）全焼する／させる
  ▶ burn は「やけどする」,「料理で焼け焦がす」の意も。
- **follow** [fάːlou] 【動】～の後についていく；従う → ～を続いて生じさせる
  【形】following 次の ▶ -ing 形尾（～している）【前】following ～のあとで
  《連語》as follows 次のとおり（≒ in the following）
  【名】follower 信奉者, 従者 ▶ -er 名尾（～する人）
- **judge** [dʒʌ́dʒ] 【動】～を判断する → ～を審査する；裁判する 【名】審査員；裁判官
  【名】judgment 判断, 審査；裁判 ▶ -ment 名尾
  【形】judicial 裁判の；司法の ▶ -al 形尾
- **live** [lív] 【動】生きている, 住んでいる ▶ live a happy life で「幸せな生活をする」。
  【形】lively [láɪvli] 生き生きとした；元気な ▶ -ly 形尾（～のような）
  【名】life 生きていること；生命 → 一生；生涯
- **remain** [rɪméɪn] 【動】[remain in ～] ～の中に留まる [remain C] ～の状態のままである
  【名】remainder 残り；余り ▶ -er 名尾（～するもの）
- **rise** [ráɪz] 【動】立ち上がる → 起床する →（煙・温度・物価などが）上がる
  [形が顔に似ている擬人化] → 太陽／月が昇る ▶ 他動詞形は raise。
- **surround** [səráʊnd] 【動】～を（取り）囲む；取り巻く
  【名】surroundings（人や場所を取り巻く地理的な）環境
  ▶ circumstances は「（影響を及ぼす）周囲」, environment は「（自然／社会の）環境」。
- **mere** [míɚ] 【形】単なる（≒ only）▶ 副詞形 merely は「単に」。
- **safe** [séɪf] 【形】安全な, 無事な（⟷ unsafe 安全でない, dangerous 危険な）【名】金庫
  【名】safety 安全, 無事 ▶ -ty 名尾
- **wide** [wáɪd] 【形】広い ⟷ narrow（幅が）狭い
  【動】widen ～を広くする ▶ -en 動尾 【名】width 広さ；幅 ▶ -th 名尾

EXERCISE A

各文の下線部分に入る適切な語を左ページの見出し語から選びましょう。

1. The circle is a _____ .
2. The river is too _____ to cross here. We should look for a narrower point.
3. Please take _____ of your grandmother. She's getting old.
4. I'm going to order a drink at the _____ .
5. I'm a _____ of a band. I play the drums.
6. We _____ in a small village. I enjoy our peaceful life here.
7. Due to the forest fire, I think that many homes will _____ down to the ground tonight.
8. Late at night, this area is not _____ , so be careful!
9. The shop is in the business _____ of the city.
10. Smoking is a bad _____ . You should stop smoking as soon as possible!

EXERCISE B

左の語の定義として正しいものを右のコラムより選び、（ ）にアルファベットを書き入れましょう。

Part 1

1. ( ) letter   a. the form or outline of an object
2. ( ) project   b. an area or section of a country or city
3. ( ) bar   c. form an opinion after careful thought
4. ( ) shape   d. not in danger
5. ( ) surround   e. the change that results when something is done
6. ( ) safe   f. a written message to someone
7. ( ) district   g. stay in the same place
8. ( ) remain   h. a straight piece of metal
9. ( ) effect   i. a planned piece of work with a specific purpose
10. ( ) judge   j. be on every side of something

Part 2

1. ( ) follow   a. be on fire
2. ( ) live   b. the speed at which something happens over a period of time
3. ( ) care   c. something that someone does regularly
4. ( ) mere   d. go after or behind
5. ( ) rate   e. move upward
6. ( ) burn   f. having a great amount of space from one side to the other
7. ( ) member   g. the effort made to do something correctly or safely
8. ( ) wide   h. have a home in a specific place
9. ( ) rise   i. small or unimportant
10. ( ) habit   j. someone who belongs to a group or organization

Unit 25

- **article** [ɑ́ɚtɪkl] 【名】(新聞・雑誌の)記事；論説, 品物, 箇条
  ▶「全体をつなぐ一つひとつのもの」のイメージ。
- **club** [klʌ́b] 【名】(社交・スポーツ・研究のために集まった)クラブ
  ▶原義は「こん棒」。杖を持つ賢者が知恵を出し合うために集まったことによる。
- **desert** 【名】(見捨てられた土地)→ 砂漠
  [(名) dézɚt] ▶ desert island は「無人島」。「デザート」は dessert。
  [(動) dɪzɚ́t] 【動】～を見捨てる − [任務を捨てる] → 軍隊から脱走する ▶ de- 否定・-sert 結合
  【名】当然の報い；当然受けるべき賞罰 ▶ 上記と別語源。
- **fear** [fíɚ] 【名】(危険への)恐れ − [被害への恐れ] → 心配 【動】～を恐れる；心配する
- **library** [láɪbreri] 【名】図書館；図書室 ▶ libr- = biblio- 本・-ary 名尾(～に関する場所)
- **mouth** [máʊθ] 【名】口, 口状のもの ▶ mouth of a river は「河口」。mouse は「ねずみ」。
- **purpose** [pɚ́pəs] 【名】目的；意図 ▶ pur- = pre- 前に・-pose 置く。「具体的な目的」は aim。
- **relation** [rɪléɪʃən] 【名】関連 ▶ -ation 名尾。in relation to ～で「～に関して」。
  【動】relate ～を関係づける ▶ re- 元の場所へ・-late 運ぶ
  《連語》be related to / with ～ ～と関係がある
  【形】relative 相対的な ▶ -ive 形尾 (⟷ absolute 絶対的な) 【名】血縁関係；親類
  【名】relationship 関係 ▶ -ship 名尾(性質)
- **summer** [sʌ́mɚ] 【名】夏；夏季 [the (high) summer] 人生の盛り
- **charge** [tʃɑ́ɚdʒ] 【動】容器に入れる → ～を充電する, 弾・火薬を入れる, ～に突入する
  責任を負わせる → ～を命ずる, ～を告発する, ～を請求する
  【名】料金 ▶ 全ての意は「容器に入れる／責任を負わせる」いずれかのイメージ。
- **count** [káʊnt] 【動】～を一つずつ数える − [勘定する] → (ある計算に基づき)～と思う
  → (前もって考慮するほど)重要である 【名】計算；総数, 重要
  《連語》count A (as / for) B A を B と思う　count on A A を当てにする
- **divide** [dəváɪd] 【動】[divide (A) into B] (A を) B に分ける ▶ di- 分離・-vide 離して置く
  【名】division 分割, 割り算 ▶ -sion 名尾 【形】individual 個々の ▶ in- 否定・-al 形尾
- **introduce** 【動】～を導入する − [集団の中に導く] → ～を紹介する ▶ intro- 中へ・-duce 導く
  [ɪntrədúːs] 【名】introduction 導入；序論, 紹介 ▶ -tion 名尾
- **preserve** [prɪzɚ́v] 【動】～を保存する, (動物などを)保護する ▶ pre- 前もって・-serve 保つ
  【形】preservative 保存力のある 【名】防腐剤 ▶ -ative 形尾
  【名】preservation 保存, 保護 ▶ -ation 名尾
- **reply** [rɪpláɪ] 【動】(よく考えて)答える 【名】答え ▶ reply は自動詞, answer は他動詞。
  《連語》in reply to ～ ～に答えて
- **report** [rɪpɔ́ɚt] 【動】～を報告する 【名】報告；レポート ▶ re- 元の場所へ・-port 運ぶ
- **permanent** 【形】(半)永久的な；絶え間ない ⟷ temporary / temporal 一時的な
  [pɚ́mənənt] ▶ permanent wave は「パーマ」。
- **sure** [ʃʊ́ɚ] 【形】確かな 【副】確かに, (返事で)もちろん；いいですとも
  《連語》be sure of ～ ～を確信する (≒ be certain of ～) ▶ 主語の確信。
  　　　 be sure to do きっと～する (≒ be certain to do) ▶ 話し手の確信。
  【副】surely 確かに；きっと ▶ -ly 副尾
- **total** [tóʊtl] 【形】(統計として)全体の → 全くの；全体の 【名】総計
  【副】totally 全く；すっかり ▶ -ly 副尾
- **wise** [wáɪz] 【形】賢明な；聡明な ▶ clever は「頭の回転が早くて抜け目なく賢い」。
  【名】wisdom 知恵 ▶ -dom 名尾(状態)

EXERCISE A

各文の下線部分に入る適切な語を左ページの見出し語から選びましょう。

1. He's a _____ old man. You should listen to his advice carefully.
2. Let me _____ you to my friend John. I think you'll like him.
3. Don't put that in your _____ . It's not food!
4. I should _____ to my friend soon. I got his letter two weeks ago.
5. For my writing class, I had to write a _____ about my summer vacation.
6. What's the _____ of your visit to this country?
7. In the _____ , the weather is very hot and dry, and there is a lot of sand.
8. _____ comes after spring.
9. I have a _____ of snakes. I hate their shape.
10. I borrowed some books from the _____ .

EXERCISE B

左の語の定義として正しいものを右のコラムより選び、（ ）にアルファベットを書き入れましょう。

Part 1

1. ( ) report   a. the warmest season
2. ( ) desert   b. complete
3. ( ) article   c. lasting for a very long time or forever
4. ( ) permanent   d. keep in its original state or condition
5. ( ) total   e. give information about something in a newspaper or on TV
6. ( ) introduce   f. a place where books are available for people to borrow
7. ( ) summer   g. an area of dry land usually covered with sand
8. ( ) purpose   h. make someone known to someone else by name
9. ( ) library   i. the reason why something is done
10. ( ) preserve   j. a piece of writing in a magazine or newspaper

Part 2

1. ( ) sure   a. a member of one's family
2. ( ) divide   b. the opening through which food passes into the body
3. ( ) wisdom   c. add things together to find the total
4. ( ) club   d. a sports team or organization
5. ( ) fear   e. separate into two or more groups
6. ( ) relative   f. knowledge gained by someone over a lifetime
7. ( ) count   g. not having any doubt
8. ( ) mouth   h. an emotion caused by feeling danger
9. ( ) reply   i. say or write an answer to a question
10. ( ) charge   j. the amount of money one has to pay for something

Unit 26

- **bit** [bít] 【名】少し；少量 ▶ bite(噛む)と同源。「噛み取られた部分」が原義。
  《連語》a (little) bit of ~ 少しの~　a bit 形容詞／副詞 [副詞的に] 少し~

- **form** [fɔ́ɚm] 【名】形；形態 → 外形；外観 → 姿 【動】~を形作る
  【形】formal 形の, 外形の → 形式的な；格式ばった → 正式の ▶ -al 形尾

- **mass** [mǽs] 【名】(形・大きさが明確でない)かたまり；集まり [the masses] 一般大衆
  《連語》a mass of ~ 多数の~ ▶「マスコミ」は mass communication。
  【形】massive 大きなかたまりの, 巨大な ▶ -ive 形尾

- **mile** [máɪl] 【名】マイル ▶ 距離の単位で約 1.6 km。

- **poverty** [pá:vɚti] 【名】不足 → 貧しさ ▶ -ty 名尾(状態)
  【形】poor 不十分な, 貧しい
  《連語》be poor at ~ ~に不足している − [才能の不足] → ~が不得意である

- **progress**
  [(名) prá:grəs]
  [(動) prəgrés] 【名】進歩 ▶ pro- = pre- 前へ・-gress 歩く。make progress で「進歩する」。× do progress
  ↔ regress 後戻り → 退化 【動】後戻りする, 退化する ▶ re- 元の場所へ
  【形】progressive 進歩的な ▶ -sive 形尾
  ↔ regressive 退行的な, conservative 保守的な

- **road** [róʊd] 【名】(町と町とを結ぶ)公道 ▶ street の項参照。

- **situation** [sɪtʃuéɪʃən] 【名】位置 − [その場の状態] → 事態 ▶ -ation 名尾。site(位置；場所)と同源。
  【動】situate ~を位置づける ▶ -ate 動尾。be situated in ~で「~に位置する」。

- **spirit** [spírət] 【名】精神, 霊；霊魂 [spirits] 蒸留酒；焼酎
  ▶ 原義は「息」。土人形の鼻の穴から神が「息を吹き込み」アダムが誕生した聖書の話に由来。酒の spirit は, 製造過程で「息」と同じような「気体」が発生するため。
  【形】spiritual 精神の, 精神的な ▶ -al 形尾

- **table** [téɪbl] 【名】食卓 − [近接関係] → 食事 ▶ be at (the) table で「食事中である」。

- **union** [júːnjən] 【名】結合 → 連合；組合 ▶ uni- 1つの。「2つ以上が結合したモノ」のイメージ。

- **cover** [kʌ́vɚ] 【動】~を覆う 【名】覆い
  ▶「本のカバー」は jacket。be covered with ~で「~で覆われている」。

- **lie** [láɪ] 【動】横たわる；横になる [lie C] ~のままである ▶ 活用は lay の項参照。
  【動】嘘をつく (≒ tell a lie) 【名】うそ ↔ truth 真実

- **present**
  [(動) prɪzént]
  [(形, 名) préznt] 【動】~を贈呈する, ~を提示／発表する 【名】現在, 贈り物 【形】現在の
  ▶ pre- 前へ・-es 存在する・-ent 形尾。「人の前に存在する」イメージ。
  《連語》be present at ~ ~に出席している
  ↔ be absent from ~ ~を欠席している
  【名】presentation 贈呈, 提示, 発表 ▶ -ation 名尾

- **return** [rɪtɚ́ːn] 【動】~に戻る；~を戻す 【名】戻すこと → 帰り ▶ re- 元の場所へ・turn 回転

- **speak** [spíːk] 【動】(対象者に向けて + 音声を出して)話す ▶ speak to 人で「人に話しかける」。
  ▶ tell は「人に内容を述べる」, talk は「(まとまりある内容を)音声を出して話し合う」, say は「セリフを言う, (標識・文章などが)示す」の意。
  speaking of/about ~ (既出の話題に続いて) ~といえば (≒ talking of/ about)

- **left** [léft] 【形】左の；左側の (↔ right 右の；右側の) 【名】左；左側

- **proper** [prá:pɚ] 【形】(自分自身の) → 特有の − [個々に属する] → 適切な

- **real** [ríːəl] 【形】本当の
  【副】really 本当に ▶ -ly 副尾 【動】realize ~を実現化する, ~に気づく ▶ -ize 動尾

- **still** [stíl] 【形／副】静止した；しんとした − [状態が変わらない] → まだ；依然として
  [程度の上昇が変わらずに続く] → [比較級を強めて] なおいっそう

EXERCISE A

各文の下線部分に入る適切な語を左ページの見出し語から選びましょう。

1. Please put the plates on the _____ . We will be having dinner soon.
2. It's wrong to _____ . You should always tell the truth.
3. Before you can enter the building, you need to fill in this _____ .
4. I need to _____ the DVD to the rental shop.
5. We walked slowly along the _____ .
6. In India, _____ is a serious social problem.
7. At the end of the road, please turn _____ .
8. I don't know the answer. But, when I _____ to my boss tomorrow, I will ask her.
9. I'm not sure if I saw a _____ person or a ghost.
10. We have walked for about a _____ . That's about 1.6 kilometers.

EXERCISE B

左の語の定義として正しいものを右のコラムより選び、(　)にアルファベットを書き入れましょう。

Part 1
1. ( ) real   a. come or go back to a place again
2. ( ) progress   b. be in a flat position
3. ( ) lie   c. movement toward a place
4. ( ) cover   d. not to the right
5. ( ) massive   e. a flat piece of wood with four legs used for putting things on
6. ( ) bit   f. very large and heavy
7. ( ) table   g. a small piece of something
8. ( ) situate   h. actually existing or happening
9. ( ) return   i. put something on the top
10. ( ) left   j. put in a specific place

Part 2
1. ( ) proper   a. a situation in which someone does not have much money
2. ( ) mile   b. correct according to social rules
3. ( ) speak   c. not moving
4. ( ) road   d. soul
5. ( ) present   e. a hard flat way for cars to be driven on
6. ( ) spirit   f. say words to express one's thoughts
7. ( ) formal   g. give something to someone
8. ( ) poverty   h. needing or using serious clothes and manners
9. ( ) still   i. an organization of workers
10. ( ) union   j. unit of measurement

Unit 27

- **breath** [bréθ]　【名】息；呼吸
  ▶breast(胸)と同源。原義は「膨らませる」。out of breath で「息を切らして」。
  【動】breathe 呼吸する；～を吸う▶breathe one's last で「息を引き取る」。
- **hill** [híl]　【名】丘；小山▶mountain よりも低く、一般にふもとからの高さが300 m以下のもの。
- **light** [láɪt]　【名】光 → 明かり；電灯【形】明るい → 色が薄い－[密度が薄い] → 軽い
- **matter** [mǽtɚ]　【名/動】(生み出すもの)┬[製品を生むもの] →(材料となる)物質
  └[結果を生むもの] → 事柄；問題－[問題となる] → 重要である
  ▶mother と同源。「生み出すもの」のイメージ。
  《連語》as a matter of fact 実際のところ(≒in fact)
- **memory** [mém(ə)ri]　【名】記憶；思い出▶memo- 思い出させる。in memory of ～で「～を記念して」。
  【動】memorize ～を記憶する▶-ize 動尾【形】memorial 記念の、記念物▶-al 形尾
- **nature** [néɪtʃɚ]　【名】自然－[本来的に存在しているもの] → 本性；性質▶nat- 生まれる・-ure 名尾
  《連語》by nature 生まれつき～である▶be 動詞と共に用いられる。
  【形】natural 自然の；天然の、(本質として)生来の▶-al 形尾
- **part** [pάːt]　【名】部分－[地理に限定] → 地域；地方 ⟷ whole 全体の、全体
  【形】partial 部分的な；一部の → 不公平な▶-al 形尾
- **position** [pəzíʃən]　【名】位置－[社会／組織の中での位置] → 立場；地位▶posi- 置く・-tion 名尾
- **spot** [spάt]　【名】小さなしみ；斑(はん)点 → 地点－[観光に限定] → 名所；観光地
- **explain** [ɪkspléɪn]　【動】～を説明する▶ex- 強意・-plain 平らな。「諸問題を完全に平らにする」イメージ。
  【名】explanation 説明▶-ation 名尾
- **draw** [drάː]　【動】～を引っ張る；引き出す、～を(線で)描く
  ▶「絵の具で描く」は paint a picture。drawing room は「居間」(≒living room)。「食堂から引き下がる場所」に由来。同じ「引く」でも pull は「支点を利用して引く」ことから、対象物そのものの位置は変化しない(例: pull a door/oar(ドアを引く／オールをこぐ))。それに対し、draw は位置が変化する(例: draw a curtain(カーテンを引く))。
  【名】drawer 引き出し [drawers] たんす▶-er 名尾(～されるもの)
- **fit** [fít]　【動】～に寸法が合う → ～を合わせる →(抽象的に)～に合う【形】適した
  ▶「色・柄が人に似合う」は suit。「色・柄が他の色・柄に合う」は match, go with。
  《連語》fit A to B A を B に合わせる　fit A with B A を B に取り付ける
- **lose** [lúːz]　【動】～を失う；なくす → ～を(取り)損なう → ～に負ける
  《連語》lose one's way 道を見失う　lose one's temper 自制心を失う
  lose weight 体重を減らす ⟷ gain weight 体重が増える
- **repeat** [rɪpíːt]　【動】～を繰り返す → ～を繰り返して言う
  【名】repetition 反復▶-tion 名尾
- **save** [séɪv]　【動】(逃れる)┬[危険から逃れる] → ～を救う
  └[損失から逃れる] →(金／時)を節約する → ～をたくわえる
- **round** [ráʊnd]　【形】丸い【前】[英]～のまわりを／に、(角などを)曲がって、～のあたりに
  【名】円；回転▶【前】の[米]用法は around。「円」もしくは「その一部」のイメージ。
- **soft** [sάːft]　【形】やわらかい ⟷ hard かたい▶hard は「密度が濃い」イメージ。
- **sudden** [sʌ́dn]　【形】突然の▶sud-＝ad- 方向・-den 行く。「こっそり行く → 思いがけない」イメージ。
  《連語》all of a sudden 突然(≒suddenly)▶suddenly は sudden の副詞形。
- **terrible** [térəbl]　【形】恐ろしい；ひどい▶-ible＝-able 形尾(可能)
  【名】terror 恐怖【形】terrific(恐ろしい)→ ものすごい；素晴らしい▶-ic 形尾
- **wrong** [rάːŋ]　【形】間違っている【副】間違って(≒wrongly) ⟷ right 正しい

EXERCISE A

各文の下線部分に入る適切な語を左ページの見出し語から選びましょう。

1. Steve can remember faces well, but he says that he has a bad _____ for names.
2. To help me find the restaurant more easily, could you _____ me a map?
3. Well done on the test! You got 29 questions right, and only one question _____ .
4. Circles are not square. They are _____ .
5. On a cold day, you can see people's _____ .
6. If you want to buy a new car, you will have to _____ some money.
7. We live on the top of a _____ .
8. My head hurts and my stomach feels _____ . I think I should go and see a doctor.
9. My new clothes _____ perfectly.
10. As a _____ of fact, I will be going to see that movie tomorrow.

EXERCISE B

左の語の定義として正しいものを右のコラムより選び、（　）にアルファベットを書き入れましょう。

Part 1

1. (　) drawer　　　　　a. smooth and pleasant to touch
2. (　) save　　　　　　b. learn well so that one can remember perfectly
3. (　) breath　　　　　c. very shocking and upsetting
4. (　) part　　　　　　d. one of the pieces that make something
5. (　) terrible　　　　e. not dark or deep in color
6. (　) spot　　　　　　f. be unable to find something
7. (　) soft　　　　　　g. a small area that is different from other areas
8. (　) memorize　　　　h. air you take into your lungs to live
9. (　) lose　　　　　　i. keep safe
10. (　) light　　　　　j. a box that slides out of a piece of furniture

Part 2

1. (　) explain　　　　a. a round area of land that is higher than the land around it
2. (　) nature　　　　 b. the thing that forms physical objects; the situation or subject that is
3. (　) round　　　　　　 being discussed
4. (　) repeat　　　　 c. be the right size or shape
5. (　) fit　　　　　　d. quickly
6. (　) hill　　　　　 e. shaped like a circle or a ball
7. (　) wrong　　　　　f. not agreeing with the facts or the truth
8. (　) position　　　 g. say something again
9. (　) matter　　　　 h. make clear or easy to understand
10. (　) suddenly　　　i. everything in the world not made by people
　　　　　　　　　　　 j. the place that something is in

Unit 28

- **court** [kɔ́ɚt]
  - 【名】(囲い(地)) → 中庭 − [囲まれた／区分された場所] → 法廷, 宮廷
  - 【形】courteous(宮廷のような) → 礼儀正しい ▶ -ous 形尾
  - 【名】courtesy 礼儀正しさ ▶ -y 名尾
- **dollar** [dɑ́:lɚ]
  - 【名】ドル ▶ アメリカ・カナダの通貨単位。記号は「＄」。1ドル＝100セント。
- **force** [fɔ́ɚs]
  - 【名】力 [the forces] 軍隊 ▶ manner の項参照。by force は「力ずくで」, air force は「空軍」, labor force は「労働力, 全労働人口」。
  - 【動】[force 人 to do] 人に力ずくで〜させる ▶ forced smile で「作り笑い」。
  - 【動】enforce 〜を強制する − [事項の強制] →(法律などを)施行する
- **mark** [mɑ́ɚk]
  - 【名】印 → 標的 − [根拠となる印] → 基準
  - 《連語》 be beside / off the mark 的外れである
  - be wide of the mark 要点とずれている
- **office** [ɑ́:fəs]
  - 【名】公職 −[一般化]→ 勤め先；会社, 事務所 ▶「サラリーマン」は office worker。
  - 【形】official 公の；公式の ▶ -al 形尾 【名】公務員
  - ▶ official duties は「公務」, the government officials は「官僚」。
  - 【名】officer 将校,(official よりも上位の)公務員 ▶ -er 名尾(〜する人)
- **problem** [prɑ́:bləm]
  - 【名】(解決すべき困難な)問題；難問 → やっかいなこと
  - 【形】problematic 問題のある；解決しがたい ▶ -ic 形尾
- **space** [spéɪs]
  - 【名】空間, 余白, 宇宙；宇宙空間 ▶ 原義は「空地」。
- **wind** [wínd]
  - 【名】風 ▶ window は「風の目(wind eye)→ 風の出入りする穴」が原義。
- **arrange** [əréɪndʒ]
  - 【動】〜をきちんと並べて整える → 手はずを整える ▶ a- 〜を・range 並べる
  - 【名】arrangement 配列；整理, 手配；取り決め ▶ -ment 名尾
- **climb** [kláɪm]
  - 【動】〜をよじ登る；登る(≒climb up)
  - ▶「上／下」に関係なく本来は「傾き」を表す。climb down(手足を使って降りる)。
- **cook** [kúk]
  - 【動】〜を(加熱して)料理する ▶「過熱しないで料理を作る」場合は fix。
- **depend** [dɪpénd]
  - 【動】[depend on / upon 〜] 〜に頼る ▶ de- 下へ・-pend ぶら下がる
  - 【形】[be dependent on / upon 〜] 〜に頼っている ▶ -ent 形尾
  - ⟷ be independent of 〜 〜から独立している ▶ in- 否定。of は「分離」の意。
- **rub** [rʌ́b]
  - 【動】〜をこする → 〜をこすって消す
  - 【名】rubber(鉛筆の文字をこすって消せるもの)→ ゴム；消しゴム ▶ -er 名尾
- **shut** [ʃʌ́t]
  - 【動】(戸などを)閉める ▶ shut は「入り口をふさぐ」, close は「空間を閉じる」。
- **view** [vjú:]
  - 【動／名】〜を注意深く見る → 〜を眺める；眺め → 視界, 視力 → 見解
  - 《連語》 view A as B「A を B として見なす」
  - ▶ stare at は「じろじろ見る」, gaze at は「じっと見る」, glare at は「にらみつける」, peer at は「まじまじと見る」, glimpse at は「ちらりと見る」, glance at は「ちらりと見て認識する」, peep at は「こっそりのぞく」, peek at は「ひそかにチラッとのぞく」。
- **wake** [wéɪk]
  - 【動】[wake up] 目が覚める [wake 〜 up] 〜を目覚めさせる
- **plain** [pléɪn]
  - 【形】平らな → 平易な；普通の → わかりやすくてはっきりした
- **smooth** [smú:ð]
  - 【形】(表面が)なめらかな − [ひっかかりがない] → 流暢(りゅうちょう)な
- **stupid** [stú:pəd]
  - 【形】(生まれつき)愚鈍(ぐどん)な；愚かな ⟷ clever(利口な), wise(賢明な)
- **violent** [váɪələnt]
  - 【形】激しい → 乱暴な；暴力的な ▶ -ent 形尾。die a violent death は「変死する」。
  - 【名】violence 激しさ, 乱暴；暴力
  - ▶ -ence 名尾。DV(家庭内暴力)は domestic violence の略。

EXERCISE A

各文の下線部分に入る適切な語を左ページの見出し語から選びましょう。

1. I'm going to _____ dinner soon. I'm planning to make Chinese food.
2. I will do it correctly! You can _____ on me!
3. When you leave, please make sure that you _____ the door.
4. Silk is very _____ .
5. What a nice _____ of the sea!
6. A cold _____ is blowing from the north.
7. If we are going to catch our flight, we will have to _____ up early.
8. The ice cream will be one _____ and ten cents.
9. No, I don't work for the army. I'm a pilot in the air _____ .
10. What time do you plan to _____ up the mountain?

EXERCISE B

左の語の定義として正しいものを右のコラムより選び、（ ）にアルファベットを書き入れましょう。

Part 1

1. (　) office　　　　a. having a lack of ability to learn and understand things
2. (　) court　　　　b. power
3. (　) stupid　　　 c. close
4. (　) force　　　　d. need someone or something for support
5. (　) space　　　　e. a building or room where people work
6. (　) climb　　　　f. the natural movement of air
7. (　) plain　　　　g. the place where a king or queen lives and works
8. (　) shut　　　　 h. move or go up
9. (　) depend　　　i. not having added or extra things
10. (　) wind　　　　j. the amount of area that can be used

Part 2

1. (　) arrange　　　a. not rough; being flat and even
2. (　) dollar　　　　b. stop sleeping
3. (　) smooth　　　c. prepare food for eating by using heat
4. (　) mark　　　　d. move into a certain order or position
5. (　) rubber　　　e. something that is difficult to deal with
6. (　) wake　　　　f. the unit of money in the US, Canada and Australia
7. (　) cook　　　　g. something used to make tires
8. (　) problem　　 h. opinion or way of thinking about something
9. (　) view　　　　i. written or printed shape or symbol
10. (　) violence　　j. the use of power to damage someone or something

Unit 29

- **butter** [bʌ́tɚ] 【名】バター ▶「マーガリン」は margarine。発音は「マージャリン」。
- **concern** [kənsə́ːn] 【名】関係 − [心が関係づけられる] → 関心(事) − [気がかり] → 心配
  【動】〜に関係がある；関心がある，〜を心配する
  《連語》be concerned with / in 〜 〜と関係している
  be concerned about 〜 〜に心配している（≒ be worried / anxious about）
  as far as S am / is / are concerned 〜に関する限り
  【前】concerning 〜 〜に関して ▶ -ing 形尾（〜している）。本来は形容詞だった。
- **lot** [lɑ́ːt] 【名】割り当て ┌ [未来の事柄の割り当て] → 運命；くじ
  └ 敷地（例：parking lot 駐車場）→ ひと山；たくさんのこと
  《連語》a lot of 可算名詞／不可算名詞 たくさんの〜
  ▶ many + 可算名詞，much + 不可算名詞。厳密には両者は肯定文以外で用いる。
- **mind** [máɪnd] 【名／動】（感情ではなく知性としての）心 − [思考する] ┐
  └ 〜を気にする；嫌がる
  ▶ Do you mind (my) smoking here? と聞かれた時，OK の場合は No，ダメなら Yes。
- **price** [práɪs] 【名】値段；価格 ▶「値」のイメージ。詳しくは rate の項参照。
- **scissors** [sízɚz] 【名】はさみ ▶ はさみの刃は blade。植木ばさみは shears。ホッチキスは stapler。
- **square** [skwéɚ] 【名】正方形；四角 →（四角形の）広場 →（面積計算で）平方
- **standard** [stǽndɚd] 【名】標準
  ▶ stand 立つ・-ard 名尾（場所）。「ある高さの位置」のイメージ。mark は「基準」。
- **tool** [túːl] 【名】工具；商売道具
- **train** [tréɪn] 【名／動】列車；行列 − [列状を保たせる] → 〜を訓練する ▶ tra- 引く（= draw）
  【名】training 訓練；訓練を受けること ▶ -ing 名尾（〜すること）
- **attend** [əténd] 【動】（張る）┌ [心を張る] → [attend to 〜] 〜に注意する；注意して聞く ┐
  ├ [気を配る] → 〜を世話する ▶ at- = ad- 方向・-tend 張る
  └ [(体を張って)お供する] → 〜に参加する；出席する
  【名】attention 注意 ▶ -tion 名尾。pay attention to 〜で「〜に注意を払う」。
  【名】attendance 出席 ▶ -ance 名尾 【名】attendant 出席人・世話人 ▶ -ant 名尾（人）
- **boast** [bóʊst] 【動】[boast of 〜] 〜を自慢する ▶ be proud of よりも「鼻にかける」感じ。
  【名】自慢
- **cost** [kɔ́ːst] 【動】（金／労力／時間が）かかる 【名】費用；代価, 犠牲
  《連語》[物 + cost + 人 + 名詞] 物が人に〜という犠牲を払わせる
  　　　at the cost of 〜 〜を犠牲にして
- **forbid** [fɚbíd] 【動】〜を禁じる（≒ prohibit）▶ for- 禁止（= not）・-bid 命令
  《連語》forbid 人 from 〜 ing 〜することを禁じる
- **melt** [mélt] 【動】（熱で）溶ける，〜を溶かす ▶ 加熱しないで溶解する場合は dissolve。
- **sew** [sóʊ] 【動】〜を縫う [sew A on / to B] A を B に縫い付ける
  【形／名】sewing 裁縫の, 裁縫
  ▶ -ing 形尾（〜している）。sewing machine で「ミシン」。
- **afraid** [əfréɪd] 【形】[be afraid of 〜] 〜を恐れる
  [be afraid of 〜 ing / be afraid that S V] 〜を心配する
- **clever** [klévɚ] 【形】（頭の回転が早く抜け目なくて）利口な ▶ wise は思慮分別のある賢さ。
- **fresh** [fréʃ] 【形】新鮮な；できたての ▶ 原義は「塩漬けにされていない」。flesh は「肉体」。
- **wild** [wáɪld] 【形】野生の → 荒々しい → 乱暴な 【名】[the wilds] 荒野

EXERCISE A

各文の下線部分に入る適切な語を左ページの見出し語から選びましょう。

1. It's important for your health to eat _____ vegetables everyday.
2. A _____ is a shape that has four sides.
3. My father sold his house for a good _____ .
4. Would you like _____ or margarine on your toast?
5. If you want to swim at the Olympics, you will have to _____ everyday.
6. The little boy was _____ of spiders.
7. I'm sorry. I won't be able to _____ your wedding.
8. Could you _____ a button onto the shirt?
9. When the weather becomes warmer, the snow will quickly _____ .
10. Sally is a very _____ girl. She always gets the best score in math tests.

EXERCISE B

左の語の定義として正しいものを右のコラムより選び、（　）にアルファベットを書き入れましょう。

Part 1

1. ( ) tool   a. a solid yellow substance made from milk
2. ( ) lot   b. make or repair something using a needle and thread
3. ( ) fresh   c. the amount of money one pays for something
4. ( ) forbid   d. feeling fear
5. ( ) sew   e. something used for a certain task
6. ( ) afraid   f. a shape with four equal sides
7. ( ) square   g. express too much pride in oneself
8. ( ) butter   h. a portion of land; a considerable amount
9. ( ) price   i. newly made; clean and pure
10. ( ) boast   j. order not to do something

Part 2

1. ( ) mind   a. change from a solid to a liquid
2. ( ) concern   b. go to and be present at an event or meeting
3. ( ) attend   c. a level of quality that is acceptable or desired
4. ( ) wild   d. living in nature without human care or control
5. ( ) standard   e. the part of a person that thinks
6. ( ) cost   f. intelligent and able to learn things quickly
7. ( ) melt   g. a feeling of worry
8. ( ) train   h. something lost or given up to get something
9. ( ) clever   i. a tool used for cutting
10. ( ) scissors   j. teach someone the skills to do something

Unit 30

- **beast** [bíːst] 【名】獣, けだもの；畜生 ▶映画『美女と野獣』は Beauty and the Beast。
- **date** [déɪt] 【名】ある特定の日；日付 → (その日付に)会う約束；デート
  【動】〜とデートする
  ▶ give と同源。one's date of birth (= DOB) で「生年月日」。
- **fancy** [fǽnsi] 【名】空想 → 思いつき → (気まぐれな)好み ▶fantasy (空想；夢想) の省略形。
  【形】空想的な - [あり得ないほど巧みな] → 手の込んだ
  【形】fantastic 空想的な - [奇想天外な] → 素晴らしい ▶fantasy 空想・-ic 形尾
- **hammer** [hǽmɚ] 【名】かなづち；ハンマー ▶「泳げない」意での「かなづち」は I can't swim at all.。
- **leaf** [líːf] 【名】(木や草の)葉
  ▶複数形は leaves。麦などの細く尖った葉は blade, 松などの針状の葉は needle。
- **morning** [mɔ́ɚnɪŋ] 【名】朝 → 午前 ▶「朝顔」は morning glory。
- **piece** [píːs] 【名】1つ, 一切れ, 断片, (曲の)小品 ▶part とは異なり,「1つの独立したもの」。
  《連語》a piece of 不可算名詞 一つの〜
- **prize** [práɪz] 【名】賞；賞品 ▶win the first prize で「1等賞をとる」。
- **shield** [ʃíːld] 【名】盾(たて)；防御物 ▶「矛(ほこ)」は pike。「矛盾」は contradiction。
- **sign** [sáɪn] 【名】印；記号 → 合図；身振り → 標識 【動】〜に署名する
  ▶ phonetic sign は「発音記号」, sign language は「手話」, traffic sign は「交通標識」。
  【形】signal 合図の, 信号の 【名】合図, 信号
  【動】〜に合図する；信号を送る ▶-al 形尾
- **station** [stéɪʃən] 【名】駅；(待合室のある)バス停留所, 署；局；(サービスをする)所
  ▶屋根のない小さな駅は [米] stop, [英] halt。fire station は「消防署」, gas station は「ガソリンスタンド」, television station は「テレビ局」。
- **boil** [bɔ́ɪəl] 【動】〜を沸かす；沸く → 〜を煮る；茹(ゆ)でる ▶soft-boiled egg は「ゆで卵」。
  ▶「直火で焼く」は grill,「オーブンで焼く」は bake,「油で炒める；揚げる」は fry。
- **cross** [krɔ́ːs] 【動】〜を交差させる；交差する → 〜を横切る；横断する 【名】十字架
- **defend** [dɪfénd] 【動】〜を守る - [不利益から守る] → 〜を弁護する
  ▶ de- 分離 → かわす・-fend 刺す
  ⇔ offend (刃を向ける) → 〜を怒らせる；感情を害する
      [反逆する] → (法律・規則を)犯す ▶ of- 方向・-fend 刺す
  【名】defense 防衛, 弁護 ⇔ offense 攻撃, 無礼, 違反 ▶fence (柵) は de- が消失。
  【名】defendant 被告人 (≒ the accused) 【形】被告の ▶-ant 名尾 (人)・形尾
- **forgive** [fɚgív] 【動】(罪・間違いを)許す ▶for- 強意・give 与える。「許可して免除する」イメージ。
  《連語》forgive A for 〜 ing A が〜したのを許す
- **spell** [spél] 【動】〜を綴(つづ)る 【名】呪文, 一続きの期間；一時期
  ▶それぞれの意は別語源。
  【名】spelling (単語の)綴り ▶-ing 名尾 (〜すること)
- **welcome** [wélkəm] 【動】〜を歓迎する 【名】歓迎 【間】ようこそ ▶wel- 喜び・-come 来る人
  《連語》You're welcome. どういたしまして
           (≒ It's my pleasure. / Not at all. / Don't mention it.)
- **mild** [máɪəld] 【形】温和な；優しい - [味が穏やか] → まろやかな
  ▶「甘口カレー」は mild curry。
- **probable** [prɑ́ːbəbl] 【形】ほぼ確実な ▶prob- 証明する (= probe)・-able 形尾 (可能)
  【副】probably 十中八九 ▶-ly 副尾。perhaps の項参照。
- **abroad** [əbrɔ́ːd] 【副】外国へ／で；海外へ／で ▶a- = ad- 方向・-broad 広い ⇔ at home 本国で

EXERCISE A

各文の下線部分に入る適切な語を左ページの見出し語から選びましょう。

1. The weather this winter has been very _____ . It hasn't been very cold at all.
2. She hit the nail into the wood with a _____ .
3. The express train doesn't stop at this _____ .
4. The brown _____ from the apple tree slowly fell to the ground.
5. It is too dangerous to _____ the road here. There are too many cars.
6. _____ to my home! You will be staying in the guest bedroom tonight.
7. My sister won first _____ in the singing contest!
8. First, _____ the water. After that, please put the water into the cup.
9. If I have the chance, I would like to study _____ someday.
10. Please write today's _____ at the top of the page.

EXERCISE B

左の語の定義として正しいものを右のコラムより選び、( )にアルファベットを書き入れましょう。

Part 1

1. ( ) probable   a. one of the flat, green parts of a plant
2. ( ) piece   b. go from one side of something to the other
3. ( ) welcome   c. an animal that is large, dangerous or unusual
4. ( ) fancy   d. a large piece of metal carried for protection
5. ( ) leaf   e. a place where buses or trains regularly stop
6. ( ) forgive   f. stop feeling anger toward someone
7. ( ) shield   g. greet someone in a friendly way
8. ( ) beast   h. an amount that is cut from a larger section of something
9. ( ) cross   i. likely to happen but not certain
10. ( ) station   j. the feeling of liking someone or something

Part 2

1. ( ) abroad   a. fight in order to keep someone or something safe
2. ( ) boil   b. something won in a contest
3. ( ) date   c. say or write the letters of a word
4. ( ) defend   d. a tool used for hitting nails
5. ( ) hammer   e. the early part of the day
6. ( ) mild   f. in or to a foreign country
7. ( ) morning   g. gentle in nature or behavior; not strong
8. ( ) prize   h. a specific day of a month
9. ( ) sign   i. a board that gives information about something
10. ( ) spell   j. become so hot that bubbles form in a liquid

Section B

Unit 1

- **tend** [ténd] 【動】[tend to do] ～する傾向がある
  【名】tendency 傾向 ▶-ency 名尾。[have a tendency to do] で [tend to do] の意。
- **baggage** [bǽgɪdʒ] 【名】[集合的に](旅行時の)手荷物(≒ [英] luggage)
  ▶[米] では luggage の方が高級なイメージを与え, 広告や店頭などで好まれる。
- **forecast** [fɔ́ɚkæst] 【名】予報 【動】～を予報する
  ▶fore- 前もって・-cast 投げる→見越す。weather forecast は「天気予報」。この意では forecast 1語でも可。
- **campaign** [kæmpéɪn] 【名】(政治的・社会的)運動, (戦略的)軍事行動
  ▶campus((大学などの)キャンパス), camp(キャンプ)と同源。原義は「野原」。野原が戦場となった時代背景から「戦いの活動」のイメージを持つ。
- **frame** [fréɪm] 【名】骨組み；枠組み → 額縁 → [身体の骨組み] → 体格
  [思考の枠組み] → 視点
- **pronounce** [prənáʊns] 【動】～を発音する, ～を公言する ▶pro- = pre- 前へ・-nounce 声に出して述べる
  【名】pronunciation 発音 ▶-ation 名尾
- **drawer** [drɔ́ːɚ] 【名】引き出し, [drawers] たんす ▶draw 引く・-er 名尾(もの)。draw の項参照。
- **revenge** [rɪvéndʒ] 【名】復讐 【動】～の仕返しをする ▶re- 再び・-venge 立証する(= vindicate)
- **status** [stéɪtəs] [stǽtəs] 【名】地位；身分－[置かれている状況] → 現状；状態
  ▶stand と同源。「立場 → 置かれている状況」のイメージ。
- **accuse** [əkjúːz] 【動】～を非難する；告訴する ▶ac- = ad- 方向 → ～に対して・-cuse 原因(= cause)
  《連語》accuse 人 of ～ 人を～の理由で非難する；告訴する
- **extend** [ɪksténd] 【動】～を伸ばす；伸びる → ～を延期する ▶ex- 外へ・-tend 伸びる
  [四方八方に伸ばす] → ～を拡大する
  ▶extend は「二次元の面の広がり」, expand は「三次元の空間の広がり」を表す。
  【形】extensive 広範囲の ▶-sive 形尾 【名】extension 延長, 拡張 ▶-tion 名尾
- **imitate** [ímɪteɪt] 【動】～をまねする
  ▶copy は可能な限り正確にまねる場合, mimic は動作や話し方などをそっくりまねて, 人をからかったり馬鹿にしたりする場合。
  【名】imitation 真似；模造品 ▶-ation 名尾
- **pardon** [páɚdn] 【動】～を許す 【名】許し；容赦(ようしゃ) ▶par- 十分に・-don 与える(= give)
  《連語》I beg your pardon. もう一度言ってもらえますか。
- **smell** [smél] 【動】～の匂いを嗅ぐ 【名】匂い；香り
  ▶芳香・悪臭にかかわらず, 本来, 匂いを表す最も中立的な語。
- **salary** [sǽləri] 【名】(年俸としての)給料；サラリー
  ▶salt(食塩)と同源。「塩代としてローマ兵に与えられた銀貨」が原義。「日給としての賃金」は wage。salary と wage をまとめたものが pay(給料)。
- **wander** [wáːndɚ] 【動】さまよう ▶roam は「家から離れて遠くまで自由に動き回る」の意。
- **hollow** [háːloʊ] 【形】空(から)の；空洞の ┌ くぼんだ；へこんだ ▶hole(穴)と同語源。
  └ うわべだけの；実質のない
- **particular** [pɚtíkjələɚ] 【形】特定の ▶part 部分・-icul = -cle 小さいもの・-ar 形尾
  《連語》be particular about ～ ～の好みがうるさい　in particular 特に
  【副】particularly 特に ▶-ly 副尾
- **tiny** [táɪni] 【形】(同種のものと比べて)極端に小さい ⟷ huge 巨大な
  ▶small は「相対的に小さい」。
- **true** [trúː] 【形】(現実のものと寸分違わず一致する) → 本当の；忠実な
  ▶real は「見かけと実質が一致」, actual は単に想像や仮定ではなく「実在」イメージ。
  【名】truth 真理 ▶-th 名尾(抽象名詞)

一生もののの一冊に！大学生のうちに読みたい本

対訳 21世紀に生きる君たちへ
司馬遼太郎 著／ドナルド・キーン 監訳
ロバート・ミンツァー 訳

定価：1,100円（本体1,000円＋税）

いつの時代になっても人間が生きていく上で欠かすことのできない構えがある。司馬遼太郎が小学校用教科書のために書きおろした、簡潔ながら力強いメッセージを日英対訳で収めたた新しい時代への道しるべ。

こども哲学 いっしょにいるって、なに？
オスカー・ブルニフィエ 著／西宮かおり 訳／重松清 監修／フレデリック・ベナグリア 絵

定価：1,760円（本体1,600円＋税）

哲学教育の本場・フランスから生まれた、世界各国でロングセラーのシリーズ。こどもの「なぜ？」を楽しく考える絵本。

岐路の前にいる君たちに
鷲田清一 著

定価：1,760円（本体1,600円＋税）

哲学者・鷲田清一が、入学・卒業式で、新しい世界に旅立つ若者へ贈った、8年分の人生哲学。不安と希望が入り交じった若い人へ向けたメッセージはそのまま、現代人が直面する仕事や人生の悩みに寄り添い、背中を押してくれます。

しぶとい十人の本屋
辻山良雄 著

定価：2,310円（本体2,100円＋税）

新刊書店「Title」を開いて8年。ふと自分の仕事がわからなくなり、全国にいる仲間のもとを訪ねると消費されず、健やかに生きるヒントが見えてきた――。読み終えるころには きっと元気が出る一冊。

誰のために法は生まれた
木庭顕 著
定価：2,035円(本体1,850円+税)

紀伊國屋じんぶん大賞2019受賞！ 追いつめられた、たった一人を守るもの、それが法とデモクラシーの基なんだ──問題を鋭く見つめ、格闘した紀元前ギリシャ・ローマの人たち、彼らが残した古典作品を深く読み解き、すべてを貫く原理を取り出してくる。中高生と語り合った5日間の記録。

断片的なものの社会学
岸政彦 著
定価：1,716円(本体1,560円+税)

人の話を聞くということは、ある人生のなかに入っていくということ。社会学者が実際に出会った「解釈できない出来事」をめぐるエッセイ。一人ひとりのなかにある記憶や感覚が立ち現れてくる。稀有な読書体験となります。「一生に一度はこういう本を書いてみたいと感じるような書でした。」──星野智幸さん

渡り鳥たちが語る科学夜話
全卓樹 著
定価：1,760円(本体1,600円+税)

「科学が照らすものは、この世の世界に降りそそぐ美しい奇跡なのだ。」──島本理

戦争まで
加藤陽子 著
定価：1,870円(本体1,700円+税)

かつて日本は、世界から「どちらを選ぶか」と三度、問われた。より良き道を選べなかったのはなぜか？「第一級資料を前にした歴史学者と中高生のおもしろく、半端なくスリリングで息を呑む対話が、選択を迫られる私たちのためのだいじな鍵がここにある」──中島京子さん

慣れろ、おちょくれ、踏み外せ
森山至貴＋能町みね子 著
定価：1,980円(本体1,800円+税)

「LGBT」に分類して整理したら終わりじゃない。クィアで考えるスタート地点にして決定版！

「彼らの決死の自己開示と深い洞察とをまとめた本書は、他の追随を許さない名著(...)我々を勇気づけ、この先10年の社会を力強く照らしてくれる」──花田菜々子さん

銀河の片隅で科学夜話
全卓樹 著
定価：1,760円(本体1,600円+税)

一日の長さは一年に0.000017秒ずつ伸びている。500億年のちは、一日の

エモい古語辞典

堀越英美 著／海島千本 イラスト

定価：1,782円（本体1,620円＋税）

新たな表現は古語から生まれる！胸がうずく、心がゆれる日本語表現を1654語厳選。春夏秋冬、月や星、草花や色、「恋」など人の心を表す美しい言葉から、怖さやおぞましさでぞくっとかむ言葉、知る人ぞ知る四字熟語、現代的の文章でも使えるみやびやかな推量語まで、創作のアイデアソースにぜひ！

最新日米口語辞典［決定版］

エドワード・G・サイデンステッカー
松本道弘 編

定価：5,280円（本体4,800円＋税）

40年以上のベストセラーとなった「読む辞典」、待望の改訂版。表現の羅列ではなく、読んで楽しめる。日常使いの口語表現を採用し、ニュアンスや使い分けをわかりやすく説明しています。今、発信したい言葉が例文付きでたっぷり盛り込まれた辞典です。

生命海流 GALAPAGOS

福岡伸一 著

定価：2,090円（本体1,900円＋税）

絶海の孤島に生息する奇妙な生物たちはどこから来たのか？特殊な進化を遂げたのはなぜか？なぜ生物たちは人間を恐れないのか？ガラパゴスの生物たちの謎を解き明かす。島の大自然を全身で感じながら、"進化の現場"と、その驚くべき生命の姿を生き生きと克明に綴った紀行ノンフィクション。

文体練習

レーモン・クノー 著／朝比奈弘治 訳

定価：3,738円（本体3,398円＋税）

バスの中で起こった他愛もない出来事が99通りの変奏によって変幻自在に書き分けられてゆく。20世紀フランス文学の急進的言語革命を率いたクノーによる究極の言語遊戯。伸條正義による美しいブックデザインもお楽しみ下さい。

お近くの書店・ネット書店でご注文ください。

朝日出版社

まつだ本です。一部さん

十皿の料理
斉須政雄 著
定価：1,980円（本体1,800円＋税）

読む度に背筋が伸びる、料理を通して仕事読本。フランス料理レストラン「コート・ドール」のシェフが語り下ろす十皿の定番料理、誠実に「仕事と自分をどう近づけ、幸せな向きあい方を実現させていったのか？」——読み継がれるべき一冊。一幅先生

絵を見る技術
秋田麻早子 著
定価：2,035円（本体1,850円＋税）

謎を解く鍵は、絵の中に隠された「線」にあった。絵の研究は「意味」と「形」の二本柱。本書では、これまであまり触れられてこなかった「造形」の面から名画を見ていきます。「読んだ後、絵を見ることが楽しくなる本！」——結城浩さん（「数学ガール」著者）

自炊者になるための26週
三浦哲哉 著
定価：2,178円（本体1,980円＋税）

さっと買って、さっと作って、このうえなく幸福になれる、日々の小さく創造的行為。"トーストを焼くだけからはじまる、"ほぼ毎日キッチンに立つ"映画研究者"の手立てを具体的に語ります。おいしさと創造力をめぐる、全くあたらしい理論＆実践の書！

だれでもデザイン
山中俊治 著
定価：2,090円（本体1,900円＋税）

デザインは、ささやかでも誰かを確実にハッピーにする！人間工学と新しい技術を考え続けたデザイナーが中高生に語る、物づくりの根幹とこれからを。偶然の出会いを大切に、隣の人の脳みそを借りて。「才能とは無関係、誰もが身につけられる方法を話します」

EXERCISE A

各文の下線部分に入る適切な語を左ページの見出し語から選びましょう。

1. The tree looks healthy, but it's _____ inside.
2. The weather _____ says it will rain later today.
3. I keep my pens and pencils in my desk _____ .
4. How do you _____ your first name?
5. The man plans to take _____ on his neighbor for stealing his bicycle.
6. Can you _____ that? I think it's gas. Perhaps it's coming from the oven.
7. I'm only going away for the weekend, so I won't take much _____ .
8. The baby's _____ fingers are so cute!
9. The train company plans to _____ the monorail line to the airport.
10. I know that you don't believe me. However, what I'm saying is _____ .

EXERCISE B

次の各文の空所に入る適切な語を (a) ~ (d) から選び、○をしましょう。

1. The continental United States _____ from the Atlantic to the Pacific oceans.
   a. wanders
   b. extends
   c. accuses
   d. smells

2. This isn't a real Rolex. It is merely an _____ .
   a. imitative
   b. imitation
   c. imitating
   d. imitator

3. Betty loves sports, _____ team sports such as basketball and football.
   a. particular
   b. particularly
   c. particularity
   d. particularize

4. Many prisoners were _____ and released.
   a. pardoned
   b. accused
   c. imitated
   d. wandered

5. Place each _____ of clothing through the security scanner.
   a. baggage
   b. contents
   c. article
   d. matter

6. Cathy couldn't help but _____ when John gave her a dozen roses.
   a. smell
   b. cry
   c. imitate
   d. wander

Unit 2

- **absence** [ǽbsəns] 【名】不在 ▶ ab- 離れて・-se 存在・-ence 名尾 ⟷ presence 存在
  【形】absent 不在の ▶ -ent 形尾 ⟷ present 存在している
  《連語》be absent from 〜 〜を欠席する ⟷ be present at 〜 〜に出席する

- **sweep** [swíːp] 【動】〜を掃く；掃除する → 〜を一掃する 【名】掃除
  ▶「拭(ふ)く」は wipe,「(ほこりなどを)はたく」は dust,「掃除機をかける」は vacuum。

- **limb** [lím] 【名】手足 − [形状の類似] → 大枝 ▶ 手足；四肢(しし)をまとめていう語。

- **hunt** [hʌ́nt] 【動】〜を狩る；狩猟する → (犯人などを)追う
  【名】hunting 狩猟, 追跡 ▶ -ing 名尾(〜すること)。job hunting は「就職活動」。

- **process** [práːses] 【名】過程・プロセス → 加工・製法 ▶ pro- 前へ・-cess 行くこと
  【動】proceed 前進する, 進行する ▶ -ceed 行く(=go)
  【名】procession 行列(の行進) ▶ -sion 名尾。「複数のものの進行」のイメージ。
  【名】procedure 手順；手続き ▶ -ure 名尾。「物事の進行過程」のイメージ。

- **quantity** [kwάːntəti] 【名】量 ▶ quant- 何らかの量・-ity 名尾 ⟷ quality 質

- **strength** [stréŋkθ] 【名】強さ → 力 ▶ -th 名尾。strong(強い)の名詞形。
  【動】strengthen 〜を強くする；強化する ▶ -en 動尾

- **bury** [béri] 【動】〜を埋める → 〜を埋葬する ⟷ cremate 〜を火葬する
  【名】burial 埋葬 ▶ -al 名尾

- **collect** [kəlékt] 【動】〜を(入念に選んで組織的に)集める；収集する
  ▶ col-=con- 共に・-lect 集める。assemble は「ある目的のために集める」の意。
  【名】collection 集めること；収集 ▶ -tion 名尾

- **deserve** [dɪzə́ːv] 【動】〜に値する ▶ de- 強意・serve 奉仕する
  《連語》deserve to do 〜して当然だ
  【名】desert [dɪzə́ːt] 当然の報い

- **educate** [édʒəkeɪt] 【動】〜を教育する
  ▶ e- 外へ → 出す・duc- 導く・-ate 動尾。「才能を導き出す」イメージ。
  【形】educational 教育に関する ▶ -al 形尾 【名】education 教育 ▶ -ation 名尾

- **justify** [dʒʌ́stəfaɪ] 【動】〜を正当化する ▶ just 正しいと思う・-ify 動尾
  【名】justification 正当化 ▶ -ation 名尾

- **lean** [líːn] 【動】[lean on / against 〜] 〜に寄りかかる；もたれる
  【形】(筋肉質で)痩せた(≒slender, slim) ⟷ fat

- **prefer** [prɪfə́ː] 【動】〜をより好む ▶ pre- 先に・-fer 運ぶ。「優先する」イメージ。
  《連語》prefer A to B　B と対照して A を好む(× prefer A than B)
  【形】preferable 好ましい ▶ -able 形尾(可能)
  【名】preference 好み ▶ -ence 名尾

- **remove** [rɪmúːv] 【動】〜を移す → 〜を取り除く ▶ re- 元の場所へ → 再び・move 動く
  【名】removal 移動, 除去 ▶ -al 名尾

- **concept** [kάːnsept] 【名】概念 ▶ con- 共に・-ceive つかむ。「心に取り入れたモノ」のイメージ。
  【名】conception 概念 ▶ -tion 名尾。計画や想像力にも適用されるという点で
  　　　　　　　　　conception は concept に比べて意味範囲が広い。
  【動】conceive 〜を心に抱く, [conceive a child] 妊娠する

- **efficient** [ɪfíʃənt] 【形】有能な；能率の良い ▶ ef- 強意・-fici 作る・ent 形尾
  【名】efficiency 能力, 能率 ▶ -ency 名尾

- **joyful** [dʒɔ́ɪfəl] 【形】喜びに満ちた；嬉しい ▶ joy 喜び；嬉しさ・-ful 形尾(満ちている)

- **slight** [sláɪt] 【形】きゃしゃな → 細い；薄い − [厚み・密度が少ない] → わずかな

- **tough** [tʌ́f] 【形】堅い → 頑丈な；丈夫な；たくましい → 手ごわい → 難しい

EXERCISE A

各文の下線部分に入る適切な語を左ページの見出し語から選びましょう。

1. For a small child, he has surprising _____ .
2. I love to _____ stamps. It has been my hobby for about 10 years and I now have hundreds!
3. I'm going to _____ the leaves into a pile.
4. Our dog likes to _____ bones in the garden, but he takes them out of the ground soon.
5. Before coming in, _____ your shoes. We want to keep the house clean.
6. I _____ ice-cream to chocolate.
7. Please _____ your opinion. If I know the reason for your opinion, I might agree with you.
8. You worked hard! You _____ a break!
9. I'm a history teacher. I try to _____ my students about events in the past.
10. Please think carefully before you answer. This is a very _____ question.

EXERCISE B

次の各文の空所に入る適切な語を (a) ~ (d) から選び、○をしましょう。

1. I had a _____ cold, but I was well enough to go to class.
    a. efficient
    b. lean
    c. slight
    d. tough

2. This bottle may be opened by _____ the child-safety seal.
    a. removed
    b. removal
    c. removes
    d. removing

3. Her _____ for chocolate cake made it nearly impossible for her to lose weight.
    a. preferring
    b. preference
    c. preferable
    d. prefer

4. After the 15-mile run, Shirley was so tired that she had no _____ to go further.
    a. strength
    b. exercise
    c. health
    d. battle

5. Many European cities have old houses that are well _____ .
    a. believed
    b. deserved
    c. justified
    d. preserved

6. Please put out all your recyclables for _____ in the morning.
    a. collect
    b. collectable
    c. collection
    d. collective

Unit 3

- **elect** [ɪlékt]
  - 【動】~を選出する ▶ e- = ex- 外へ → 出す・-lect 集める
  - 【名】election 選挙 ▶ -tion 名尾。「総選挙」は general election。
- **conscience** [kάːnʃəns]
  - 【名】良心 ▶ con- 共に → 共通して・sci- 知る・-ence 名尾
  - 【形】conscientious 良心的な ▶ -ous 形尾
- **cure** [kjúɚ]
  - 【動】[cure 人 of 病気] 人の病気を治療する 【名】治療
  - ▶「病気の治療」が cure,「怪我の治療」が heal。ここでの of は「分離」のイメージ。
- **bribe** [bráɪb]
  - 【名】賄賂(わいろ) 【動】~に賄賂を贈る(≒ offer a bribe to)
  - ⟷ take a bribe 賄賂を受け取る ▶ rebate は「本来戻されるべき正当なもの」。
  - 【名】bribery 汚職 ▶ -ery 名尾
- **subject** [sʌ́bdʒɪkt]
  - 【名】(神からの投下物)→ 主題 ┬ [話の主題] → 話題 ▶ sub- 下へ・ject 投げる
    - ├ [教育課程の主題] → 科目
    - └ [主題を持って行動するもの] → 主体 – [文中の主体となるモノ] → 主語
  - 《連語》be subject to ~ ~に従属している ▶「下に置かれている」イメージ。
  - 【形】subjective 主観的な, 主語の ▶ -tive 形尾 ⟷ objective 客観的な
- **track** [trǽk]
  - 【名】跡；足跡 – [何度も通ってできた跡] ┬ 小道, 轍(わだち)
    - └ [輸送路の発達] → 鉄道線路
  - 【動】(足)跡を追う(≒ keep track of)
- **wealth** [wélθ]
  - 【名】富, 財産 ▶ weal- 幸せな(= well)・-th 名尾
- **annoy** [ənɔ́ɪ]
  - 【動】~を(一時的に)いらいらさせる；悩ます
  - ▶ harass は「絶えず悩ませる」, bother は「ある状態を邪魔することで悩ませる」。
  - 《連語》be annoyed at ~ ~に腹立たしく思う
- **cheat** [tʃíːt]
  - 【動】~をだます → ごまかす；カンニングする 【名】不正行為, 詐欺(師)
  - ▶ カンニングは和製英語。「ずるい」を意味する cunning から。
- **decrease** [dɪkríːs]
  - 【動】~を減らす；減る 【名】減少 ▶ de- 下へ・crease 成長する
  - ⟷ increase ~を増やす；増える 【名】増加 ▶ in- 積み重ねて(= on)
- **fade** [féɪd]
  - 【動】色あせる → 衰える ┬ 姿を消す；見えなくなる
    - └ (花が)しぼむ
  - 《連語》fade away 消える(≒ fade out)
- **hire** [háɪɚ]
  - 【動】[英](物を)有料で貸借する, [米](人を)雇う
- **sword** [sɔ́ːd]
  - 【名】剣；刀 ▶ The pen is mightier than the sword.(ペンは剣よりも強し)
- **survive** [sɚváɪv]
  - 【動】~を切り抜けて生き残る；~より長生きする
  - ▶ sur- 上へ → 越えて・vive 生きる(= live)
  - 【名】survival 生き残ること ▶ -al 名尾
- **weave** [wíːv]
  - 【動】~を織る；編む ▶ weave は「糸を織り機で織る」, knit は「編み棒を使って糸を編む」, sew は「針と糸で縫う」の意。
- **constant** [kάːnstənt]
  - 【形】絶え間ない；一定の
  - ▶ stand と同源。「動かない → 変化がない」イメージ。
- **modest** [mάːdəst]
  - 【形】謙虚な；適度な
  - ▶ mod- 計る → 尺度。「自分の尺度(= 領分)に合った」イメージ。
- **recent** [ríːsnt]
  - 【形】つい最近の
  - 【副】recently つい最近(≒ lately) ▶ -ly 副尾
- **absolutely** [ǽbsəluːtli]
  - 【副】絶対に,(返事で)その通りですよ ▶ -ly 副尾
  - 【形】absolute 絶対的な ⟷ relative 相対的な
- **nevertheless** [nèvɚðəlés]
  - 【副】それにもかかわらず(≒ nonetheless)
  - ▶ never 決して~ない・the それほど・less 少ない。「それほど少ない内容ではないが → 補足説明しなければならない」イメージ。

EXERCISE A

各文の下線部分に入る適切な語を左ページの見出し語から選びましょう。

1. Is there a medicine to _____ my sickness?
2. A train runs along a _____ .
3. There has been a _____ in the number of students this year. We hope to get more next year.
4. Don't _____ on the test! If you get caught, you will be in a lot of trouble.
5. We plan to _____ 20 people for the new office.
6. Although Carl speaks great French, he says that he's not very good. I think he's very _____ .
7. A _____ is a dangerous weapon.
8. The country will _____ a new leader this year.
9. I did nothing wrong. My _____ is clear.
10. I heard that two people were able to _____ the plane accident. They were very lucky.

EXERCISE B

次の各文の空所に入る適切な語を (a) ~ (d) から選び、○をしましょう。

1. It has not been decided who the president will _____ as new sales manager.
    a. hire
    b. fade
    c. survive
    d. cheat

2. I have an important appointment on Friday, so I _____ cannot come to the party.
    a. absolutely
    b. particularly
    c. nevertheless
    d. recently

3. The _____ thing about my new job is that I have to travel two hours to get to the office.
    a. annoy
    b. annoyance
    c. annoyed
    d. annoying

4. The population has been _____ each year since the mid-2000s.
    a. hiring
    b. fading
    c. decreasing
    d. weaving

5. There is no _____ in continuing to buy from companies that refuse to offer a discount on large orders.
    a. subject
    b. point
    c. wealth
    d. object

6. Be careful when washing this sweater as the color may _____ .
    a. decrease
    b. extend
    c. fade
    d. imitate

Unit 4

☐ **skyscraper** [skáɪskreɪpɚ]	【名】	超高層ビル；摩天楼(まてんろう) ▶sky 空・scraper こするもの
☐ **humble** [hʌ́mbl]	【形】	謙虚な ▶hum- 大地。「自分の頭を地面につける」イメージ。
☐ **collar** [kɑ́:lɚ]	【名】	襟(えり) ▶color(色)[kʌ́lɚ] との発音の違いに注意。
☐ **flood** [flʌ́d]	【名】	洪水【動】〜を氾濫させる ▶flow(流れる)と同源。
☐ **immediate** [ɪmí:diət]	【形】	即座の ▶im- = in- 否定 → 欠如・medi- 中間(= middle)・-ate 形尾
	【副】	immediately 即座に ▶-ly 副尾
☐ **ounce** [áʊns]	【名】	(重さの単位)オンス
		▶日常生活での重量単位(日常オンス)として 1 / 16 ポンド(≒ 28g)，貴金属の重量単位(金衡オンス)として 1 / 12 金衡ポンド(≒ 31g)。
☐ **principle** [prínsəpl]	【名】	原理；原則 → 主義
		▶prin- 第一・cip- 取る・-ple 名尾。principal と同音。
☐ **spite** [spáɪt]	【名】	[in spite of 〜] 〜にもかかわらず ▶spite の原義は「軽蔑」。in spite of は「(〜を軽蔑して；無視して)→ 〜にもかかわらず」。
☐ **value** [vǽlju]	【名】	価値；[values] 価値観【動】〜を評価する；尊重する
	【形】	valuable 貴重な；高価な【名】貴重品 ▶-able 形尾(可能)
	【形】	invaluable この上なく貴重な ▶in- 否定。「価値がはかれないほど貴重な」。
☐ **argue** [ɑ́ɚgju]	【動】	〜を論じる，言い争う ▶根拠を挙げて議論し，白黒をつけること。
	【名】	argument 議論 ▶-ment 名尾
☐ **beg** [bég]	【動】	[beg 人 for 物 / beg 物 from 人] 人に物を請う
		▶beg (人) (物) の形は不可。
	【名】	beggar 乞食 ▶-ar 名尾(〜の人)
☐ **aim** [éɪm]	【名】	狙い；(具体的な)目的【動】[aim at 〜] 〜に照準を合わせる；狙う [aim to do] 〜することに狙いを定めている；〜することを目標としている
		▶purpose は単に「決意した目標」。object は「努力目標」，objective は「達成可能と思われる目標」，goal は「最終的な目標」。
☐ **descend** [dɪsénd]	【動】	降りる →(祖先から)伝わる ▶de- 下へ・-scend 登る ⟷ ascend 上がる
	【名】	descent 降りること，下り坂，血統 ⟷ ascent 登ること，上り坂
	【名】	descendant 子孫 ▶-ant 名尾(〜する人) ⟷ ancestor 祖先
☐ **govern** [gʌ́vɚn]	【動】	〜を統治する(≒ rule) →(感情などを)抑える(≒ control)
	【名】	government 政治；[the Government] 政府 ▶-ment 名尾
	【名】	governor 州知事 ▶-or = -er 名尾(〜する人)
☐ **harm** [hɑ́ɚm]	【動】	〜に害を与える；危害を加える【名】害；危害
	《連語》	do harm to 〜 / do 〜 harm 〜に害を与える
	【形】	harmful 有害な ▶-ful 形尾(満ちている) ⟷ harmless 無害な
☐ **damp** [dǽmp]	【形】	湿気の多い ▶humid は「湿気で蒸し蒸しする」，moist は「適度に湿った」。
☐ **succeed** [səksí:d]	【動】	[succeed to 〜] (地位・財産などを)引き継ぐ
		[succeed in 〜] 〜に成功する ▶suc- 付随して → 続いて・-ceed 行く
		▶原義は「続いて行く → 追いつく」。succeed to は「先人の地位に追いつく」，succeed in は「追いついた結果，その地位のまっただ中にいる」イメージ。
	【名】	success 成功【形】successful 成功した ▶-ful 形尾(満ちている)
	【名】	succession 継続，継承 ▶-sion 名尾【形】successive 連続する ▶-ive 形尾
☐ **dull** [dʌ́l]	【形】	(刃物が)鋭くない；切れ味の悪い →(思考が)鋭くない；鈍い → [(思考に)面白みがない] →(変化がなく)単調な；退屈な
☐ **rude** [rú:d]	【形】	(粗野で)無礼な ▶impolite は「言葉など社会的礼儀をわきまえていない」。
☐ **mighty** [máɪti]	【形】	強力な；強大な ▶might(肉体的・精神的に大きな)力・-y 形尾

EXERCISE A

各文の下線部分に入る適切な語を左ページの見出し語から選びましょう。

1. My boyfriend proposed to me when we were on the top of a _____ in New York.
2. The old man was so poor that he had to _____ for money from strangers.
3. I'm very sorry. I didn't mean to do any _____ .
4. I usually enjoy reading. However, this story is really _____ .
5. This plan will never _____ ! We need to think of some new ideas.
6. When we started to _____ the mountain, the weather became worse.
7. He's wearing a shirt that has a white _____ .
8. In _____ of the rain, we decided to leave the house.
9. My _____ reaction was shock and horror when I heard the news.
10. The people in the house next to ours often _____ . We can sometimes hear them shouting.

EXERCISE B

次の各文の空所に入る適切な語を (a) ~ (d) から選び、○をしましょう。

1. She is a direct _____ of George Washington.
    a. descend
    b. descendant
    c. descended
    d. descending

2. A _____ hotel will cost you only $50 a night in Seattle.
    a. dull
    b. mighty
    c. modest
    d. recent

3. The poverty is so bad in India that many children are _____ on the street for money.
    a. arguing
    b. begging
    c. descending
    d. harming

4. The _____ party is planning to take the nation in new direction.
    a. governor
    b. governed
    c. government
    d. governing

5. The president of the United States _____ the country for four years.
    a. argues
    b. succeeds
    c. governs
    d. values

6. The police hope to _____ what happened to cause the fire.
    a. arrange
    b. determine
    c. propose
    d. succeed

Unit 5

- ☐ **comfort** [kámfɚt]
  - 【動】～を元気づける；慰める 【名】（元気づけによる）慰め → 快適さ
  - ▶ com- 強意・-fort 強い。consolation は「落胆時に寄せられる同情や励まし」での慰め。
  - 【形】comfortable 快適な ▶ -able 形尾（可能）

- ☐ **devil** [dévl]
  - 【名】悪魔 ▶「悪口を言う人」が原義。

- ☐ **fault** [fɔ́:lt]
  - 【名】欠点；欠陥（≒ defect）→ 誤り；過失
  - 《連語》be at fault 間違っている　find fault with ～ ～のあら探しをする

- ☐ **ladder** [lǽdɚ]
  - 【名】はしご ▶ the ladder of success は「成功のはしご」という比喩表現。

- ☐ **deaf** [déf]
  - 【形】耳が聞こえない 【名】[the deaf] 耳の聞こえない人たち
  - 《連語》turn a deaf ear to ～ ～に少しも耳を貸さない

- ☐ **rust** [rʌ́st]
  - 【名/動】錆（さび）；錆付く－[錆付くと動きが鈍くなることから]
  - →（能力などの）鈍化；衰え；（能力などが）鈍る
  - 【形】rusty 錆びた；錆び付いた，（能力などが）鈍くなった；衰えた ▶ -y 形尾

- ☐ **replace** [rɪpléɪs]
  - 【動】[replace A with B] A を B と取り替える ▶ re- 元の場所へ・-place 置く
  - 【名】replacement 交換；取替え ▶ -ment 名尾

- ☐ **holy** [hóʊli]
  - 【形】神聖な ▶ the Holy Bible で「聖書（the Bible, the Good Book）」の意。

- ☐ **blame** [bléɪm]
  - 【動】～を非難する 【名】非難
  - ▶ blasphemy（神への冒涜（ぼうとく））の短縮形。「不敬な言動を発する」イメージ。
  - 《連語》blame A for B / blame B on A　A に B の責任を負わせる

- ☐ **compose** [kəmpóʊz]
  - 【動】～を構成する，（曲・文などを）作る，～を落ち着かせる
  - ▶ con- 共に・pose 置く。「複数のものをまとめて置く」イメージ。同種のもので構成されている場合は consist of, 異質のものの場合は be composed of。
  - 《連語》A be composed of B　A が B で構成されている
  - 【名】composition 構成，作曲；作文 ▶ -tion 名尾
  - 【名】composer 作曲家 ▶ -er 名尾（～する人）

- ☐ **interrupt** [ìntərʌ́pt]
  - 【動】～を妨げる；中断する ▶ inter- 二者間の（＝between）・-rupt 壊す（＝break）
  - 【名】interruption 妨害；中断 ▶ -tion 名尾

- ☐ **recommend** [rèkəménd]
  - 【動】～を推薦する；勧める ▶ advise とは異なり，recommend 人 that S + V の形は不可。正しくは recommend A for / to / as B。
  - 【名】recommendation 推薦, 推薦状（≒ a letter of recommendation）

- ☐ **swallow** [swɑ́:loʊ]
  - 【動】～を（噛まずに）飲み込む－[噛み砕かない]→（話を）鵜呑みにする
  - 【名】ツバメ ▶ 食べ物を丸呑みする代表的な鳥の一つが「ツバメ」。

- ☐ **encounter** [ɪnkáʊntɚ]
  - 【動】～に出くわす 【名】偶然の出会い
  - ▶ en- 中へ・counter 反対の → 対抗して

- ☐ **insist** [ɪnsíst]
  - 【動】[insist on ～] ～を（強く）主張する
  - ▶ in- 上に（＝on）・-sist 立つ（＝stand）。「あくまでも自分の立場に立つ」イメージ。
  - 【名】insistence（強い）主張 ▶ -ence 名尾

- ☐ **prohibit** [proʊhíbət]
  - 【動】[prohibit A from doing] A が～するのを禁止する ▶ pro- 前・-hibit 保つ
  - 【名】prohibition 禁止 [the Prohibition] [米] 酒類製造販売禁止 ▶ -tion 名尾

- ☐ **extraordinary** [ɪkstrɔ́ɚdəneri]
  - 【形】異常な ▶ extra- 範囲外の・-ordinary 通常の

- ☐ **evaluate** [ɪvǽljueɪt]
  - 【動】～を評価する ▶ -ate 動尾。estimate（見積もる → 評価する）より綿密さを表す。
  - 【名】evaluation 評価 ▶ e- ＝ ex- 強意・value 価値・-ation 名尾

- ☐ **thorough** [θɚ́roʊ]
  - 【形】完全な；徹底的な ▶ 前置詞 through と同源。「全体を通して」のイメージ。
  - 【形/名】thoroughbred（育ちが完全な）→（馬が）純血種の ▶ -bred 育ち

- ☐ **miserable** [mízərəbl]
  - 【形】惨（みじ）めな；非常に不幸な ▶ -able 形尾（可能）
  - 【名】misery 惨めさ ▶ miser 惨め・-y 名尾

EXERCISE A

各文の下線部分に入る適切な語を左ページの見出し語から選びましょう。

1. Please don't _____ me while I'm busy. I can help you later.
2. Churches are _____ places because they are linked to God and religion.
3. The battery in my alarm clock has died. I'll need to _____ it with a new one.
4. My car is really old. It has some _____ on its doors.
5. At the end of each school year, the teacher has to _____ the students by giving them a grade.
6. Be careful when you climb the _____ . You don't want to fall!
7. Although Steve is _____ in one ear, he can play the piano very well.
8. Even in the coldest temperatures, these boots provide warmth and _____ .
9. Mozart began to _____ music at a very young age.
10. After losing the important tennis match, I felt _____ .

EXERCISE B

次の各文の空所に入る適切な語を (a) 〜 (d) から選び、○をしましょう。

1. Ask your teacher to _____ a good dictionary to use in class.
    a. compose
    b. encounter
    c. recommend
    d. interrupt

2. This _____ of Bach's is considered to be one of the best in the history of music.
    a. compose
    b. composer
    c. composing
    d. composition

3. I thought we could share the bill, but my dad _____ on paying for everything.
    a. insisted
    b. recommended
    c. interrupted
    d. prohibited

4. When you visit Europe, make sure that you take time to _____ as many new things as possible.
    a. interrupt
    b. swallow
    c. encounter
    d. blame

5. If you want to climb the _____ of success, you have to be willing to work harder than the average person.
    a. fault
    b. ladder
    c. recommendation
    d. rust

6. I lost my wallet on the way back home on Friday, and spent the weekend feeling _____ .
    a. deaf
    b. extraordinary
    c. miserable
    d. thorough

Unit 6

- **agriculture** [ǽgrɪkʌltʃɚ]
  - 【名】農業, 農学 ▶ agri- 田畑・-culture 耕すこと
  - 【形】agricultural 農業の ▶ -al 形尾
- **beard** [bíɚd]
  - 【名】あごひげ ▶ 口ひげは mustache, ほおひげは whiskers, 無精ひげは stubble。
- **convenience** [kənvíːnjəns]
  - 【名】便利さ, 便利なもの；文明の利器 ⟷ inconvenience 不便, 不都合
  - ▶ con- 共に → 一緒に・-veni 来る・-ence 名尾。「色々なものが集まる」イメージ。
  - 【形】convenient 便利な；好都合な ▶ -ent 形尾
  - 《連語》when it is convenient for / to you 都合のよいときに
- **glory** [glɔ́ːri]
  - 【名】栄光；壮麗（そうれい）▶「光輝く」イメージ。
  - 【形】glorious 栄光ある；壮麗な ▶ -ous 形尾 【動】glorify 栄光を称える ▶ -ify 動尾
- **colleague** [káːliːg] 【名】同僚 ▶ col- = co- 共に・-league 選ばれた者
- **wrist** [ríst] 【名】手首 ▶ turn と同語源。「ぐるりと回る身体部位」のイメージ。
- **religion** [rɪlídʒən]
  - 【名】宗教；信仰
  - 【形】religious 信心深い ▶ -ous 形尾
- **whip** [wíp]
  - 【動】〜を鞭（むち）打つ −[馬を操る]→ 〜を急に動かす 【名】鞭
  - ▶「強くかき回して泡立たせる」の意もある。鞭を打つ「激しさ・素早さ」に由来。
- **gallon** [gǽlən] 【名】ガロン ▶ 液量単位で, 1ガロン ≒ 4クォート ≒ 3.8リットル。gal. と略す。
- **trap** [trǽp] 【名】罠 → 計略 【動】〜を罠にかける；罠を仕掛ける
- **reveal** [rɪvíːl]
  - 【動】（隠れているものを）現す（≒ disclose）
  - ▶ re- 元の場所へ → 取る・-veal 覆い（= veil）
- **amuse** [əmjúːz]
  - 【動】〜を面白がらせる ▶ muse（じっと見つめる → 物思いにふける）と同源。
  - 【形】amusing 面白い ▶ -ing 形尾 【形】amused 面白がって ▶ -ed 形尾
  - 【名】amusement 楽しみ；娯楽 ▶ -ment 名尾。「遊園地」は amusement park。
- **strip** [stríp] 【動】[strip A of 服／果実や樹木の皮] A から〜を剥（は）ぎ取る
- **float** [flóʊt] 【動】（物・人が水面に）浮かぶ →（考えなどが）心に浮かぶ ▶ flow と同源。
- **imagine** [ɪmǽdʒən]
  - 【動】〜を想像する ▶ 目的語には to do ではなく, doing を用いる。image の派生語。
  - 【名】imagination 想像；想像力 ▶ -tion 名尾 【形】imaginary 想像上の ▶ -ary 形尾
  - 【形】imaginative 想像力に富む ▶ -tive 形尾（性質）
  - 【形】imaginable 想像し得る ▶ -able 形尾（可能）
- **multiply** [mʌ́ltəplaɪ]
  - 【動】〜を掛ける → 〜を増やす ▶ multi- たくさん・-ply 重ねる
  - 《連語》multiply A by B　A を B で掛ける ⟷ divide A by B　A を B で割る
  - 【形／名】multiple 多数の, 倍数 ▶ -ple 形尾（重なりの）
  - 【名】multiplication 掛け算 ▶ -ation 名尾 ⟷ division 割り算
- **stick** [stík]
  - 【動】（突き）刺す →（体の一部を）突き出す −[引っかかる]
  - → 〜をはりつける −[考えが頭や心にくっつく]→（こびりついて）離れない
  - 【名】（突き刺さるもの）→ 棒切れ → 杖
  - 《連語》stick to A「A にくっつく」→ A に固執する
  - 【形】sticky ねばねばする；べとべとする, 粘着性の ▶ -y 形尾
- **risk** [rísk]
  - 【名】（何かを得るために自ら進んで背負う）危険；危険性
  - 《連語》run the risk of doing 〜する危険を冒す
  - ▶「何かを得る目的に向けてリスクを動かす」イメージ。
  - 【形】risky 危険な ▶ -y 形尾
- **earnest** [ɚ́ːnəst]
  - 【形】真剣な；本気の
  - 《連語》in earnest 本気で
- **vague** [véɪg]
  - 【形】（輪郭などが）ぼんやりした → 曖昧（あいまい）な
  - ▶「思考がさまよう」イメージ。vagabond（放浪者）も同源。

EXERCISE A

各文の下線部分に入る適切な語を左ページの見出し語から選びましょう。

1. I'm growing a _____ . Do you like it?
2. If you _____ 4 by 4, you get 16.
3. I have a _____ memory of meeting the woman, but I don't remember her clearly.
4. I'm a farmer. I work in _____ .
5. When the man retired from his job, his _____ made a speech about him.
6. When I got a watch for my birthday, I put it on my _____ .
7. Will this big heavy ship really _____ ?
8. If you want to make the horse go faster, _____ it!
9. To _____ his grandchildren, the old man told a funny story.
10. There is a _____ store near my house. It's open 24 hours a day, 7 days a week.

EXERCISE B

次の各文の空所に入る適切な語を (a) ~ (d) から選び、〇をしましょう。

1. What do you get if you _____ seven by seven?
    a. multiply
    b. awaken
    c. delay
    d. harvest

2. Jane thought it very _____ when George came to the formal party wearing jeans and a T-shirt.
    a. amused
    b. amusing
    c. amusement
    d. amuses

3. Would you call me back at your _____ ?
    a. conveniences
    b. conveniently
    c. convenience
    d. convenient

4. While traveling in Australia, Kaori spoke English in order to make herself _____ .
    a. expected
    b. supposed
    c. imagined
    d. understood

5. Although I couldn't remember his name, his face was quite _____ .
    a. earnest
    b. familiar
    c. serious
    d. vague

6. Could you give me a hand opening this window? It always gets _____ in wet weather.
    a. stuck
    b. floated
    c. trapped
    d. revealed

Unit 7

- **dawn** [dɔ́:n] 【名】夜明け 【動】夜が明ける，[dawn on ～] ～にわかり始める
  ▶ dawn on は光が射すと物事の実像が見え始めることに由来。

- **discipline** [dísəplən] 【名 / 動】躾(しつけ)→ [躾をする] → 訓練する ─┐
  └→ [あるべき行為の躾] → 規律 ─ [学問上躾ける範囲] → 学問分野
  ▶ disciple (弟子) から生まれた語。原義は「教え → 躾(しつけ)」。

- **furniture** [fə́:nɪtʃə] 【名】家具，備品 ▶ -ure 名尾。「一つの家具」は a piece of furniture。
  【動】[furnish A with B] A に B を備え付ける；供給する

- **hut** [hʌ́t] 【名】(泊まれる程度の手軽な)小屋 【動】～を小屋に泊まらせる；泊まる
  ▶ cabin は「主に森林や山岳地帯にある木造の小さな家」。

- **adequate** [ǽdɪkwət] 【形】(ちょうど) 十分な ▶ ad- 方向・-equ 等しい (= equal)・-ate 形尾

- **range** [réɪndʒ] 【名】列；連なり，範囲；領域 ▶ mountain range で「山の連なり → 山脈」。
  【動】～を列に並べる，(範囲などが)及ぶ
  《連語》range A from B　A から B に及ぶ

- **shallow** [ʃǽloʊ] 【形】浅い → 浅はかな ⟷ deep 深い 【名】[the shallows] 浅瀬

- **trial** [tráɪəl] 【名】試み ─ [罪の有無の解明を試みる] → 審理；裁判 ▶ -al 名尾
  ▶ experiment は「証明のための慎重な試み」，test は「一定基準に達しているかの検査」。
  【動】try ～を試みる，～を審理する；裁判にかける
  《連語》try doing 試しに～してみる　try on ～ ～を試着する

- **complain** [kəmpléɪn] 【動】[complain of/about ～] ～の不満を言う
  ▶ plaint (嘆き；苦情 → 告訴状) と同源。

- **dig** [díg] 【動】～を掘る ▶ excavate は dig よりも形式ばった語で，特に「遺跡などを発掘する」。

- **encourage** [ɪnkə́:rɪdʒ] 【動】～を勇気づける → ～を促進する ▶ en- 動詞化接頭辞・courage 勇気
  ⟷ discourage 落胆させる，(人の行為を) 思い留まらせる ▶ dis- 分離
  《連語》encourage 人 to do 勇気づけて～させる ▶ この to do は allow の項参照。
  ⟷ discourage 人 from ～ ing 落胆させて～させない
  【名】encouragement 勇気づけ，促進 ▶ -ment 名尾 ⟷ discouragement 落胆

- **lend** [lénd] 【動】～を無料で貸す ⟷ borrow ～を無料で借りる
  ▶「有料で貸す⟷有料で借りる」は共に rent。

- **pour** [pɔ́ə] 【動】～を注ぐ ─ [注いだ液体が容器一杯になる] → 流れ出る ─┐
  └→ [川があふれ出るほど雨が降る] → (雨が) 激しく降る

- **roar** [rɔ́ə] 【動】(猛獣が)吼(ほ)える；大声を出す；(雷などが)轟(とどろ)く
  【名】うなり声；轟き；大笑い
  ▶「猛獣が吼えるような低く太く轟く音」のイメージ。

- **burst** [bə́:st] 【動】(内部からの圧力によって)破裂する；～を破裂させる 【名】破裂
  《連語》burst out laughing どっと笑い出す　burst into tears どっと泣き出す

- **trust** [trʌ́st] 【動】～を信頼する → (信頼して) ～に預ける (≒ entrust) 【名】信頼；委託
  【名】trustworthy 信頼できる ▶ -worth 価値・-y 形尾

- **quarrel** [kwɔ́rəl] 【動】口論する 【名】口論 ▶ conflict は「意見や利害などの衝突」。
  【形】quarrelsome けんか好きな ▶ -some 形尾 (～の傾向がある)

- **curious** [kjúəriəs] 【形】好奇心の強い ─ [好奇心をそそるようなもので] → 奇妙な
  ▶ care (注意) と同源。
  【名】curiosity 好奇心 ▶ -ity 名尾

- **frequent** [frí:kwənt] 【形】頻繁な ▶「ぎっしり詰まった，混んだ」が原義。
  【副】frequently 頻繁に ▶ -ly 副尾 【名】frequency 頻度；頻発 ▶ -ency 名尾

- **whole** [hóʊl] 【形】全体の 【名】全部
  《連語》as a whole / on the whole 全体として；概して

EXERCISE A

各文の下線部分に入る適切な語を左ページの見出し語から選びましょう。

1. After a long _____ , the woman was sent to prison for ten years.
2. Could you _____ some water into my cup?
3. There will be a wider _____ of choices in the future.
4. Did you hear the lion _____ ? He was so loud that he woke me up.
5. My parents often _____ me to try new things. I started playing the piano thanks to my mom.
6. I ate a _____ cake all by myself, and I now feel sick.
7. After I bought a house, I had to buy some _____ to put inside it.
8. The dog decided to _____ a hole in the garden. He seems to love killing my flowers.
9. I love shopping, so I take _____ trips to the shopping mall.
10. I don't like to swim in deep water. I much prefer to swim where the water is _____ .

EXERCISE B

次の各文の空所に入る適切な語を (a) ~ (d) から選び、○をしましょう。

1. Bill received a lot of _____ from his co-workers when he was promoted to manager.
    a. encouragement
    b. encouraging
    c. encouraged
    d. encourage

2. Before the toast, Maggie _____ out four glasses of champagne.
    a. digged
    b. poured
    c. stuck
    d. deserved

3. The library will _____ up to ten books to each student.
    a. lending
    b. lender
    c. lent
    d. lend

4. Randy has not yet won the _____ of all his employees, even though he has been the boss for over five years.
    a. hut
    b. discipline
    c. stage
    d. trust

5. In a _____ letter, Joanna mentioned that she would no longer be taking a trip to Europe in the summer.
    a. permanent
    b. shallow
    c. frequent
    d. recent

6. I'm _____ to know if I have passed the exam.
    a. curious
    b. adequate
    c. sure
    d. possible

Unit 8

☐ **empire** [émpaɪɚ]	【名】	帝国 ▶「皇帝(emperor)によって統治された領土」が原義。
	【名】	emperor 皇帝 ▶ em- 中に・-per 命令する・-or = -er 名尾(〜する人)
	【形】	imperial 帝国の ▶ -al 形尾
☐ **fate** [féɪt]	【名】	運命 ▶「不運」のイメージ。
	【形】	fatal 致命的な；運命を左右する ▶ -al 形尾
☐ **flour** [fláʊɚ]	【名】	小麦粉 ▶「花」を意味する flower と同音。
☐ **boundary** [báʊndri]	【名】	(同一の世界を仕切る)境界；境界線 ▶ border の項参照。
☐ **applaud** [əplɔ́ːd]	【動】	(賞賛して)拍手する ▶ ap- = ad- 方向・-laud 拍手する
	【名】	applause 拍手 ▶ acclaim は「大声・拍手で喝采して強い賛成の意を表明する」。
☐ **slave** [sléɪv]	【名】	奴隷 ▶ 中世ラテン語 Sclavus(スラブ人)が原義。中世に奴隷にされたことから。
	【名】	slavery 奴隷の身分；奴隷制度 ▶ -ry 名尾
☐ **stock** [stάːk]	【名】	切り株 − [残っているもの] → 在庫品；貯蔵品 ┐ └→ [株分け；利益を分配するもの] → 株(式) (≒ [英] share)
	《連語》	in stock 在庫あり ⇔ out of stock 在庫切れ
☐ **tragedy** [trǽdədi]	【名】	悲劇 ⇔ comedy 喜劇 ▶「落語」は comic storytelling, comic monologue。
	【形】	tragic 悲劇の, 悲劇的な ▶ -ic 形尾 ⇔ comic 喜劇の, 喜劇的な
☐ **bend** [bénd]	【動】	(ひもを縛った弓をひく) − [弓の形状の類似] → 〜を曲げる ┐ ┌→ 身をかがめる；かがむ → 〜を屈服させる └ [ある方向に曲がる；向ける] → (努力・注意などを)向ける
	【形】	bent 曲がった ▶ 過去分詞形が形容詞に。bend は bind(縛る)と同源。
☐ **calculate** [kǽlkjəleɪt]	【動】	〜を計算する − [人の援助を計算する] ┐ └→ [calculate on 〜] 〜を当てにする
	▶ calculate は「高度で複雑な計算をする」, count は「指折り数える」。
	【名】	calculation 計算, 予想 ▶ -ation 名尾 【名】 calculator 計算機 ▶ -or 名尾(物)
☐ **invent** [ɪnvént]	【動】	〜を創造する；発明する
	▶ in- 接触(= on)・-vent 来る。「神の創造物がやって来て人に接触する」イメージ。
	【名】	invention 発明 ▶ -tion 名尾 【名】 inventor 発明家, 創案者 ▶ -or = -er 名尾(人)
	【名】	inventory 品目一覧表 ▶ -ory 名尾。「死後見つけられた動産目録」が原義。
☐ **mend** [ménd]	【動】	(欠点を除いて)〜を直す
	▶ amend の頭部が省略。同様の省略法に story(話, 物語, 階) − history(歴史), fence(囲い；フェンス) − defense(防御), sport(娯楽) − disport(気晴らし)など。
☐ **represent** [rèprɪzént]	【動】	〜を表示する − [一部で全体を表す] → 〜を代表する
	【形/名】	representative 代表的な, 代表者, [米] 下院議員 ▶ -ative 形尾
☐ **retire** [rɪtάɪɚ]	【動】	[retire from 〜] 〜から引退する；定年退職する
	▶「仕事を止める」は quit one's job
	【名】	retiree 定年退職者 ▶ -ee 名尾(〜される人)
☐ **basin** [béɪsn]	【名】	水鉢；たらい ▶ 詳しくは bowl の項参照。
☐ **flavor** [fléɪvɚ]	【名】	風味 【動】 〜に風味をつける
	▶ savor は「美味しいことを暗示する味わいと匂い」。
☐ **bitter** [bítɚ]	【形】	(舌を刺すように)苦い → (風が肌を突き刺すように)つらい
☐ **faint** [féɪnt]	【形】	かすかな；ぼんやりした 【名】 失神 【動】 失神する
☐ **lazy** [léɪzi]	【形】	(根っからの)怠け者の ▶ idle は「やることがなく暇な」のイメージ。
☐ **neat** [níːt]	【形】	きちんとした；(服装が)こざっぱりした
	▶ tidy は「こまめに手入れして整理・整頓・清潔さが行き届いていること」を表す。

EXERCISE A

各文の下線部分に入る適切な語を左ページの見出し語から選びましょう。

1. To make a loaf of bread or a cake, you have to use some _____ .
2. At the end of a classical music concert, I always _____ the musicians because they work so hard.
3. I washed my face in the _____ in the bathroom.
4. My friend's room is really _____ . It's clean and tidy!
5. One day, I hope to _____ my country in the Olympics.
6. Could you _____ my old shoes? They have some holes in them.
7. He has decided to _____ from his job early. He wants to have more free time.
8. There is a fence that marks the _____ between the two farms.
9. If you add some sugar, it will improve the _____ .
10. This chocolate is too _____ for most children, but my daughter likes it.

EXERCISE B

次の各文の空所に入る適切な語を (a) ~ (d) から選び、○をしましょう。

1. Do you know who is supposed to have _____ the television?
   a. invents
   b. invented
   c. invention
   d. inventing

2. Keep your knees _____ as you do this exercise.
   a. bend
   b. bending
   c. bent
   d. bends

3. His main goal was to be on the Olympic team as a _____ of his country.
   a. representative
   b. represented
   c. representing
   d. representational

4. This new soft drink is quite _____ . I'm sure it will be very popular.
   a. flavored
   b. flavorful
   c. flavorless
   d. flavoring

5. Everything was _____ and tidy in Richard's apartment.
   a. efficient
   b. dull
   c. lazy
   d. neat

6. The cake will get bigger as it _____ .
   a. mends
   b. applauds
   c. bakes
   d. boils

Unit 9

- **arrow** [ǽroʊ] 【名】矢 → 矢印 ▶「弓」は bow。
- **source** [sɔ́ɚs] 【名】源；出どころ ▶「物事の発生源になっているところ」のイメージ。
- **conflict** [kάnflıkt] 【名/動】紛争 → 衝突する, 矛盾する ▶ con- 共に → 互いに・-flict 打つ（= strike）
- **jealous** [dʒéləs] 【形】嫉妬深い
  - ▶ -ous 形尾。envious は「憎む気持ちよりもそれにあやかりたい」イメージ。
  - 【名】jealousy 嫉妬 ▶ -y 名尾
- **examination** [ɪgzæmənéɪʃən] 【名】調査, 試験, 診察 ▶ -ation 名尾。「試験」の意では, くだけた語として exam。
  - 【動】examine 〜を調べる ┬ [性質や能力を調査] → 〜に試験をする
  - └ [健康状態の調査] → 〜を診察する
  - 【名】examinee 受験生 ▶ -ee 名尾（〜される人）
- **cupboard** [kΛ́bɚd] 【名】食器戸棚 ▶「食器に関係なく小さな戸棚や押入れ」。p は発音しないので注意。
- **nuisance** [nú:sns] 【名】迷惑な人／もの／行為, 嫌なこと ▶ nuis- 害する・-ance 名尾
- **state** [stéɪt] 【名/動】（立っている；動かない）→ 状態 → [立場] ┬ 地位；身分；階級
  - ┌ [立場を位置づける] → 〜を述べる
  - └ [立場の違いが存在する所] → 国家 – [行政区画] → 州
  - 【形】stately 威厳のある；堂々とした ▶ -ly 形尾。state は stand と同源。
  - 【名】statement 陳述（ちんじゅつ）；声明 ▶ -ment 名尾
  - 【名】statesman（特に立派な, 尊敬される）政治家 ▶「政治屋」は politician。
- **stress** [strés] 【名/動】圧迫 [精神的圧迫] → 緊張；ストレス ┐
  - └ [重きを置く] → 強調, 〜を強調する ▶ distress（苦痛）の dis- が省略。
- **tongue** [tΛ́ŋ] 【名】舌 – [手段と行為との近接関係] → 言葉遣い,（特定の）言語
  - 《連語》hold the / one's tongue 口をつぐんでいる
  - on the tip of one's tongue 喉まで出かかって；思い出せないで
- **accustom** [əkΛ́stəm] 【動】〜を慣らす ▶ ac- = ad- 方向 → 〜に対して・custom 習慣
  - 《連語》be accustomed to 〜 〜に慣れている
- **bind** [báɪnd] 【動】〜を縛る；拘束する → 〜を束縛する →（人々・国を）結びつける
  - 《連語》be bound to do 〜 きっと〜する
  - ▶「ある運命に束縛されている」イメージ。
- **dip** [díp] 【動】〜をちょっと浸す 【名】ちょっと浸すこと ▶ soak は「どっぷり浸ける」。
- **envy** [énvi] 【動】〜をうらやましく思う；ねたむ 【名】ねたみ ▶ en- 中まで・-vy 見る
  - 【形】envious うらやんで ▶ -ous 形尾 《連語》envious of 〜 〜をうらやんで
- **heal** [hí:l] 【動】（特に切り傷や精神的な傷などを）治療する；治る
  - ▶「病気を治す」は cure。
- **invite** [ɪnváɪt] 【動】〜を招く → [invite 人 to do] 人に〜を求める ▶ allow の項参照。
  - 【名】invitation 招待；招待状 ▶ -ation 名尾
- **artificial** [ɑːtəfíʃ(ə)l] 【形】人工の ▶ art 技芸・-fici 作る・-al 形尾。「人工知能」は artificial intelligence (AI)。
  - 【名】artifice 技巧；術策
- **correct** [kərékt] 【形】正しい 【動】〜を訂正する ▶ cor- 強意・-rect まっすぐ（= straight）
  - ⟷ incorrect 正しくない；間違った ▶ in- 否定
  - 【名】correctness 正確さ；適切さ ▶ -ness 名尾 【名】correction 訂正 ▶ -tion 名尾
- **ideal** [aɪdí:l] 【形】想像上の → 理想的な 【名】理想 ▶ idea 観念・-al 形尾
  - 【名】idealism 理想主義 ▶ -ism 名尾（主義） 【形】idealistic 理想主義的な ▶ -istic 形尾
- **moral** [mɔ́rəl] 【形】（一般社会の善悪の基準に従い）道徳的な；道徳の 【名】[morals] 道徳
  - ▶ ethical は「学問的で体系的な道徳規範」, virtuous は「高い道徳基準を有している」。
  - ⟷ immoral 道徳に反する ▶ im- = in- 否定
  - 【名】morality 道徳；道徳性 ▶ -ity 名尾

EXERCISE A

各文の下線部分に入る適切な語を左ページの見出し語から選びましょう。

1. I keep all of my plates on the second shelf of this _____ .
2. Although the woman was much richer than her friends, they were not _____ of her success.
3. Have you studied for the _____ ?
4. She's so beautiful and rich. I _____ her!
5. When I was eating lunch, I bit my _____ . It now feels very painful.
6. I plan to _____ lots of people to come to my party.
7. No, they are not real flowers. They are _____ .
8. He shot his last _____ at the target.
9. If you continue to rest, your injuries will _____ soon.
10. Could you _____ my spelling? I'm sure that I've made lots of mistakes.

EXERCISE B

次の各文の空所に入る適切な語を (a) ~ (d) から選び、○をしましょう。

1. During the 1980s, the Japanese economy was the _____ of the rest of the world.
   a. arrow
   b. envy
   c. nuisance
   d. source

2. When traveling abroad, give yourself a few days to become _____ to your new surroundings.
   a. accustomed
   b. correct
   c. ideal
   d. bound

3. The results of this year's _____ show that over 20% of students need to study English grammar harder.
   a. examining
   b. examiner
   c. examinee
   d. examination

4. Look at these lovely old leather-_____ books.
   a. binds
   b. bound
   c. binding
   d. bind

5. Though relatively harmless, pop-up windows are quite a _____ to many Internet surfers.
   a. conflict
   b. fear
   c. danger
   d. nuisance

6. A number of household appliances now have _____ intelligence.
   a. artificial
   b. correct
   c. moral
   d. ideal

Unit 10

- **ambition** [æmbíʃən]
  - 【名】野心；大望
  - ▶ambi- 歩き回る・-tion 名尾。原義は「(票を求めて)歩き回ること」。
  - 【形】ambitious 野心／大望を抱いた▶-ous 形尾

- **patient** [péɪʃənt]
  - 【形／名】忍耐強い－[病気に耐えている]→患者, 病人▶pati- 苦しみ・-ent 形尾
  - 【名】patience 忍耐；辛抱強さ▶-ence 名尾

- **estimate** [éstəmət]
  - 【動】〜を評価する－[価値を推定する]→〜を見積もる【名】見積もり
  - ▶esteem(価値を置く→高く評価する)と同源。

- **loyal** [lɔ́ɪəl]
  - 【形】忠実な▶royal は「王室の；王者らしい」。
  - 【名】loyalty 忠実さ；忠誠心▶-ty 名尾

- **height** [háɪt]
  - 【名】高さ→[heights] 高地－[人間の高さ]→身長▶high の名詞形。
  - 【動】heighten 〜を高くする▶-en 動尾

- **available** [əvéɪləbl]
  - 【形】利用できる▶-able 形尾(可能)
  - 【動】[avail oneself of 〜] 〜を利用できる(≒help oneself to)

- **surface** [sə́ːfəs]
  - 【名】表面；うわべ▶sur- 上・face 顔

- **beat** [bíːt]
  - 【動】〜を繰り返し叩く→〜を打ち負かす【名】続けざまに打つこと, 鼓動
  - ▶「げんこつや重い物で繰り返し叩く」は pound, 「平手で叩く」は slap。

- **confess** [kənfés]
  - 【動】〜を白状する▶con- 強意・-fess 発声して認める
  - 【名】confession 自白▶-sion 名尾

- **hate** [héɪt]
  - 【動】〜を憎む【名】憎しみ▶dislike ＜ hate ＜ detest の順に意味が強くなる。
  - 【形】hateful 憎むべき；憎悪に満ちた▶-ful 形尾(満ちている)
  - 【名】hatred 憎悪▶-red 名尾(性質・状態)

- **hesitate** [hézəteɪt]
  - 【動】[hesitate to do] 〜することをためらう；躊躇(ちゅうちょ)する
  - ▶hesit- 付着する→固執する・-ate 動尾。「従来の考えに固執する」イメージ。
  - 【形】hesitant ためらっている▶-ant 形尾 【名】hesitation ためらい▶-tion 名尾

- **pause** [pɔ́ːz]
  - 【動】一休みする【名】一休止▶stop は一時的かどうかには言及しない。

- **record** [(動) rɪkɔ́ːd] [(名) rékəd]
  - 【動】記録する；登録する；録音／録画する【名】記録
  - ▶re- 元の場所へ→再び・-cord 心(＝heart)

- **resemble** [rɪzémbəl]
  - 【動】〜に似ている▶re- 元の場所へ・-semble 〜のように見える(＝seem)。
  - 受け身・進行形は不可。ただし「だんだん似てきている」なら進行形も可。
  - 【名】resemblance (外面的に)似ていること；類似点▶-ance 名尾

- **stir** [stə́ː]
  - 【動】〜をかき回す→〜を動かす－[気持ちを動かす]
  - →[stir up 〜] 〜を駆り立てる【名】かき回すこと, (かすかな)動き

- **generous** [dʒénərəs]
  - 【形】(生まれが良い)┬[物惜しみしない]→気前の良い▶gener- 生まれ・-ous 形尾
  -               └[優しい；心が広い]→寛大な
  - 【名】generosity 気前の良さ, 寛大さ▶-ity 名尾

- **wrap** [rǽp]
  - 【動】〜を(紙, 綿(製品), 毛(織物)などで)包む→〜を包み隠す
  - ▶cover は「ふたや紙, 布などで覆う」, pack は「輸送や保管のために包装する」。

- **peculiar** [pɪkjúːlɪə]
  - 【形】(ひときわ際立って)独特の→妙な
  - ▶-iar 形尾。strange は「なじみがない」, eccentric は「正常なことから大幅に外れている」, odd は「規則正しさや予定から外れている」ことを強調。
  - 《連語》be peculiar to 〜 〜に特有である
  - 【名】peculiarity 特性, 風変わりなこと▶-ity 名尾

- **aloud** [əláʊd]
  - 【副】声を出して▶「大声で」の意では loudly が用いられる。

- **meanwhile** [míːnwaɪl]
  - 【副】その間に(も)→一方では(≒meantime)
  - ▶mean- 中間(＝middle)・while 時間(＝time)。「2つの時点の中間」のイメージ。

EXERCISE A

各文の下線部分に入る適切な語を左ページの見出し語から選びましょう。

1. Please read the book _____ .
2. Although many did not believe him, his most _____ friends thought he was telling the truth.
3. She has lots of _____ habits including never leaving home without a hat.
4. You have to _____ the soup while it boils.
5. Tickets for the new movie are now _____ at the cinema.
6. It was very _____ of you to give me such a nice present.
7. When I buy Christmas presents at a department store, the staff will often _____ them for me.
8. You can't have everything you want right now. Please be _____ !
9. The man didn't _____ that he stole the car. However, the police still thought he did it.
10. I _____ my best friend at tennis. I won easily.

EXERCISE B

次の各文の空所に入る適切な語を (a) ~ (d) から選び、○をしましょう。

1. It has been claimed that the police forced the man into _____ .
    a. pausing
    b. hesitating
    c. confessing
    d. beating

2. If the shirt doesn't fit, you won't _____ to return it, will you?
    a. hesitate
    b. stir
    c. beat
    d. record

3. The workers had to _____ how many cans of paint they needed to do the job.
    a. estimate
    b. hesitate
    c. beat
    d. resemble

4. Travel to India declines from July to September, the _____ months of the year.
    a. most hesitant
    b. wettest
    c. most frequent
    d. most generous

5. When I was a small boy, my father always read _____ to me before bed.
    a. together
    b. aloud
    c. perfectly
    d. ordinarily

6. Martin is always _____ in sharing his knowledge of gardening with his neighbors.
    a. generous
    b. ambitious
    c. hateful
    d. patient

Unit 11

- □ **crop** [krάːp] 【名】作物；収穫物 → 収穫量
- □ **carriage** [kǽrɪdʒ] 【名】馬車 − [文明の発達] → [英] 車両（＝ [米] car）
  - ▶ carri- 運ぶ（＝carry）・-age 名尾
- □ **despair** [dɪspέər] 【名】絶望 【動】絶望する；断念する ▶ de- 否定・-spair 希望
  - 【形】desperate 絶望的な → 気違いじみた → 必死の ▶ -ate 形尾
- □ **industry** [índəstri] 【名】（人の本質）→ 勤勉 − [勤勉さから生まれたモノ] → 産業；工業
  - ▶ in- 中に・dust- 建てる・-y 名尾。「人の中に建てられたモノ；本質」が原義。
  - 【形】industrial 産業の；工業の ▶ -al 形尾 【形】industrious 勤勉な ▶ -ous 形尾
  - 【動】industrialize 産業化する；工業化する ▶ -ize 動尾
- □ **pack** [pǽk] 【名/動】（運べるように包装された比較的大きい）包み；荷物
  - → ～を梱包する → 一包み；一箱 − [まとまったもの] → 一団, 一味, 群れ
- □ **property** [prάːpərti] 【名】財産, 不動産 ▶ proper 固有の・-ty 名尾（性質・状態）
- □ **idle** [áɪdl] 【形】のらくらしている；怠惰（たいだ）な ▶ 詳しくは lazy の項参照。
- □ **soil** [sɔ́ɪl] 【名】土, 土壌；土地
  - ▶ soil は「植物生育の土壌」, ground は「ある程度広がりのある土地」。
- □ **ill** [íl] 【形】[米] 吐き気がする；気分が悪い（≒[英] sick），
  - [英] 病気で（≒[米] sick）
  - ▶ 名詞の前では, [米]・[英] 共に sick が通常（例：a sick person, a sick child）。
  - 《連語》speak ill of ～ ～を悪く言う ⇔ speak well of ～ ～をよく言う
  - 【名】illness 病気 ▶ -ness 名尾
- □ **congratulate** [kəngrǽtʃəleɪt] 【動】（人を）祝福する ▶ con- 共に・gratul- 喜ぶ・-ate 動尾
  - 【名】congratulations 祝いの言葉,「おめでとう」▶ -tion 名尾。必ず複数形で。
- □ **entertain** [ὲntərtéɪn] 【動】～を楽しませる；もてなす ▶ enter- 間 → 人と人との間・-tain 張る → 保つ
  - 【名】entertainment もてなし；歓待, 娯楽 ▶ -ment 名尾
- □ **neglect** [nɪglékt] 【動】（注意すべきものを）無視する → ～を怠ける
  - ▶ disregard は「意図的に無視／軽視する」, ignore は「認めたくなく無視する」。
  - 【形】negligent 怠慢な ▶ -ent 形尾 【名】negligence 怠慢 ▶ -ence 名尾
- □ **obey** [oʊbéɪ] 【動】～に従う ×obey to ～ ⇔ disobey ～に従わない ▶ dis- 反対
  - 【形】obedient 従順な ▶ -ent 形尾 【名】obedience 従順さ ▶ -ence 名尾
  - ▶ package は「小型／中型の包装物」, packet は「手紙などの束や小包など小さな束」。
- □ **repair** [rɪpéər] 【動】（複雑なものを）修理する 【名】修理
  - ▶ re- 元の場所へ・-pair 揃える。mend は「小さいものを修理する」, [米] fix は「各部品を正しい位置に固定する」イメージ。
- □ **suspect**
  - [(動) səspékt] 【動】～とうすうす感じる；疑う 【名】容疑者
  - [(名) sʌ́spekt] ▶ sus- 下に・-pect 見る。「相手の言動の下にある意図まで見る」イメージ。
  - 【形】suspicious 怪しい；不審な ▶ -ous 形尾 【名】suspicion 疑惑 ▶ -cion 名尾
- □ **weigh** [wéɪ] 【動】重さがある ― [重点を置く] → よく考える ▶ way（道, 方法）と同音。
  - [重石になってのしかかる] → [weigh on ～] ～を苦しめる
  - 【名】weight 重さ；体重,（心の）重荷, 重要さ ▶ -t 名尾
- □ **alike** [əláɪk] 【形】似ている；同様な 【副】同様に ▶ similar は「異なったもの同士の類似性」。
- □ **gradual** [grǽdʒuəl] 【形】段階的な, 徐々の
  - ▶ grad- 段階・-al 形尾。「段階を一歩一歩進む」イメージ。
  - 【名】grade 階段；等級, 学年；学位 【副】gradually 段階的に；徐々に ▶ -ly 副尾
- □ **noble** [nóʊbəl] 【形】高貴な, 貴族の 【名】[nobles] 貴族
  - ▶ no- 知っている・-ble ＝ -able 形尾（可能）。「よく知られ得るほど生まれが良い」。
- □ **ripe** [ráɪp] 【形】（果物が）熟した ▶ mature（成熟した）は人に用いられることが多い。

EXERCISE A

各文の下線部分に入る適切な語を左ページの見出し語から選びましょう。

1. Are the bananas _____ enough to eat yet?
2. After losing his job and his family, the man fell into _____ .
3. I would like to _____ you on your win. Well done!
4. The twins look so _____ . I keep mixing them up.
5. The king was a very _____ man. He was always kind and honest.
6. In that part of the country, the main _____ that the farmers grow is tobacco.
7. I'm not sure, but I _____ that it was your brother who stole the ring. He needs the money!
8. The bus leaves in 10 minutes! Please quickly _____ your clothes into your bag.
9. I have a headache and a sore throat. I think that I'm _____ .
10. Could you _____ my car? It was damaged in an accident.

EXERCISE B

次の各文の空所に入る適切な語を (a) ~ (d) から選び、○をしましょう。

1. Joan was an _____ and willing worker.
    a. industrialize
    b. industrial
    c. industry
    d. industrious

2. Robbie denied that he had been _____ his homework for the past several weeks.
    a. despairing
    b. entertaining
    c. suspecting
    d. neglecting

3. I _____ that Jim and Linda will get married this summer as they have been dating for several years.
    a. congratulate
    b. entertain
    c. suspect
    d. obey

4. George is _____ with people who work at Apple Computer Company.
    a. familiar
    b. alike
    c. similar
    d. common

5. The attackers said that they were taking _____ on the gang of teenagers who had broken into the public library.
    a. negligence
    b. despair
    c. repair
    d. revenge

6. Jim _____ up his things and headed to the airport.
    a. neglected
    b. repaired
    c. packed
    d. weighed

Unit 12

- **agent** [éɪdʒənt] 　【名】代理人；代理店, 業者 ▶ age- 行う（=act）・-ent 名尾
  　【名】agency 代理店,（行政）機関 ▶ -cy 名尾（地位）。「代理する地位」のイメージ。
- **trick** [trík] 　【名】計略；たくらみ → 悪戯（いたずら）－［騙（だま）すこと］
  　　　　　　　　　　　　　　　　　→ 手品；トリック
  　【動】〜をだます ▶「巧妙な行い」のイメージ。
- **fool** [fú:l] 　【名】ばか者 ▶「ふいご（＝火力を強くする送風装置）で中身が空っぽ」が原義。
  　《連語》make a fool of / out of 〜 〜を笑いものにする
  　【形】foolish バカな ▶ -ish 形尾
- **passage** [pǽsɪdʒ] 　【名】通過；通路, 経過,（文・楽曲の）一節 ▶ 詳しくは pass の項参照。
- **soldier** [sóʊldʒɚ] 　【名】（陸軍の）軍人；兵士 ▶「海兵」は sailor,「空士（＝空軍の兵士）」は airman.
- **skill** [skíl] 　【名】（努力や訓練によって後天的に身につけた）技術；腕前
  　【形】skilled（経験が積み重ねられて）熟練した ▶ -ed 形尾（〜された）
  　【形】skillful 上手な ▶ -ful 形尾（〜に満ちている）
- **weapon** [wépən] 　【名】武器 ▶ 棒切れから核兵器まであらゆるものを含む。
- **awake** [əwéɪk] 　【形】目が覚めて（⟷ asleep 眠って）▶ a- 強意・wake 目覚める。
  　【動】awaken 〜を目覚めさせる ▶ -en 動尾
- **row** [róʊ] 　【名】（横にまっすぐ並んだ）列,（数学の行列やコンピュータの横並びの）行
  　▶「（数学の行列やコンピュータの）列（＝縦並び）」は column,「順番に並ぶ縦の列」は line.
  　《連語》in a row 一列に並んで → 連続して
  　▶ この in は in the form of（〜の形で）の略。
- **decay** [dɪkéɪ] 　【動】腐る；衰える；〜を腐敗させる 【名】腐敗；衰弱
  　▶ a decayed tooth は「虫歯」。「虫歯になる」は get a cavity.
- **graduate** [grǽdʒʊeɪt] 　【動】[graduate from 〜] 〜を卒業する ▶ gradu- 学位（＝grade）・-ate 動尾。
  　　　　　　　　　　　「〜から学位をとる」イメージ。gradual の項参照。
- **manage** [mǽnɪdʒ] 　【動】〜を上手く取り扱う━（人や組織を）管理する；経営する
  　　　　　　　　　　　　　　　　　→ [manage to do] 何とか〜する ▶ man- 手・-age 動尾
  　【名】management 管理；経営者側 ▶ -ment 名尾 ⟷ labor 被雇用者側
  　【名】manager 経営者；（部長・課長などの）管理職；支配人 ▶ -er 名尾
- **pinch** [píntʃ] 　【動 / 名】〜をつねる → 〜を苦しめる；苦痛－［苦痛を感じる事態］→ 危機
- **steer** [stíɚ] 　【動】〜を操縦する → 〜を（ある方向へ）向ける
  　▶「（自動車の）ハンドル」は steering wheel.「車輪（wheel）を操縦するもの」。
- **translate** [trænsléɪt, trǽnzleɪt] 　【動】[translate A into B] A を B に翻訳する ▶ trans- 越えて・-late 運ぶ
  　【名】translation 翻訳 ▶ -tion 名尾 【名】translator 翻訳家 ▶ -or＝-er 名尾（〜する人）
- **wipe** [wáɪp] 　【動】〜を拭く；拭う
  　▶「こすって消す」は rub,「固いものでゴシゴシこする」は scrub.
  　【名】wiper 拭く人；（自動車の）ワイパー ▶ -er 名尾（〜する人／もの）
- **ashamed** [əʃéɪmd] 　【形】恥じて；恥じ入る ▶ -ed 形尾（〜される）。「引っ込み思案ではにかむ」は shy.
  　【名】shame 恥, [a shame] 残念なこと
- **coarse** [kɔ́ɚs] 　【形】下品な；粗末な ▶ course（進行, 経過, 課程）と同音。
- **honest** [ɑ́:nəst] 　【形】正直な, 誠実な ⟷ dishonest 不正直な, 不誠実な ▶ dis- 否定
  　▶ honor と同源。「名声どおりに, 言動において嘘や不正がない」イメージ。
  　【名】honesty 正直, 誠実 ▶ -y 名尾 【副】honestly 正直に, 誠実に ▶ -ly 副尾
- **male** [méɪl] 　【形】男性の；雄性の 【名】男性；雄性 ▶ masculine（男らしい）と同源。
  　⟷ female 女性；雌性, 女性の；雌性の ▶ feminine（女性らしい）と同源。
  　▶ 生物全般に用いられ,「人」については生物学的および統計学上の性別を表す場合に使用。

EXERCISE A

各文の下線部分に入る適切な語を左ページの見出し語から選びましょう。

1. After I _____ from university, I hope to find a job working for the government.
2. The man's jokes are very _____ . They are too dirty!
3. The man wearing the uniform is a _____ in the army.
4. A gun is a very dangerous _____ .
5. After you wash your hands, please _____ them with a towel.
6. Could you _____ this into English for me?
7. He's a very _____ man. I don't think he would ever lie or cheat.
8. I might not be very clever, but I'm not a _____ .
9. To be good at archery, you need a lot of _____ .
10. Could you _____ the boat along the river for a while? I need to take a break.

EXERCISE B

次の各文の空所に入る適切な語を (a) ~ (d) から選び、○をしましょう。

1. We both kept on _____ ourselves to prove that it wasn't all a dream.
    a. pinching
    b. managing
    c. steering
    d. wiping

2. In just five years, Simon had _____ to become the top salesman in the company.
    a. translated
    b. managed
    c. steered
    d. decayed

3. Bill was rather _____ and always said things to upset the other office staff.
    a. obedient
    b. coarse
    c. ashamed
    d. male

4. Tooth _____ is terrible, and it can also be the cause of other diseases.
    a. decayed
    b. decays
    c. decaying
    d. decay

5. This novel has been _____ from French into nearly 50 languages.
    a. recorded
    b. tricked
    c. translated
    d. repaired

6. After puzzling over the problem for hours, the committee finally _____ on a solution.
    a. pinched
    b. managed
    c. wiped
    d. hit

Unit 13

- ☐ **bunch** [bʌ́ntʃ] 【名】(果物の)房 → (同種のものの)束 → 一団；一味
- ☐ **charm** [tʃɑ́ːm] 【名】魔力 → まじない；お守り － [魔法のように作用する] → 魅力
  【動】～を魅了する ▶「チャームポイント」は charming feature。
- ☐ **excess** [ɪksés, ékses] 【名】過多；過度【形】余分の ▶ to excess で「過度に」。
  【動】[exceed in ～] ～を超過する ▶ ex- 外へ → 範囲を越えて・-ceed 行く
  【形】excessive 過度の ▶ -ive 形尾【副】excessively 過度に ▶ -ly 副尾
- ☐ **inward** [ínwəd] 【形】内の；内的な【副】中へ ▶ in- 中へ・-ward 方向 ⟷ outward 外の, 外へ
- ☐ **heap** [híːp] 【動】～を積み上げる(≒ heap up)【名】(積まれたものの)山
  《連語》heaps of 複数名詞 どっさりの～
- ☐ **sense** [séns] 【名/動】感覚 ┬ [識別するもの] → 良識；分別, ～を感知する
  └ [語句や文脈から感じられるモノ] → 意味
  【形】sensory 感覚の；知覚の ▶ -ory 形尾【名】sensibility 感受性 ▶ -ity 名尾
  【形】sensitive 敏感な, 感じやすい ▶ -ive 形尾
  【名】sensitivity 感じやすさ ▶ -ity 名尾
  【形】sensible 良識のある；分別のある ▶ -ible=-able 形尾(可能)
- ☐ **tuition** [tuɪ́ʃən] 【名】授業料, 授業；教授 ▶ tui- 世話する・-ition 名尾。特に小人数や個別の指導を指す。同源の tutor は「家庭教師；個別指導教員」
- ☐ **rob** [rɑ́ːb] 【動】[rob 人 of 物] 人を脅して物を奪い取る ▶ この of は「分離」のイメージ。
  【名】robber 強盗 ▶ -er 名尾(～する人)【名】robbery 強盗事件 ▶ -ery 名尾
- ☐ **asleep** [əslíːp] 【形】眠っている ⟷ awake 目が覚めている ▶ 名詞の前では sleeping。
- ☐ **approve** [əprúːv] 【動】(あるモノの良さを証明する)→ ～を承認する
  ▶ a- = ad- 方向・prove 証明する
  《連語》approve of ～ ～を(個人的なレベルで)承認する
  【名】approval 賛成；承認 ▶ -al 名尾
- ☐ **bite** [báɪt] 【動】～を噛む；噛みつく【名】噛むこと
  ▶ chew は「歯で噛み砕いたり磨り潰したりする」。
- ☐ **combine** [kəmbáɪn] 【動】～を結合させる；結合する ▶ com- 共に・-bine 2つ一緒に
  【名】combination 結合 ▶ -tion 名尾
- ☐ **drown** [dráʊn] 【動】～を溺死させる ▶ drown は溺れ「死ぬ」であり、単に「溺れる」の意を表す時は nearly drown または be nearly drowned。
- ☐ **promote** [prəmóʊt] 【動】(前進させる) ┬ [物事を進める] → ～を促進する ▶ pro- 前へ・-mote 動く
  └ [地位を進める] → ～を昇進させる ▶「～に昇進する」は be promoted to ～。
  【名】promotion 促進, 昇進 ▶ -tion 名尾
- ☐ **exhaust** [ɪgzɔ́ːst] 【動】～を使い果たす → ～を疲れ果てさせる
  《連語》be exhausted from ～ ～で疲れ果てる(≒ be tired from)
  ▶「体力・気力を使い果たして何もできない」イメージ。
- ☐ **urge** [ə́ːdʒ] 【動】(押す) － [言葉で圧力をかける] → ～を強く主張する
  《連語》urge 人 to do 人に～するようにしきりに促す
  【形】urgent 緊急の ▶ -ent 形尾。【名】urgency 緊急 ▶ -ency 名尾
- ☐ **offend** [əfénd] 【動】～を怒らせる；感情を害する, (法律・規則を)犯す ▶ defend の項参照。
  【形】offensive 攻撃的な → 不愉快な ▶ -sive 形尾 ⟷ defensive 防御の
- ☐ **latter** [lǽtə] 【形】[the latter] 後者の ⟷ [the former] 前者の ▶ late の項参照。
- ☐ **proud** [práʊd] 【形】～を誇りに思っている → うぬぼれた ▶ pro- 前・-ud 存在する
  《連語》be proud of ～ ～を誇りに思う (≒ take pride in)
- ☐ **stiff** [stíf] 【形】硬直した；強硬な ▶「曲げたり形を変えたりしがたい」イメージ。

EXERCISE A

各文の下線部分に入る適切な語を左ページの見出し語から選びましょう。

1. I'm very _____ of my new car. Isn't it beautiful?
2. Little children often fall _____ very quickly. I wish I could do that.
3. I will _____ him to think about his decision again. I really don't want him to quit his job.
4. Don't be scared. My dog is just friendly. He doesn't _____ .
5. Could I have a _____ of bananas and a bag of oranges?
6. I want to go to university. However, the _____ is very high and I have little money.
7. I went on a long run yesterday. This morning when I woke up, my legs were really _____ .
8. Which do you prefer, summer or winter? I prefer the _____ to the former.
9. The gang wanted to _____ the rich old man of his money.
10. She loves her boyfriend. However, her parents don't _____ of him.

EXERCISE B

次の各文の空所に入る適切な語を (a) ~ (d) から選び、○をしましょう。

1. Madonna will visit Japan early next year to _____ her new album.
    a. promote
    b. promotion
    c. promoting
    d. promoted

2. This new copier _____ when the machine gets too hot and shuts off automatically.
    a. approves
    b. combines
    c. senses
    d. urges

3. The man left all his dirty clothes in a _____ on the floor.
    a. heap
    b. tuition
    c. excess
    d. charm

4. Don't be _____ . Bill acts that way with everyone.
    a. offended
    b. promoted
    c. urged
    d. approved

5. The number of _____ victims increases sharply in the summer months when people crowd the beaches.
    a. floating
    b. slipping
    c. drowning
    d. biting

6. When finished boiling the pasta, pour off any _____ water.
    a. quantity
    b. excess
    c. degree
    d. number

Unit 14

- **advice** [ədváɪs] 【名】忠告；助言▶「1つの忠告；助言」は a piece / word / bit of advice.
  【動】advise ～に忠告する；助言する
- **request** [rɪkwést] 【名】要請；リクエスト【動】(願望を丁重に述べて)～を要請する；頼む
- **liquid** [líkwɪd] 【名】液体【形】液体の▶「固体」は solid,「気体」は gas.
- **mud** [mʌ́d] 【名】泥▶(as) clear as mud で「(話や説明などが)ちっともわからない」。
  【形】muddy 泥の；泥だらけの▶-y 形尾
- **questionnaire** [kwèstʃənéɚ] 【名】アンケート▶-aire 名尾(～に関するもの)
  【名】question 質問【動】～を質問する▶-tion 名尾
  【動】quest ～を探究する【名】探究▶que- は「探し求める」イメージ。
- **steady** [stédi] 【形】安定した▶stead- 立っている(= stand)→ 立場▶-y 形尾
  【副】ぐらつかないように、着実に▶hold ～ steady でよく用いられる。
  【副】steadily 着実に▶-ly 副尾
- **spit** [spít] 【名】つば【動】つばを吐く▶動詞の活用に注意(spit < spat < spit)。
- **thunder** [θʌ́ndɚ] 【名】雷, 雷鳴▶ゴロゴロと雷のなる音が thunder, ピカッと光る稲妻が lightning.
- **transportation** [trænspɚtéɪʃən] 【名】輸送▶-ation 名尾
  【動】transport (大量に)輸送する▶trans- 越えて・-port 運ぶ
- **behave** [bɪhéɪv] 【動】(適切に)振る舞う
  《連語》behave oneself 行儀よくする
  【名】behavior (適切な)振る舞い▶-or = -er 名尾(～すること)
- **compete** [kəmpíːt] 【動】[compete with ～]～と競争する
  ▶戦闘／競争動詞と結びつく with は「対抗」(= against)のイメージ。
  【形】competitive 競争が激しい；競争力がある【名】competition 競争
- **curse** [kɚ́ːs] 【動】～を呪う ↔ bless ～に(十字を切って)神の加護を祈る【名】呪い
- **excite** [ɪksáɪt] 【動】～を興奮させる▶感情動詞は be + -ed で「～する」の意となる。
  【形】excited 興奮した▶-ed 形尾(～された)
  【形】exciting 興奮させる；興奮させるような▶-ing 形尾(～している)
  【名】excitement 興奮▶-ment 名尾
- **fold** [fóʊld] 【動】～を折りたたむ–[手足を折りたたむ]→(腕や足を)組む
  ↔ unfold 開く；広げる→(秘密を)打ち明ける,(物語が)展開する
- **improve** [ɪmprúːv] 【動】～を改善する▶「不満や欠陥のあるものを改善する」イメージ。
  【名】improvement 改良▶-ment 名尾
- **ruin** [rúːɪn] 【動】～を破滅させる；～を台無しにする【名】荒廃；破滅, [ruins] 廃墟
  ▶「物を壊す」最も一般的な語は destroy.
- **bold** [bóʊld] 【形】大胆な → ずうずうしい▶bald(頭がはげた)は [bɔ́ːld]。
- **eager** [íːgɚ] 【形】熱望して；熱心な
  ▶願望の達成に熱心なあまり、しばしば焦りのニュアンスを持つ。
  《連語》be eager to do しきりに～したがっている
- **intense** [ɪnténs] 【形】(光・温度などが)強烈な →(感情・行動などが)激しい
  【形】intensive 激しい；徹底的な▶-sive 形尾
  【動】intensify ～を激しくする▶-fy 動尾
- **prompt** [prɑ́ːmpt] 【形/動】即座の；迅速な–[すぐに行なうよう急ぎ立てる]→ ～を促す
  ▶pro- 前・-mpt 取り出す。「(事前に取り出された)→ すぐに動き出せる」イメージ。
  《連語》prompt(人)to do (人に)～するよう促す
  【副】promptly 即座に；迅速に▶-ly 副尾

EXERCISE A

各文の下線部分に入る適切な語を左ページの見出し語から選びましょう。

1. When you take the photograph, make sure that you hold the camera _____ .
2. During a storm, after a flash of lightening, you can often hear _____ .
3. Thank you for your _____ reply. I'm really glad you could write back to me so quickly.
4. The new company employee is very _____ to learn about our business.
5. Because of the serious economic problems, the government was under _____ pressure.
6. I shouldn't have walked in the field. My shoes are so dirty. They are covered in _____ .
7. That racehorse will go to America to _____ in the Derby.
8. Please _____ your clothes before you put them into your suitcase.
9. The car, the train and the airplane are all types of _____ .
10. After I tried the new product, a staff member asked me to fill in a _____ .

EXERCISE B

次の各文の空所に入る適切な語を (a) ~ (d) から選び、○をしましょう。

1. Please visit your _____ before you register for classes.
    a. advisor
    b. advising
    c. advice
    d. advisory

2. You should be _____ to do as you are told by your mother.
    a. intense
    b. excited
    c. bold
    d. prompt

3. John is _____ waiting for the end of the semester so he can take a vacation.
    a. boldly
    b. promptly
    c. intensely
    d. eagerly

4. The Shinkansen is one of the most dependable _____ systems.
    a. stream
    b. passage
    c. transportation
    d. ground

5. If you _____ badly, you will not be allowed to have dessert after dinner.
    a. compete
    b. behave
    c. ruin
    d. improve

6. Jane was very _____ when she heard that she had got the job.
    a. excited
    b. behaved
    c. cursed
    d. ruined

Unit 15

- **wound** [wúːnd] 【動】〜を傷つける；負傷する 【名】傷；怪我 ▶「事故による怪我」は injury。
  【形】wounded 負傷した；怪我をしている ▶ -ed 形尾(〜された)
- **require** [rɪkwáɪɚ] 【動】〜を(当然のこととして)要求する ▶ re- 元の場所へ・-quire 求める
  【名】requisition 要求 ▶ -tion 名尾 【名】requirement 必要条件 ▶ -ment 名尾
- **horizon** [həráɪzn] 【名】地平線；水平線 ▶ 原義は「境界(線)」。
  【形】horizontal 水平の ▶ -al 形尾 ⟷ vertical 垂直の ▶ vertic- 頂点・-al 形尾
- **mechanic** [mɪkǽnɪk] 【名】機械工 ▶ mechan- 機械(= machine)・-ic 形尾(〜に関する)→ 名尾
  【形】mechanical 機械的な ▶ -al 形尾 【名】mechanism 仕組み ▶ -ism 名尾
  【名】machine 機械 ▶ -ism 名尾 【名】machinery 機械類 ▶ -ery 名尾
- **shore** [ʃɔ́ɚ] 【名】(海側から見た)岸；海岸
  ▶「大陸から見た海岸」は coast。beach は「砂や小石の多い海や湖の平らな岸」。
- **merchant** [mɚ́tʃənt] 【名】[米] 商人, [英] 卸売商, 貿易商 ▶ march- 商売する・-ant 名尾(〜する人)
  【動/名】merchandise/merchandize 〜を商取引する, (集合的に)商品
- **beverage** [bévərɪdʒ] 【名】(水以外の)飲み物 ▶ コーヒー・紅茶・ビール・牛乳など。
- **virtue** [vɚ́tʃu] 【名】(男)→(力) − [by virtue of 〜] 〜の力で；〜のおかげで
  [力で一族を守ることが正義であったことから] → 美徳, 長所
  ▶「美徳」の意での反意語は vice(悪徳),「長所」の意での反意語は fault(短所)。
  【形】virtuous 高潔な；徳の高い ▶ -ous 形尾 ⟷ vicious 悪意のある；不道徳な
- **admire** [ədmáɪɚ] 【動】〜に感心する；〜を賞賛する ▶ ad- 方向・-mire 感嘆する
  【形】admirable 見事な ▶ -able 形尾(可能)
  【名】admiration 感嘆；賞賛 ▶ -arion 名尾
- **confuse** [kənfjúːz] 【動】[confuse A with B] A を B と間違える ▶ con- 一緒に・fuse 注ぐ
  【形】confusing 紛らわしい ▶ -ing 形尾(〜している)
  【名】confusion 混同；混乱 ▶ -sion 名尾
- **enclose** [ɪnklóʊz] 【動】〜を囲む；同封する ▶ en- 中へ・close 閉じる
  【名】enclosure 囲い込み → 囲われた土地；構内, 同封されたもの ▶ -ure 名尾
- **approach** [əpróʊtʃ] 【動】〜に接近する →(問題などに)取り組む 【名】接近, 研究；方法
  ▶ ap- = ad- 方向・-proach 近い。通常, 他動詞(×approach to)。同様の注意すべき他動詞は discuss(×discuss about), marry(×marry with), reach(×reach at)等。
- **locate** [lóʊkeɪt] 【動】〜を配置する − [配置場所の判明] → 〜の場所を突き止める
  《連語》be located at / on / in 〜 〜に位置している
  【名】location 場所；位置 ▶ -tion 名尾
- **qualify** [kwɑ́ːləfaɪ] 【動】〜に資格を与える；[qualify as 〜] 〜の資格を得る
  ▶ qual- 質(= quality)・-ify 動尾(与える)。qualify as 〜 は qualify oneself as 〜 の略。
  【形】qualified 資格のある ▶ -ed 形尾(〜された)
  【名】qualification 資格 ▶ -ation 名尾
- **rot** [rɑ́ːt] 【動】腐る →(道徳的に)腐敗する 【形】rotten 腐った, 腐敗した
- **complicated** [kɑ́ːmpləkeɪtəd] 【形】複雑な(≒ complex) ▶ -ed 形尾(〜された)
  【動】complicate 〜を複雑にする ▶ -ate 動尾 ⟷ simplify 〜を簡単にする
- **firm** [fɚ́m] 【形】堅い(≒ hard)→ しっかりした → 厳格な(≒ strict)
- **loose** [lúːs] 【形】緩い；たるんだ − [束縛されていない] → 〜から解放された；自由の
- **moderate** [mɑ́ːdərət] 【形】適度な(≒ modest)→ 節度のある
  ▶ moder- 尺度にあった・-ate 形尾
- **nasal** [néɪzəl] 【形】鼻の；鼻に関する(≒ rhinal) ▶ -al 形尾
  【名】鼻 − [近接関係] → 嗅覚 【形】nosy 詮索好きな ▶ -y 形尾
  ▶「高い鼻」は a long / large nose,「低い鼻」は a short / small nose。

EXERCISE A

各文の下線部分に入る適切な語を左ページの見出し語から選びましょう。

1. I work on cars every day. I'm a _____ .
2. I _____ Mr. Suzuki. I think that he's a really great man.
3. Computers are very _____ machines. I don't understand them at all.
4. After taking a heavy fall, blood flowed from a _____ on the man's leg.
5. The school rules _____ the students to wear a uniform.
6. The woman married a _____ who often traveled overseas for business.
7. When you send your application materials, please don't forget to _____ your photo.
8. The hiker was thankful to find a _____ in his bag.
9. My tooth is a little _____ . I think that I should go and see a dentist.
10. She won't be able to _____ as a teacher until next year.

EXERCISE B

次の各文の空所に入る適切な語を (a) ~ (d) から選び、○をしましょう。

1. Did the concierge tell you where the museum is _____ ?
   a. locates
   b. locating
   c. location
   d. located

2. A _____ engineer studies how machines and engines work.
   a. mechanized
   b. mechanical
   c. mechanic
   d. mechanism

3. The old house is _____ away and will soon have to be destroyed.
   a. rotting
   b. jumping
   c. loosening
   d. enclosing

4. Share prices on the New York Stock Exchange made a _____ rise today unlike yesterday's dramatic jump.
   a. complicated
   b. loose
   c. firm
   d. moderate

5. The man seems to understand the traditional _____ of hard work.
   a. nasal
   b. horizon
   c. virtue
   d. wound

6. Look at that cute baby riding in the _____ .
   a. enclosure
   b. carriage
   c. bottle
   d. nest

Unit 16

☐ **bay** [béɪ]	【名】	湾；入り江 ▶ cove ＜ bay ＜ gulf の順に大きくなる。	
☐ **confidence** [kάnfədəns]	【名】	信頼 ─[自分を信頼する] → 自信, 確信 └ 打ち明け話 ▶ con- 強意・-fide 信頼（＝faith）する・-ence 名尾	
	【動】	[confide in ～] ～を信頼する；秘密を打ち明ける	
	【形】	confident 自信のある；確信している ▶-ent 形尾	
	【形】	confidential 内密の ▶-al 形尾	
☐ **rejoice** [rɪdʒɔ́ɪs]	【動】	喜ぶ；うれしく思う ▶ be glad の方がより口語的な語。joy と同源。	
☐ **deed** [díːd]	【名】	行為 ▶ do の名詞形。「意図的な行為」を表す。	
	【副】	indeed 本当に ▶ in- 中に・deed 行為。「実際に行なった行為の中で」から。	
☐ **define** [dɪfáɪn]	【動】	～を定義する；定める ▶ de- 強意・-fine 境界線を定める→（そこで）終える	
	【形】	definite 明確な, 限定された ▶-ite 形尾	
	【形】	definitive 決定的な ▶-ive 形尾	
	【名】	definition 定義 ▶-tion 名尾	
	【副】	definitely 明確に → もちろんですとも ▶-ly 副尾	
☐ **inferior** [ɪnfíːriɚ]	【形】	[be inferior to ～] ～よりも劣っている ▶ この to は senior の項参照。 ⟷ [superior to ～] ～よりも優れている	
	【名】	inferiority 劣っていること ▶-ity 名尾 ⟷ superiority 優れていること	
☐ **ache** [éɪk]	【動】	ずきずき痛む →（心が）うずく 【名】痛み ▶ headache（頭痛）など, [身体部位名詞 + -ache] の形で「～痛」の意。	
☐ **rake** [réɪk]	【名】	（落ち葉や枯れ草などをかき集めるための）熊手, 草かき ▶ (hay) fork は主に「干草を下からすくい上げる」ために用いられる。	
☐ **stomach** [stʌ́mək]	【名】	胃, 腹 ▶「腹が痛い」は have a pain in one's stomach, have a stomachache。	
☐ **stuff** [stʌ́f]	【名】	材料；素材 【動】 ～に物を詰め込む ▶「ぬいぐるみ」は stuffed animal。	
☐ **arrest** [ərést]	【動】	～を逮捕する 【名】逮捕 ▶ ar- = ad- 方向 → ～に対して・-rest 休む → 留める 《連語》 under arrest 逮捕されて ▶ ここでの under は「状況下」のイメージ。	
☐ **crash** [krǽʃ]	【動】	～を押しつぶす；粉砕する 【名】押しつぶすこと；粉砕 ▶ clash（(金属などが)ガチャンとぶつかる, ガチャンという音）との違いに注意。	
☐ **earn** [ɚ́ːn]	【動】	（働いてお金などを）得る；稼ぐ →（名声などを）得る ▶ gain は労働や努力の結果, 金を得ることを必ずしも意味せず「利益として得る」。 《連語》 earn one's living by ～ ～で生計を立てる（≒ earn one's daily bread by ～）	
☐ **hinder** [híndɚ]	【動】	[hinder A from doing] A が～することを妨害する ▶ hind- 後ろに（＝behind）・-er 引き止めておく	
	【名】	hindrance 妨害 ▶-ance 名尾	
☐ **participate** [pɑɚtísəpeɪt]	【動】	[participate in ～] ～に参加する（≒ take part in） ▶ parti- 部分・-cipate つかむ（＝catch）	
	【名】	participation 参加 ▶-ation 名尾	
☐ **tap** [tǽp]	【動】	～を軽く叩く 【名】 ～を軽く叩くこと ▶「[英] (水道などの)蛇口, 栓」（＝ [米] faucet）を意味する tap は別語源。	
☐ **awkward** [ɔ́ːkwɚd]	【形】	ぎこちない → 落ち着かない → 厄介な ▶ awk- 分離・-ward 方向 ▶ awkward age は「思春期」。この時期は世間慣れせず, 言動が落ち着かないから。	
☐ **grand** [grǽnd]	【形】	壮大な；雄大な → 堂々とした；威厳のある ▶ magnificent は「豊かで美しい」, stately は「建物などが大きく堂々としている」様。	
	【名】	grandeur 雄大；壮大, 威厳；崇高さ ▶-eur 名尾	
☐ **mad** [mǽd]	【形】	気が狂った → 頭にきて, 熱狂して ▶ mud は「泥」。	
☐ **rapid** [rǽpəd]	【形】	（流れなどが）速い 【名】[rapids] 急流 ▶ 詳しくは quick の項参照。	
	【名】	rapidity 急速 ▶-ity 名尾	

EXERCISE A

各文の下線部分に入る適切な語を左ページの見出し語から選びましょう。

1. Please help me _____ a toy into each of these bags. We need to give one to each customer.
2. I tried my best, but I'm sure that my essay will be _____ to yours.
3. How does the dictionary _____ the word?
4. In fall, I use a _____ to clean up the leaves in my garden.
5. We sailed for an hour in the _____ .
6. My son is at a very _____ age. He doesn't know if he's an adult or a child.
7. When do you think that the police will _____ the killer? I hope they catch him soon.
8. I don't have enough _____ in myself.
9. Can anyone _____ in the basketball game?
10. My boss lent me his car. I really hope that I don't _____ it.

EXERCISE B

次の各文の空所に入る適切な語を (a) ~ (d) から選び、○をしましょう。

1. We would ask that you keep all information about company employees _____ .
    a. confident
    b. confide
    c. confidant
    d. confidential

2. The suspect should have been _____ , but he escaped from the police.
    a. arrested
    b. crashed
    c. participated
    d. stuffed

3. These heavy boxes are a bit _____ for one person to carry, so please ask for help.
    a. grand
    b. mad
    c. awkward
    d. rapid

4. _____ by a knee injury, Jane was unable to complete the marathon.
    a. Stuffed
    b. Hindered
    c. Crashed
    d. Tapped

5. The construction site of the new building was _____ off so that only workers could enter.
    a. screened
    b. flagged
    c. hindered
    d. framed

6. Use only a _____ to mark your answers.
    a. rake
    b. hammer
    c. pencil
    d. knife

Unit 17

- **department** [dɪpάːtmənt] 【名】(組織の)部門；課, 省, (大学などの)学科
  ▶ de- 分離・part 部分・-ment 名尾。「各部分に分かれたもの」のイメージ。department store(デパート)は,「一つひとつの売り場が集まった店」のイメージ。

- **essence** [ésns] 【名】本質 ▶ 原義は「存在；実体」。霊的実体を最も重要な「本質」と考えた。
  【形】essential 本質的な ▶ -al 形尾 【副】essentially 本質的に ▶ -ly 副尾

- **feather** [féðɚ] 【名】(1本の)羽, 羽毛 ▶ ボクシングの「フェザー級」は featherweight。

- **haste** [héɪst] 【名】急ぎ ▶ hurry(急ぐこと)より形式ばった語。hurry の項参照。
  《連語》in haste 急いで；慌てて(≒ in a hurry) make haste 急ぐ
  【動】hasten(分別を忘れて)急ぐ ▶ -en 動尾
  【形】hasty 急ぎの → 軽率な ▶ -y 形尾

- **ingredient** [ɪŋgríːdijənt] 【名】構成要素；成分 → 材料 ▶ in- 中に・-gredi 入る・-ent 名尾(状態)
  ▶ ingredient は特に料理の材料。material は物質の材料。

- **resign** [rɪzάɪn] 【動】〜を辞職する ▶ re- 元の場所へ → 元の状態へ・sign 印をつける → 署名する。「定年で辞職する」の意は retire。retire の項参照。
  【名】resignation 辞職 ▶ -ation 名尾

- **mistake** [mɪstéɪk] 【名】誤り；間違い 【動】〜を誤解する；間違える ▶ mis- 間違って・take 取る
  《連語》mistake A for B A と B とを間違える(≒ take A for B) ▶ for は「交換」。

- **pile** [páɪl] 【名】(積み重ねた)山；たくさん 【動】[pile up 〜] 〜を積み重ねる
  ▶ 物のきちんとした積み重ねを言う。雑然と積み上げたものは heap。
  《連語》a pile of 〜, piles of 〜 たくさんの〜

- **scorn** [skɔ́ɚn] 【動】〜をあざける 【名】あざけり；あざけりの的
  【形】scornful 軽蔑的な ▶ -ful 形尾(満ちている)

- **throat** [θróʊt] 【名】喉 ▶ 「喉が痛い」は sore の項参照。

- **bow** [báʊ] 【動】[bow to 〜] 〜にお辞儀する 【名】お辞儀 − [形状の類似] → 弓
  ▶ bow(お辞儀する)[baʊ], bow(弓)[boʊ]。前者は bough(大枝)と同音。

- **deceive** [dɪsíːv] 【動】〜をだます ▶ de- 下へ → 悪い方向へ・-ceive つかむ(= catch)
  【名】deceit(悪意を持って)だますこと；詐欺
  【形】deceitful 人をだますような；惑わせるような ▶ -ful 形尾(満ちている)。
  【名】deception だますこと ▶ -tion 名尾。必ずしも悪意があるとは限らない。

- **establish** [ɪstǽblɪʃ] 【動】〜を設立する → 〜を確立する
  ▶ stand と同源。found は「設立の基盤を作ること」に意味の中心があり, establish のようにその後の「確固たるものにする」存続を意味しない。
  【名】establishment 設立 ▶ -ment 名尾

- **load** [lóʊd] 【動】〜に荷物を積む → 〜に(弾丸を)装填する,(プログラムを)読み込む
  【名】積み荷 ▶ 「容器に内容物を詰める」イメージ。

- **pretend** [prɪténd] 【動】〜のふりをする
  ▶ 1. (代)名詞, 2. to do, 3. that S + V の3通りの目的語(節)を取ることができる。

- **upset** [ʌpsét] 【動/名】〜をひっくり返す；転覆 − [気持の転倒] ─
  └→ 〜をうろたえさせる；狼狽 − [冷静さを失わせる] → 〜を不快にさせる

- **yield** [jíːld] 【動/名】(代金を与える) ─ [与えられた側から] → (利益を)生む；産出(額)
  └ [権利を与える] → 〜を譲る → [yield to 〜] 〜に屈服する

- **female** [fíːmeɪl] 【形】女性の；雌性の 【名】女性；雌性 ▶ 詳しくは male の項参照。

- **opposite** [άːpəzət] 【形】[英] 反対側の(≒ [米] across from) 【名】反対のもの
  ▶ 「左右対称」の静的イメージ。移動を好む米国人は, 同じ「反対側」でも(心的な)移動を感じさせる across from(〜から横切って)を用いる。

- **strict** [stríkt] 【形】厳しい ▶ 「締め付ける」イメージ(例：strict rules(厳しい規則))。

EXERCISE A

各文の下線部分に入る適切な語を左ページの見出し語から選びましょう。

1. My five-year-old son likes to _____ that he's driving a car.
2. It is very important for you come to class on time. The teacher is very _____ about the rules.
3. After his wife died, the man married again in _____ .
4. Look at this pretty white _____ . The bird which it comes from must be very beautiful.
5. When I forgot her birthday, I _____ my mother. I will never forget her birthday again!
6. We sat at _____ ends of the table.
7. I can't go to school today because I have a sore _____ .
8. Due to the football team's terrible results, the manager decided to _____ from his job.
9. A week after the wedding, the woman realized that she had made a terrible _____ .
10. All of the teachers are _____ . There isn't a single male.

EXERCISE B

次の各文の空所に入る適切な語を (a) ~ (d) から選び、○をしましょう。

1. Would you mind _____ those books over there before putting them in the truck?
    a. upsetting
    b. piling
    c. yielding
    d. loading

2. Sally enjoys _____ to be a movie star when she plays with her friend.
    a. pretending
    b. bowing
    c. hastening
    d. establishing

3. Someone must have made a _____ when they entered his data.
    a. haste
    b. mistake
    c. resignation
    d. deception

4. Don't answer the exam questions in _____ or you may fail.
    a. essence
    b. haste
    c. deceit
    d. upset

5. He said good night _____ and ran from the room without saying another word.
    a. essentially
    b. strictly
    c. hastily
    d. deceptively

6. He was often _____ by his peers for bad manners.
    a. scorned
    b. established
    c. deceived
    d. mistaken

Unit 18

- **anxiety** [æŋzáɪəti] 【名】心配, 切望 ▶ anxie- 首を絞める → もだえ苦しむ・-ty 名尾
  【形】[be anxious about ～] ～を心配している -[うまくいって欲しい]
  → [be anxious to do ～] ～を切望している ▶ -ous 形尾

- **companion** [kəmpǽnjən] 【名】仲間；付き添い
  ▶ com- 共に → 分け合って・-pan パン・-ion 名尾

- **curve** [kə́ːv] 【名】曲線
  ▶ carve は「彫刻する」。curve の u を U 字型カーブと見て「曲線」と覚えよう。

- **clothing** [klóʊðɪŋ] 【名】衣料品；衣類 ▶ clothe 衣服を着る・-ing 名尾。靴や帽子なども含む集合名詞。

- **envelope** [énvəloʊp] 【名】封筒
  ▶ en- 中に・-velop 包む。envelop(包む)も同様のイメージ。

- **lid** [líd] 【名】(箱・鍋などの)蓋 ▶「瓶(びん)のふた」は top。「まぶた」は eyelid。

- **noun** [náʊn] 【名】名詞
  ▶ 代名詞(pronoun), 形容詞(adjective), 動詞(verb), 副詞(adverb), 前置詞(preposition), 接続詞(conjunction), 間投詞(interjection)と合わせて 8 品詞と呼ばれる。

- **kneel** [níːl] 【動】膝(ひざ)まづく
  【名】knee 膝 ▶ knee は「膝頭」, lap は座った時の「腰から両膝頭までの部分」。

- **victory** [víktəri] 【名】勝利 ▶ 単に「勝利」を表す。triumph は「華々しく圧倒的な勝利」。
  【形】victorious 勝利を得た ▶ -ous 形尾
  【名】victor 勝利者 ▶ -or = -er 名尾(～する人)

- **worship** [wə́ːʃəp] 【名】(慣例的に決まった場所での)礼拝；崇拝 【動】～を礼拝する；崇拝する
  ▶ wor- 価値がある(= worth)・-ship 名尾(状態)。adore は「個人的な神への崇敬」。

- **advertise** [ǽdvətaɪz] 【動】～を広告する ▶ ad- 方向・-vert(視線を)向ける・-ise 動尾
  【名】advertisement 広告 ▶ -ment 名尾。「注目されるもの」のイメージ。省略形は ad。

- **disgust** [dɪskʌ́st] 【動】(胸・心情を)むかむかさせる 【名】(むかむかするほどの)嫌悪
  ▶ dis- 分離・-gust 味 → 好み。「好みに合わない」イメージ。
  【形】disgusting (人を)むかむかさせている ▶ -ing 形尾(～している)

- **freeze** [fríːz] 【動】凍る → 動かなくなる ▶ "Freeze!" は「(凍りついたように)動くな！」の意。
  【形】frozen 凍った, (恐怖などで)体が動かなくなった ▶ -en 形尾(～された)
  【形】freezing 凍るような -[寒気] → ぞっとするような ▶ -ing 形尾(～している)

- **guess** [gés] 【動】～を推量する ▶ I guess ～ の形で単に「私は(たぶん)～だと思う」の意。

- **insult** [【動】ɪnsʌ́lt / 【名】ínsʌlt] 【動】～を侮辱する 【名】侮辱
  ▶ in- 上に(= on)・-sult とぶ。「(相手の上にとぶ)→(とびかかって有利に闘う)→面子を潰す」イメージ。

- **review** [rɪvjúː] 【動】(新刊書などを)批評する, [米] ～を復習する, ～を再調査する
  【名】批評, 復習, 再調査 ▶ re- 元の場所へ・view 見る。「繰り返し見る」イメージ。

- **swear** [swéə] 【動】～を誓う -[みだりに神の名を口にする] → 冒涜(ぼうとく)する

- **appropriate** [əpróʊpriət] 【形】適切な ▶ ap- = ad- 方向・-propri 適切な(= proper)・-ate 形尾
  【副】appropriately 適切に ▶ -ly 副尾

- **refer** [rɪfə́ː] 【動】(元の場所へ戻す) [話題を元へ戻す] → [refer to ～] ～に言及する
  [目を元の場所へ戻す] → [refet to ～] ～を参照する ▶ re- 元の場所へ・-fer 運ぶ
  【名】reference 言及, 参照 ▶ -ence 名尾
  【名】referee 審判員 ▶ -ee 名尾(～される人)
  【名】referendum 国民投票 ▶ -dum 名尾(～されるもの)

- **significant** [sɪgnífɪkənt] 【形】意義のある；重大な ▶ -ant 形尾
  【動】signify ～を(合図・言動などで)示す ▶ sign 合図・-ify 動尾
  【名】significance 意義；重大さ ▶ -ance 名尾

EXERCISE A

各文の下線部分に入る適切な語を左ページの見出し語から選びましょう。

1. Every Sunday, people go to church to _____ God.
2. Don't forget to put the _____ back on the jar.
3. Did you read the _____ of the new book by Dr. Smith in the newspaper?
4. The driver lost control on a _____ and the vehicle hit a tree.
5. At this temperature, water won't _____ . It's too warm.
6. Is it a _____ , a verb or an adjective?
7. After the man won the Olympic 100 meter race, he said that it was his greatest _____ .
8. Jeans are not _____ clothes to wear at a formal party.
9. I put the letter in an _____ . Then, I went to the post office and mailed it.
10. Can you _____ how old I am? I won't give you any hints.

EXERCISE B

次の各文の空所に入る適切な語を (a) ~ (d) から選び、○をしましょう。

1. This company regularly _____ in major magazines and on TV.
   a. advertisements
   b. advertising
   c. advertises
   d. advertisers

2. I feel _____ when I see people smoking on the street.
   a. disgust
   b. companion
   c. insult
   d. significance

3. Don't put off _____ your work until the last minute since you may have to make several improvements.
   a. reviews
   b. reviewed
   c. review
   d. reviewing

4. Although she is a Christian, she prefers not _____ in a church and prays at home.
   a. disgusting
   b. worshipping
   c. referring
   d. reviewing

5. If you don't know the answer, please _____ to the textbook.
   a. refer
   b. advertise
   c. swear
   d. guess

6. Both children were terribly _____ by the divorce of their parents.
   a. insulted
   b. upset
   c. envied
   d. sworn

Unit 19

- **angle** [ǽŋgl]
  - 【名】角度 – [物事を見る角度] → 観点
  - 【名】triangle 三角形 ▶ tri- 3

- **consist** [kənsíst]
  - 【動】[consist of 〜] 〜から構成されている [consist in 〜] 〜に存在する
    ▶ con- 共に・-sist 立つ（=stand）。「いくつかの要素がまとまって立つ → 成り立つ」イメージ。consist of は compose の項参照。
  - 【形】[consistent with 〜] 〜と一貫した；一致した ▶ -ent 形尾
  - 【名】consistency 一貫性 ▶ -ency 名尾

- **scatter** [skǽtɚ]
  - 【動】〜をまき散らす
    ▶ shatter（粉々に割る）と同源。scatter-brained で「注意散漫な」。
  - 【形】scattered 散らばった ▶ -ed 形尾（〜された）

- **solemn** [sɑ́:ləm]
  - 【形】（心に焼きつくほど）厳粛な → 荘厳な ▶ grave は「重々しく威厳のある」。
  - 【名】solemnity 厳粛, 荘厳 ▶ -ity 名尾

- **knee** [ní:]
  - 【名】膝（ひざ）▶ 脚の膝関節の部分。lap は腰かけた時の腰から膝にかけての部分。

- **theory** [θí:əri]
  - 【名】理論；学説 →（個人的な）理屈；持論
  - 【形】theoretical 理論的な ▶ -ical 形尾 【名】theorist 理論家 ▶ -ist 名尾（専門家）

- **tremble** [trémbl]
  - 【動】（恐れや極度の疲れで思わず）震える；振動する 【名】震え

- **sacrifice** [sǽkrəfaɪs]
  - 【名】生贄（いけにえ）；犠牲 【動】〜を捧げる；犠牲にする
    ▶ sacri- 神聖な・-fice 動尾

- **toe** [tóʊ]
  - 【名】足の指 ▶「手の指」は finger。「手の親指」は特に thumb という。

- **vessel** [vésəl]
  - 【名】容器 – [液体を運ぶ器] → 管 – [海上で人を運ぶ器] → 大型船
    ▶「船」の意では ship, boat の方が日常的。「血管」は blood vessel。

- **cheer** [tʃíɚ]
  - 【動】[cheer 〜 up] 〜を元気づける – [その手段として] → 〜に喝采を送る
  - 【名】励まし, 喝采 ▶ [英] "Cheers!" で（健康を祝して）「乾杯！」の意。
  - 【形】cheerful 快活（かいかつ）な；楽しい ▶ -ful 形尾（満ちている）

- **delight** [dɪláɪt]
  - 【動】〜を大いに喜ばせる 【名】大喜び；大好物
  - 《連語》be delighted at / with 〜 〜に大喜びする
  - 【形】delightful とても嬉しい ▶ -ful 形尾（満ちている）

- **inquire** [ɪnkwáɪɚ]
  - 【動】〜を尋ねる ▶ in- 中に・-quire 捜し求める
  - 【形】inquisitive あれこれとうるさく知りたがる；詮索好きな ▶ -ive 形尾
  - 【名】inquiry 調査；質問 ▶ -y 名尾 【名】inquisition 取調べ ▶ -tion 名尾

- **pray** [préɪ]
  - 【動】〜を祈る → 〜を懇願する ▶「えじき, 獲物」を意味する prey と同音。
  - 《連語》pray to A for B B のために A に祈る
  - 【名】prayer 祈り；祈る人 ▶ -er 名尾（〜すること／人）。

- **revise** [rɪváɪz]
  - 【動】（書物を）改訂する；（意見などを）修正する ▶ re- 元の位置へ・-vise 見る
  - 【名】revision 改訂, 修正 ▶ -sion 名尾

- **suck** [sʌ́k]
  - 【動】〜を吸う；しゃぶる 【名】吸うこと ▶ lick は「舌を使って舐める」。

- **tempt** [témpt]
  - 【動】〜を誘惑する；魅了する
    ▶ 聖書で悪魔(the Devil)がイエス(Jesus)を誘惑する時に "tempt a boy to do something wrong"（少年に何か悪さをするようそそのかす）と tempt が用いられていることから, 悪魔は the tempter とも表現される。
  - 【名】temptation 誘惑 ▶ -tion 名尾

- **exact** [ɪgzǽkt]
  - 【形】正確な ▶ ex- 外に・-act 導く。
  - 【副】exactly 正確に →（返事で）その通り ▶ -ly 副尾

- **pale** [péɪl]
  - 【形】（顔や肌に血の気がなく）青白い →（色の）薄い

- **solar** [sóʊlɚ]
  - 【形】太陽の ▶ sol- 太陽・-ar 形尾（〜に関する）⟷ lunar 月の ▶ lun- 月
  - 《連語》solar battery 太陽電池 ▶ solar cell（太陽電池）が集まった蓄電器。

EXERCISE A

各文の下線部分に入る適切な語を左ページの見出し語から選びましょう。

1. Education does not just _____ of learning lots of facts.
2. The people who were worshiping in the church looked very _____ . None of them were smiling.
3. In the future, the world will get much more energy from _____ power.
4. While we were watching TV, my granddaughter sat on my _____ .
5. Many scientists believe in The Big Bang _____ , which describes how the universe was created.
6. She wanted to _____ the seeds so the flowers would grow.
7. My little _____ is very painful. I wonder if I have broken it.
8. Let's _____ to God for world peace.
9. Are you all right? Your face looks very _____ .
10. The people started to _____ loudly when their favorite movie star arrived.

EXERCISE B

次の各文の空所に入る適切な語を (a) ~ (d) から選び、○をしましょう。

1. John's friends came to _____ him on as he ran in the marathon.
    - a. delight
    - b. pray
    - c. cheer
    - d. revise

2. When will you be finished with the _____ version of the budget?
    - a. revise
    - b. revises
    - c. revising
    - d. revised

3. The judge read the verdict in a clear and _____ voice.
    - a. exact
    - b. pale
    - c. solar
    - d. solemn

4. Remember that in the States you will _____ the waiter if you don't leave a tip.
    - a. curse
    - b. excite
    - c. tempt
    - d. insult

5. Everyone hoped that the war wouldn't _____ long and be over in a few weeks.
    - a. delight
    - b. tempt
    - c. revise
    - d. last

6. Many middle-aged people are so out of shape that they can't bend and touch their _____ .
    - a. toes
    - b. nose
    - c. knees
    - d. mouth

Unit 20

- **bush** [búʃ] 【名】低木, やぶ
  《連語》[米] beat around the bush 遠回しに言う（≒ [英] beat about the bush）▶「獲物をおびき出すのにやぶの周り (around)／あたり (about) を何度も打つ」という「遠回しなやり方」に由来。

- **contrast**
  [(名) kɑ́:ntræst]
  [(動) kəntrǽst]
  【名】（似ているところの）対照 【動】～を対照させる
  ▶「違いを比較する」は compare。
  《連語》in contrast to/with ～「～と対照的に」by/in contrast これに対して

- **broad** [brɔ́:d] 【形】幅広い
  【動】broaden ～を広げる ▶ -en 動尾 【名】breadth 幅広さ ▶ -th 名尾

- **handkerchief** [hǽŋkətʃəf] 【名】ハンカチ
  ▶日本とは異なり, 英米では鼻をかむために用いることが多い。

- **fruitful** [frú:tfəl] 【形】よく実のなる → 実りが多い；良い成果を生む ▶ -ful 形尾（満ちている）
  【名】fruit 果物；果実, 成果 ▶ bear fruits で「植物／努力が実を結ぶ」。

- **thirst** [θə́:st] 【名】（喉の）渇き → 渇望 ▶「空腹, 飢え」は hunger。hunger の項参照。
  【形】thirsty 喉の渇いた ▶ -y 形尾

- **nut** [nʌ́t] 【名】木の実；ナッツー[木の実のように堅いもの] → 留めねじ；ナット

- **paste** [péɪst] 【名／動】（すり潰してこねたもの）→（パンなどの）生地
  →（肉, 魚などの）ペースト →（のりで／ PC の画面上で）貼り付ける

- **shame** [ʃéɪm] 【名】恥 ▶ 英語の shame は「道徳上の不名誉や屈辱（感）, 苦痛（感）からくるもの」。うっかり間違えて「恥をかく」は feel embarrassed で×feel shame。
  《連語》What a shame (that) S V S が V であるのは残念だ
  【形】shameful 恥ずべき ▶ -ful 形尾（満ちている）
  【形】shameless 恥知らずの ▶ -less 形尾（～のない）

- **dismiss** [dɪsmís] 【動】（考えを）捨てる, ～を退社させる, ～を解散させる
  ▶ dis- 分離・-miss 送る。「送り出す → 容器の中から内容物を送り出す」イメージ。

- **sacred** [séɪkrəd] 【形】神聖な
  ▶「神聖で侵すことができない」という意では sacrosanct は sacred の強意語。

- **explode** [ɪksplóʊd] 【動】爆発する ▶ 進行形不可。複数の爆弾が連続して爆発する場合のみ進行形は OK。
  例：The bombs are exploding one after another.（次々に爆発している）
  【名】explosion 爆発 →（爆発的な）急増 ▶ -sion 名尾
  【形／名】explosive 爆発性の, 爆薬 ▶ -sive 形尾

- **text** [tékst] 【名】原典；原文 → 本文 − [授業で使われるもの] → 教科書（= textbook）
  ▶「携帯電話のメール；携帯メール」は text message。

- **omit** [oʊmít] 【動】～を省く（≒ leave out）▶ o- = ad- 方向・-mit 送る。「除外する」イメージ。
  【名】omission 省略 ▶ -sion 名尾

- **perceive** [pəsí:v] 【動】～を知覚する；理解する
  ▶ per- 貫通 −[全体を通じて] → 完全に・-ceive つかむ → 把握する
  【名】perception 知覚；理解 ▶ -tion 名尾

- **assess** [əsés] 【動】～を算定する；査定する
  【名】assessment 算定；査定 ▶ -ment 名尾

- **calm** [kɑ́:m] 【形】（動きがなく）静かな → 冷静な
  ▶ quiet は「物音がしないことや動きが少ないこと」, silent は「声や音の無さ」に重点。

- **false** [fɔ́:ls] 【形】間違った；偽の ▶ wrong には false が持つ「人を欺く」のイメージはない。

- **polite** [pəláɪt] 【形】礼儀正しい ▶ polish（磨く）と同源。⟷ impolite 無作法な

- **raw** [rɔ́:] 【形】生の；未加工の
  ▶ fresh は「野菜等が生で新鮮な」, crude は「資源等が天然のまま」。

EXERCISE A

各文の下線部分に入る適切な語を左ページの見出し語から選びましょう。

1. He drank lots of water because he was dying of _____ .
2. He was tall and had _____ shoulders.
3. The joint project was _____ for both companies.
4. Do you think that the statement is true or _____ ?
5. In _____ to her brother, she's a very quiet person.
6. The judge will _____ the case because of a lack of evidence.
7. This reading _____ is very difficult.
8. The police have been warned that a terrorist bomb will _____ later today.
9. Please stop crying. Here's a _____ to wipe your eyes.
10. Do you like _____ eggs? I prefer to eat them boiled.

EXERCISE B

次の各文の空所に入る適切な語を (a) ~ (d) から選び、○をしましょう。

1. Smoking is widely _____ as contributing to lung cancer.
    a. exploded
    b. contrasted
    c. omitted
    d. perceived

2. Ruby's three years in jail are a _____ part of her life that she would like to forget.
    a. shameful
    b. raw
    c. polite
    d. false

3. Since the 1850s the increase in food production and effective medicine has led to a population _____ .
    a. explosion
    b. explodes
    c. explosive
    d. exploded

4. _____ has become almost as popular as making telephone calls.
    a. Texture
    b. Text
    c. Textile
    d. Texting

5. My _____ of Tom changed when I saw him cheating on the test.
    a. perception
    b. contrast
    c. shame
    d. omission

6. This test only _____ your reading and listening ability.
    a. assesses
    b. pastes
    c. perceives
    d. explodes

Unit 21

- **bargain** [bάɚgən] 【名】売買契約 − [買い手有利な取引] → 特売品 【動】(商談)交渉する
- **cloth** [klɔ́:θ] 【名】布 − [材料と製品の近接関係] → [clothes] 衣服
  ▶ garment は商品としての衣服。
  【名】clothing (集合的に) 衣類 ▶-ing 名尾
- **ditch** [dítʃ] 【名】(灌漑(かんがい)や排水のための)溝, どぶ
- **electricity** [ɪlɛktrísəti] 【名】電気 ▶-ity 名尾。「静電気」は static electricity。
  【形】electric 電気の, 電動の ▶-ic 形尾 【形】electrical 電気に関する ▶-al 形尾
- **courage** [kɚ́ːrɪdʒ] 【名】(精神的な)勇気 ⟷ cowardice 臆病 ▶ brave は「(行動に現れる)勇気」。
  【形】courageous 勇気のある；勇敢な (≒ brave) ▶-ous 形尾
  【動】[encourage ~ to do] ~を勇気づける；促進させる ▶ en- 動詞化接頭辞
  ⟷ [discourage ~ from doing] ~を落胆させて…させない ▶ dis- 分離
  【名】encouragement 勇気づけ；促進 ▶-ment 名尾 ⟷ discouragement 落胆
- **ray** [réɪ] 【名】光線 → 放射線 ▶「放射能」は radioactivity。「X線, レントゲン写真」は X-ray, 「紫外線」は ultraviolet rays (= UV)。
- **prison** [prízn] 【名】刑務所, 投獄(とうごく) ▶ pris- つかむ。comprise (包含する) と同源。
  【名】prisoner 囚人, 捕虜 ▶-er 名尾 (~する人)
  【動】imprison ~を投獄する ▶ im- 中に 【名】imprisonment 投獄 ▶-ment 名尾
- **rival** [ráɪvəl] 【名】競争相手；ライバル 【形】競争相手の；ライバルの
  ▶ river と同源。「川の両岸で水利権を争う競争相手」が「競争相手」の意に。
- **yard** [jάɚd] 【名】ヤード(長さの単位), 庭；構内
  ▶ 各々の意は別語源。「ヤード」は 1 yard = 3 feet = 36 inches ≒ 0.9144m。一方, backyard (裏庭), schoolyard (校庭) など, 「庭」の意の yard はしばしば複合語を作る。
- **voyage** [vɔ́ɪɪdʒ] 【名】船旅 → 空の旅 → 宇宙旅行
- **astonish** [əstάːnɪʃ] 【動】~をびっくりさせる ▶ 驚きの度合いは surprise の項参照。
  【名】astonishment 非常な驚き ▶-ment 名尾
- **civilize** [sívəlaɪz] 【動】~を文明化する ▶ civil 一般市民の・-ize 動尾 (~化する)。ローマ時代, 未開人をローマ人のように市民化して教養を持たせたことによる。
  【形】civil 一般市民の ▶ the Civil War で「アメリカの南北戦争」。
- **disappoint** [dɪsəpɔ́ɪnt] 【動】~を失望させる ▶ dis- 否定・-appoint 指名する
  【名】disappointment 失望 ▶-ment 名尾
- **overcome** [oʊvɚkʌ́m] 【動】(敵に)打ち勝つ →(困難, 障害, 誘惑などを)克服する (≒ get over)
  ▶ over- 越える・come 正常な状態に移行する
- **manufacture** [mænjəfǽktʃɚ] 【動】~を製造する 【名】製造 ▶ manu- 手・-fact 作る・-ure 名尾
  【名】manufacturer メーカー ▶-er 名尾 (~する人)
- **reflect** [rɪflékt] 【動】~を反射する − [壁などに光で像が現れる] → ~を映す
  ┌ [影響がはね返って結果が現れる] → ~を反映する
  └ [頭の中で考えが何度もはね返る] → ~を熟考する (≒ reflect on)
  ▶ re- 元の場所へ・-flect 曲げる
  【名】reflection 反射, 反映, 熟考 ▶-tion 名尾
- **solve** [sάːlv] 【動】~を解く；解決する ▶ 原義は「溶かす, 結びを解く」。
  【名】solution 溶解, 解決；解答 ▶-tion 名尾
- **bare** [béɚ] 【形】(本来身につけているものがなくて)むき出しの → ありのままの
  【副】barely かろうじて ▶-ly 副尾。上記 bare とは別語源。
- **delay** [dɪléɪ] 【動】~を延期する 【名】延期 ▶ de- 分離・-lay 運ぶ
- **grateful** [gréɪtfəl] 【形】感謝している ▶ grate- 感謝の祈り・-ful 形尾 (満ちている)
  【名】gratitude 感謝 ▶-tude 名尾 【動】gratify ~を満足させる ▶-ify 動尾

EXERCISE A

各文の下線部分に入る適切な語を左ページの見出し語から選びましょう。

1. A mirror can _____ light.
2. The police officer showed great _____ to catch the criminal.
3. This T-shirt was a _____ ! It was half of its usual price.
4. There was a train _____ because of the strong wind. We had to wait an hour to leave.
5. I don't think he will ever _____ this problem. He's trying very hard, but it's too difficult.
6. The killer was sent to _____ for 10 years.
7. In summer, our _____ bill is very high. I think that we're using the air conditioner too much.
8. I'm very _____ for your help. Thank you so much!
9. A _____ of light came through my window at dawn.
10. The player used to be on my favorite team. However, he now plays for a _____ team.

EXERCISE B

次の各文の空所に入る適切な語を (a) ~ (d) から選び、○をしましょう。

1. Shipment of the requested _____ equipment will be made upon payment.
    a. electricity
    b. electrical
    c. electrics
    d. electronically

2. The new video game sold out in 10 minutes, to the _____ of many children who were waiting in line.
    a. disappointment
    b. solution
    c. reflection
    d. rival

3. The Romans hoped to _____ all the tribes of Europe.
    a. civilize
    b. delay
    c. reflect
    d. solve

4. _____ companies are now looking for ways to decrease costs without reducing the number of employees.
    a. Manufacturer
    b. Manufacture
    c. Manufacturing
    d. Manufactured

5. Could you tell me how I can _____ with local salespeople to get a cheaper price?
    a. astonish
    b. solve
    c. rival
    d. bargain

6. In the African bush, natives live in narrow _____ made of mud and grass.
    a. huts
    b. ditches
    c. streams
    d. roads

Unit 22

- ☐ **barrel** [bǽrəl] 【名】(胴のふくれた)樽(たる) − [ひと樽の量] → バレル(容量の単位)
  ▶ しばしば石油の容量を表すのに用いられる。1バレル ≒ 42米ガロン ≒ 159リットル。
- ☐ **brunch** [brʌ́ntʃ] 【名】朝昼兼用の食事；ブランチ ▶ breakfast と lunch との合成語。
- ☐ **distinguish** [dɪstíŋgwɪʃ] 【動】[distinguish A from B / between A and B] A と B とを区別する
  ▶ -ish 動尾。後者は distinguish [the difference] between A and B の略。
  【形】distinct 全く異なる；目立った ▶ dis- 分離・-stinct 突き刺す
  【形】distinctive 他と特徴が異なった；独特の ▶ -ive 形尾
  【名】distinction 区別 ▶ -tion 名尾
- ☐ **flame** [fléɪm] 【名】炎 − [温度が焦点化] → 激情 【動】めらめらと燃える
  【形】flammable 可燃性の ▶ -able 形尾(可能)
- ☐ **knot** [nɑ́:t] 【名】結び目 → ノット(速度の単位) 【動】結ぶ
  ▶ ノットの意は, 距離を示すために一定間隔で測定索に結び目をつけたことから。
- ☐ **oar** [ɔ́ːr] 【名】櫂(かい)；オール ▶「鉱石, 原鉱」を意味する ore と同音。
- ☐ **shelf** [ʃélf] 【名】棚 ▶ 複数形は shelves。
- ☐ **treasure** [tréʒɚ] 【名】宝物 【動】〜を秘蔵にする；大事にする
  【名】treasury 宝庫 → 国庫 ▶ the Department of the Treasury で「[米]財務省」。
- ☐ **witness** [wítnəs] 【名】目撃者 → 証人 【動】〜を目撃する, 〜を証言する
- ☐ **conquer** [kɑ́ŋkɚ] 【動】〜を征服する ▶ con- 共に → 一緒にする・-quer 求める。「ノルマン人の大征服」は Norman Conquest。これを機に, 英語は大きく姿を変えた。
  【名】conquest 征服 ▶ -est 名尾 【名】conqueror 征服者 ▶ -or ≒ -er 名尾(〜する人)
- ☐ **dive** [dáɪv] 【動】飛び込む → 潜水する 【名】飛び込み, 潜水 ▶ deep と同源。原義は「沈む」。
  【形】diver 潜水夫；ダイバー ▶ -er 名尾(〜する人)
- ☐ **practice** [prǽktəs] 【動】〜を実践する(≒ make 〜 into practice), 〜を練習する(≒ do practice)
  ▶ practice medicine/law で「医者／弁護士を開業する」。
  【名】実践 − [繰り返し実践] → 練習 − [規則的に実践] → 常習行為；習慣
  ▶ make it a practice to do で「よく〜している」。
- ☐ **punish** [pʌ́nɪʃ] 【動】[punish(人)for 〜](人を)〜で罰する ▶ pun- = pen- 尖ったもの・-ish 動尾
  【名】punishment 罰すること；処罰 ▶ -ment 名尾
- ☐ **rid** [ríd] 【動】[get rid of 〜] 〜から(害虫などを)取り除く
- ☐ **spill** [spíl] 【動】〜をこぼす；こぼれる ▶ 不規則活用に注意(spill < spilled < spilt)。
  ▶ It is no use crying over spilt milk.
  (こぼれたミルクに嘆いても無駄だ(= 覆水盆に返らず／後悔先に立たず))
- ☐ **wreck** [rék] 【動】〜を難破させる 【名】(船, 車などの)残骸
  ▶ turn と同源。「渦巻く荒波で追い立てられる」イメージ。
  【形】wrecked 難破した ▶ -ed 形尾(〜られた)
  【名】wrecker [米]レッカー車 ▶ -er 名尾(〜するもの)。「難破物を運ぶもの」。
- ☐ **brave** [bréɪv] 【形】勇敢な ⟷ coward/cowardly 臆病な；小心な
  ▶ courageous は「くじけず恐れない精神的な勇気」を強調。bold は「向こう見ずな勇気」。
  【名】bravery 勇敢さ ▶ -ery 名尾 ⟷ cowardice 臆病；小心
- ☐ **elastic** [ɪlǽstɪk] 【形】弾力性のある；しなやかな
  ▶ [英] elastic band で「輪ゴム」(= [米] rubber band)。
- ☐ **extreme** [ɪkstríːm] 【形】極端な ▶ 接頭辞 extra-(範囲外の)と同源。
  【副】extremely 極端に ▶ -ly 副尾
- ☐ **punctual** [pʌ́ŋktʃuəl] 【形】時間に正確な ▶ punc- 点(= point)・-al 形尾
  【副】punctually 時間／期日通りに；きちんと ▶ -ly 副尾
  【名】punctuality 時間／期日厳守；几帳面 ▶ -ty 名尾

EXERCISE A

各文の下線部分に入る適切な語を左ページの見出し語から選びましょう。

1. I was a _____ to an accident. I saw everything that happened.
2. Let's watch the man _____ into the swimming pool! He's very good at it.
3. We only have one _____ for our boat. We're waiting for the second one.
4. We have a meeting at 3 o'clock. It's very important that you are _____ .
5. Could you tie a _____ in this rope for me?
6. Be careful! If you put too much wine in the glass, you might _____ some!
7. When I finished reading it, I put the book back on the _____ with the other books.
8. The pub ordered an extra _____ of beer.
9. Well, it's too late for breakfast. Let's make _____ !
10. The twins look so similar. It's really difficult to _____ between them.

EXERCISE B

次の各文の空所に入る適切な語を (a) ~ (d) から選び、○をしましょう。

1. The medicine was taken off the _____ when it was found to be dangerous.
    a. oars
    b. knots
    c. barrels
    d. shelves

2. What a _____ you found when you hired Shelia for the position of secretary.
    a. treasure
    b. treasurer
    c. treasury
    d. treasuring

3. Acupuncture has been _____ in China for over 4,000 years.
    a. punished
    b. conquered
    c. wrecked
    d. practiced

4. _____ shot out of the burning building and lit up the night sky.
    a. Feathers
    b. Storms
    c. Flames
    d. Leaves

5. Would you mind getting _____ of that garbage?
    a. distinguished
    b. spilled
    c. rid
    d. wrecked

6. Before Billy went on a date, he promised not to _____ his father's car.
    a. wreck
    b. treasure
    c. punish
    d. spill

Unit 23

☐ **rent** [rént]	【動】(土地, 家を)有料で借りる／貸す 【名】賃貸料, 賃借料	
	▶ borrow の項参照。	
☐ **circumstance** [sə́ːkəmstæns]	【名】[circumstances] 周囲の事情；(付帯)状況	
	▶ circum- 周囲に・stance 立っているもの。surround の項参照。	
☐ **cough** [káːf]	【名】咳 【動】咳をする ▶「くしゃみ」は sneeze。	
☐ **duty** [d(j)úːti]	【名】(長期に渡る)義務 − [社会的義務] → 関税	
	▶ obligation は個々の義務を指し, 通常「1回限りのもの」を言う。	
	【形】dutiful 任務に忠実な ▶ -ful 形尾(満ちている)	
☐ **feast** [fíːst]	【名】ごちそう；宴会 【動】(目などを)楽しませる	
☐ **grace** [gréɪs]	【名】優美；優雅さ	
	【形】graceful 優美な ▶ -ful 形尾(満ちている) ⟷ graceless 優雅さのない	
	【形】gracious (目下の者に)優しい ▶ -ous 形尾 【副】gracefully 優美に ▶ -ly 副尾	
☐ **host** [hóʊst]	【名】主人, 主催国／地, 司会者 ▶「見知らない人を歓待する者」のイメージ。	
☐ **reserve** [rɪzə́ːv]	【動】〜を取っておく → [米] 〜を予約する (≒ [英] book が一般的)	
	【形】reserved 取っておいて, 予約して − [意思を留めて] → 控え目な	
	▶ -ed 形尾(〜された)	
	【名】reservation 予約 ▶ -ation 名尾。make a reservation で「予約する」。	
☐ **transfer** [trænsfə́ː]	【動】〜を移動させる → 〜を転勤させる, 〜を乗り換えさせる	
	▶ trans- 越えて・-fer 運ぶ。[be transferred to 〜] で「〜に転勤する；乗り換える」の意。	
☐ **swift** [swíft]	【形】すばやい → 短時間に行われる；迅速(じんそく)な	
	▶ 動作で swift → quick → rapid の順に速い。rapid のみ人には用いない。	
☐ **tax** [tǽks]	【名】税；税金 【動】〜に課税する；重荷を課する	
	▶「消費税」は consumption tax,「贈与税」は transfer [donation / gift] tax,「相続税」は death [inheritance] tax,「所得税」は income tax。また、tax-free は「免税の」の意。	
	【名】taxation 課税；徴税 ▶ -tion 名尾	
☐ **attract** [ətrǽkt]	【動】〜を引きつける；魅惑する ▶ at- = ad- 方向・-tract 引く	
	【形】attractive 魅力的な ▶ -tive 形尾	
	【名】attraction 引き付けるもの；魅力, (遊園地などの)アトラクション	
☐ **defeat** [dɪfíːt]	【動】〜を打ち破る 【名】打破, 敗北	
	▶ defeat に「打破」と「敗北」の2つの相反する意味があるのは, defeat に反義語が存在しないことによる。この点で, win ⟷ lose とは異なる。似たような例に rent(有料で貸す／借りる), writing(書くこと／書かれたもの)等。	
☐ **excuse** [ɪkskjúːz]	【動】〜を許す；〜の言い訳をする (≒ excuse oneself for)	
	【名】お詫び；言い訳	
	▶ 発音注意：【動】[ɪkskjúːz] ／【名】[ɪkskjúːs]。	
	《連語》excuse oneself from 〜 〜を辞退する	
☐ **hurt** [hə́ːt]	【動】〜を傷つける 【名】傷 ▶ hurt, injure, wound すべて精神的な傷にも使える。	
☐ **postpone** [poʊstpóʊn]	【動】〜を延期する (≒ put off) ▶ post- 後に・-pone 置く	
	《連語》postpone A till/to B A を B まで延期する	
☐ **sink** [síŋk]	【動】沈む 【名】(台所の)流し ▶ 不規則活用に注意 (sink < sank < sunk)。	
☐ **cruel** [krúːəl]	【形】残酷な (≒ brutal)	
	【名】cruelty 残酷 ▶ -ty 名尾	
☐ **patriotic** [peɪtriɑ́ːtɪk]	【形】愛国的な；愛国心が強い ▶ patriot 愛国者・-ic 形尾	
	【名】patriot 愛国者 ▶ patri- 父・-ot 名尾(人)。「同じ父を持つもの」のイメージ。	
	【名】patriotism 愛国心 ▶ -ism 名尾(主義)	
☐ **thin** [θín]	【形】薄い → 細い；痩せた ⟷ thick 厚い；濃い → 太い	

EXERCISE A

各文の下線部分に入る適切な語を左ページの見出し語から選びましょう。

1. The old man _____ his back when he fell.
2. While the children were raising their country's flag, they sang a _____ song.
3. After her promotion, she wants to _____ to the head office.
4. Could I _____ a table for 6 p.m., please?
5. Could you _____ my absence from class next week? I have to go to the hospital.
6. If we do nothing, the boat will _____ !
7. Due to the bad weather, they decided to _____ the soccer game until next week.
8. The horrible man was _____ to his dog. He should never be able to have a pet again.
9. The _____ of tonight's party is Mr. Jones, the president of the company.
10. We _____ this apartment for $600 a month.

EXERCISE B

次の各文の空所に入る適切な語を (a) ~ (d) から選び、○をしましょう。

1. Would you mind if we _____ discussing the new budget until next week?
    a. reserved
    b. attracted
    c. postponed
    d. transferred

2. Suzie _____ an apartment on Walnut Street.
    a. attracts
    b. excused
    c. rents
    d. postponed

3. Joanne's heart _____ when she heard the news that she didn't get the scholarship.
    a. sank
    b. excused
    c. defeated
    b. hurt

4. Due to the decreasing birth _____ , the number of university applicants is also decreasing.
    a. rate
    b. date
    c. duty
    d. circumstance

5. Mark is a gentleman as well as a _____ host.
    a. graciously
    b. graciousness
    c. grace
    d. gracious

6. My hometown is working hard to _____ more tourists.
    a. rent
    b. transfer
    c. attract
    d. reserve

Unit 24

- ☐ **merry** [méri] 【形】陽気な ▶近年 "Merry Christmas!" は "Happy Holidays!" が妥当とされる。
- ☐ **colony** [kάːləni] 【名】植民地 ▶col- = -cult 耕す・-y 名尾。移住者による開拓地が「植民地」の意へ。
  - 【形】colonial 植民地の ▶-al 形尾
  - 【動】colonize 〜を植民地化する，〜を植民地に移住させる ▶-ize 動尾
  - 【名】colonization 植民地化 ▶-ation 名尾
- ☐ **dozen** [dʌ́zn] 【名】ダース；12個 ▶数詞に続くときは単複同形(例：three dozen (of) eggs)。
  - 《連語》dozens of 複数名詞 たくさんの〜
- ☐ **ease** [íːz] 【名】安楽；容易さ 【動】〜を楽にする →(痛みなどを)和らげる
  - 【形】easy 安楽な；容易な ▶-y 形尾 【副】easily 安楽に；容易に ▶-ly 副尾
- ☐ **grain** [gréin] 【名】穀物, 穀物の粒 → [a grain of 〜] 少量の〜
- ☐ **instrument** [ínstrəmənt] 【名】(組み立てたもの) ┬ 器具 − [精密に組み建てられたもの] → 精密機器
  - └ [音楽分野] → 楽器 (= musical instrument)
  - 【形】instrumental 機器の → 手段となる → 役に立つ ▶-al 形尾
- ☐ **audience** [άːdiəns] 【名】(講演，コンサートなどの)聴衆, ラジオの聴取者, テレビの視聴者, 読者
  - ▶audi- 聴く・ence 名尾。「本の読者」の意は, 昔は読み書きが高位の人たちのものであったことに由来。つまり, 庶民は本の内容を「聴く」立場であった。
- ☐ **origin** [όrədʒən] 【名】起源 ▶ori-(太陽が)昇る・-gin 生まれ；源。「物事が生ずる源」のイメージ。
  - 【形】original 最初の → 本来の → 独自の ▶-al 形尾
  - 【名】originality 独創性 ▶-ity 名尾
- ☐ **tie** [tái] 【動】〜を結ぶ − [相手と結びつく；同等の位置になる] → 〜と同点になる
  - 《連語》tie up with 〜 〜にしっかりとくくる
  - ▶この up は「2つのものが近づく → 挟まれた空間が「上」に伸びる；なくなる」イメージ。同じ「空間の閉鎖」概念は catch up with 〜(〜に追いつく)等にも生きている。
- ☐ **lung** [lʌ́ŋ] 【名】肺 ▶aqualung は「(スキューバダイビングなどで潜水用に用いる)水中呼吸器」。
- ☐ **wheel** [wíːl] 【名】車輪 ▶「ハンドル」は steering wheel。
- ☐ **crush** [krʌ́ʃ] 【動】〜を押し潰す；粉砕する；つぶれる 【名】押しつぶすこと；粉砕
  - ▶crash は「大きな音を立てて壊れる」, clash は「(金属などが)がちゃんとぶつかる」。
- ☐ **expose** [ikspóuz] 【動】〜を(光などに)さらす − [人目につく] → 〜を暴露する
  - 【名】exposure さらすこと；暴露 ▶-ure 名尾
- ☐ **interfere** [ìntəfíə] 【動】[interfere in 〜] 〜に干渉する, [interfere with 〜] 〜の邪魔をする
  - ▶inter- 二者間の・-fere 打撃を与える。interfere in 〜は「〜の中に強く立ち入る」, interfere with 〜は「〜に対してぶつかる」イメージ。この with は compete の項参照。
  - 【名】interference 妨害, 干渉 ▶-ence 名尾
- ☐ **modify** [mάːdəfai] 【動】(部分的に)修正する；変更する ▶mod- 様相・-ify 動尾
  - 【名】modification 修正；変更 ▶-ification 名尾(-ify で終わる動詞を名詞化)
- ☐ **praise** [préiz] 【動】〜を誉める 【名】誉めること, 賞賛 ▶prize(賞品)は [práiz]。
- ☐ **sweat** [swét] 【動】汗をかく 【名】汗 ▶perspiration は蒸気状の汗。
- ☐ **immense** [iméns] 【形】計り知れない → 巨大な ▶im- = in- 否定・mense 計る
  - ▶huge は「外見に不恰好なほど大きい」, enormous は「並外れて大きい」イメージ。
- ☐ **precious** [préʃəs] 【形】(金銭では計れない程)貴重な ▶類義語 valuable は「金銭などで計り得る」場合。
- ☐ **rare** [réə] 【形】珍しい ▶「(肉が)生焼けの」を意味する rare は同音同綴語。
  - 【副】rarely めったに〜しない ▶-ly 副尾

EXERCISE A

各文の下線部分に入る適切な語を左ページの見出し語から選びましょう。

1. Can you play a musical _____ ? I used to be able to play the violin.
2. It's very _____ for the weather in June to be this cold. I hope it warms up soon.
3. Most of the people in the _____ really enjoyed the concert.
4. Could you help me _____ this knot?
5. I love my family, so my family photographs are _____ to me.
6. Please don't _____ with my work. I have to finish this report by 5 p.m. today!
7. The clever student passed the test with _____ .
8. After five minutes of running, I had to wipe _____ from my face.
9. When driving, make sure that you hold the steering _____ with both hands.
10. He wanted to wish everyone a _____ Christmas.

EXERCISE B

次の各文の空所に入る適切な語を (a) ~ (d) から選び、○をしましょう。

1. Bill was _____ for his contributions to the advertising project.
    a. modified
    b. eased
    c. praised
    d. interfered

2. Throughout the 19th century, European nations tried to _____ the world.
    a. colonialist
    b. colonial
    c. colony
    d. colonize

3. A good mother never _____ her children to extreme danger.
    a. eases
    b. crushes
    c. exposes
    d. modifies

4. Could you tell me about the _____ use of this word?
    a. originate
    b. origin
    c. original
    d. originally

5. Water is becoming an increasingly _____ resource.
    a. precious
    b. immense
    c. particular
    d. noble

6. He slipped into the driver's seat and started the _____ .
    a. mechanic
    b. engine
    c. instrument
    d. wheel

Unit 25

- **anger** [ǽŋgɚ] 【名】(一時的な激しい)怒り ▶rage は「自制力を失うほど激しく, 粗暴な怒り」。
  【形】angry 怒った, [be angry at 〜] 〜に怒る ▶-y 形尾
- **twilight** [twáɪlaɪt] 【名】(日の出前・日没後の)薄明かり；たそがれ時 ▶twi- 2・light 光
- **caution** [kɔ́ːʃən] 【名】(危険に陥らないようにした)用心(≒precaution)
  ▶cau- 注意を払う・-tion 名尾。「前もって」のイメージを強くする場合は precaution。
  【形】cautious(危険に陥らないように)用心深い(≒precautious) ▶-ous 形尾
- **flesh** [fléʃ] 【名】(人間・動物の)肉；肉体 ▶「(食肉用の)肉」は meat。
- **severe** [səvíɚ] 【形】(思いやりがなく)厳しい → (苦痛などが)ひどい
- **insect** [ínsɛkt] 【名】(脚や羽がある)昆虫 ▶「(細長く柔らかい, 脚のない)這う虫」は worm。
  【名】insecticide 殺虫剤 ▶-cide 名尾(切る；落とす → 殺す)
- **literature** [lítərətʃɚ] 【名】文学；文献 ▶literat- 読み書きができる(=literate)・-ure 名尾
  【形】literal 文字通りの ▶-al 形尾 【形】literary 文学の ▶-ary 形尾
  【形】literate 読み書きができる, 文学の ▶-ate 形尾
  ⟷ illiterate 読み書きができない ▶il-=in- 否定。「非識字率」は illiterate rate。
- **liberty** [líbɚti] 【名】(権利としての)自由 ▶-ty 名尾。freedom は「元々束縛のない自由」。
  【形】liberal 自由な −[モノに束縛されない] → 気前のよい
  ▶liber- 自由な・-al 形尾
  【動】liberate 〜を解放する ▶-ate 動尾
- **pity** [píti] 【名】(下の者に対するうわべだけの)哀れみ 【動】〜を気の毒に思う
  ▶「相手と対等な立場に立って同情する」は sympathize。
- **reputation** [rɛpjətéɪʃən] 【名】評判；名声 ▶-ation 名尾
  【動】repute 〜を評する ▶re- 元の場所へ → 再び・-pute 計算する → 見積もる
  【形】reputable 立派な ▶-able 形尾(可能)
- **avoid** [əvɔ́ɪd] 【動】〜を避ける ▶avoid がどのような対象でも用いられるのに対し, evade は「義務を逃れる」。avoid 〜 ing は「〜しないようにする。」
- **crack** [krǽk] 【動】パン／ピシッと音を立てる；ひびが入る 【名】ひび；割れ目
- **explore** [ɪksplɔ́ɚ] 【動】〜を探検する → 〜を調査する ▶ex- 外に・-plore 大声を出す
  【名】exploration 探検；調査 ▶-ation 名尾 【名】explorer 探検家 ▶-er 名尾(人)
- **insure** [ɪnʃɚ] 【動】〜に保険をかける ▶in- 中に・sure 確かに。ensure は「〜を保証する」の意。
  【名】insurance 保険；保険金 ▶-ance 名尾
- **hunger** [hʌ́ŋgɚ] 【名】空腹 → 飢え；飢餓 ▶「喉の渇き」は thirst。
  【形】hungry 空腹の, 飢えた ▶-y 形尾。「飢え死にする」は starve to death。
- **preach** [príːtʃ] 【動】説教する → 教えを広める
  【名】preacher 説教者；伝道者 ▶-er 名尾(〜する人)。「牧師」は pastor, minister。
- **remind** [rɪmáɪnd] 【動】[remind 人 of 〜] 人に〜を思い出させる
  ▶re- 元の場所へ → 再び・mind 気づく
- **guilty** [gílti] 【形】(違反行為)→ 有罪の −[後ろめたさ] → 罪の意識がある ▶-y 形尾
  ⟷ innocent 無罪の, 無邪気な ▶in- 否定・-noc 傷つける・-ent 形尾
  【名】guilt 有罪, 罪の意識
- **sincere** [sɪnsíɚ] 【形】誠実な；心からの ▶sin- 共に・-cere ふるいわけた → 残った重要なモノ；心
  【名】sincerity 誠実 ▶-ity 名尾
  【副】sincerely 心から
  ▶-ly 副尾。[米] Sincerely yours / [英] Yours sincerely は手紙の結語。
- **upright** [ʌ́praɪt] 【形】直立した −[性格がまっすぐ] → 正直な ▶up- 上方・-right まっすぐ

EXERCISE A

各文の下線部分に入る適切な語を左ページの見出し語から選びましょう。

1. It's important to _____ your house against fire.
2. In the _____ , I couldn't see their faces clearly.
3. Could you _____ me what time the meeting starts?
4. Yes, we're sure he's _____ of stealing the money. He confessed to the police that he did it.
5. The tourists decided to _____ the desert because the weather was too hot!
6. After looking at my computer monitor all day, I got a _____ headache.
7. I don't feel any _____ for him. If he hadn't stolen the car, he wouldn't been in trouble.
8. She is studying English _____ at a university in Tokyo.
9. If you have to drive in the heavy rain, please drive with _____ .
10. Firefighters have a _____ for being brave.

EXERCISE B

次の各文の空所に入る適切な語を (a) ~ (d) から選び、○をしましょう。

1. John _____ seeing his teacher until he was finished with his final paper.
    a. explored
    b. avoided
    c. insured
    d. reminded

2. Sam's father _____ at a church on 5th Avenue on Sunday mornings.
    a. preaches
    b. explores
    c. cracks
    d. avoids

3. The growing _____ of the company is due largely to its excellent customer service.
    a. anger
    b. caution
    c. insurance
    d. reputation

4. Always act with extreme _____ when you are working with dangerous chemicals.
    a. flesh
    b. reputation
    c. insurance
    d. caution

5. There is real _____ about the amount of money that has been wasted by the government.
    a. anger
    b. crack
    c. flesh
    d. literature

6. John still feels _____ about breaking up with his girlfriend.
    a. strict
    b. reputable
    c. literal
    d. guilty

Unit 26

- **cage** [kéɪdʒ] 【名】鳥かご，(動物の)檻(おり) ▶ 容器としての「かご」は basket。
- **debt** [dét] 【名】借金 − [心情的に借りているモノ] → 恩義
  《連語》be in debt to ～ / be in one's debt ～に借金している，～に恩義を感じている
  【形】indebted 借金がある；恩義がある ▶ in- 中に・-ed 形尾(～された)
- **wicked** [wíkəd] 【形】(道徳的に)邪悪な；ひどい ▶ evil よりもさらに強い意。
- **grave** [gréɪv] 【名】墓 → 墓穴 ▶ tomb は「石のある大掛かりな墓や霊廟、記念墓地など」。
- **lodging** [lɑ́:dʒɪŋ] 【名】宿；[lodgings] 貸間；下宿 ▶ lodge 泊める・-ing 名尾(～する所)
- **apologize** [əpɑ́:lədʒaɪz] 【動】[apologize(to 人)for ～]（人に）～で(弁明して)謝罪する ▶ -ize 動尾
  【名】apology 謝罪 ▶ apo- 分離・-logy 言葉。「罪から逃れるために話す」が原義。
- **threaten** [θrétn] 【動】～を脅す ▶ -en 動尾。menace は「顔つき、態度、動作などで相手をおどす」。
  【名】threat 脅し → 脅威となるもの
- **sake** [séɪk] 【名】[for the sake of / for one's sake of～] ～のために
  [for goodness(') sake] お願いだから(≒ for God's/pity's sake)
- **trade** [tréɪd] 【名/動】商売；商う → ～を取引する → 貿易；貿易する
  ▶ bargain は「取引のための話し合いをする」、barter は「金を通さずに物々交換する」。
  【名】trader 貿易業者 ▶ -er 名尾(～する人)
- **bleach** [blí:tʃ] 【動】～を(薬品で)漂泊する；脱色する → ～をしみ抜きする
  【名】漂白剤 ▶「しみ抜きする」は remove stains とも。
- **disturb** [dɪstə́:b] 【動】～をかき乱す；妨害する
  【名】disturbance かき乱すこと；妨害 ▶ -ance 名尾
- **flow** [flóʊ] 【動】流れる ▶ 活用は flow < flowed < flowed。flood(洪水)と同源。
  【動】overflow 溢れ出る → 氾濫(はんらん)する ▶ over- 越えて
- **inform** [ɪnfɔ́ərm] 【動】[inform 人 of ～] 人に～を知らせる
  ▶「～」に that 節や疑問詞節 [疑問詞 + to do] を置くときは、前置詞の of を省略する。
- **occur** [əkə́:] 【動】[occur to 人] ～に起こる − [心に生じる] → ～に思い浮かぶ
  ▶ [A occur to B] は [B hit on / upon A] に書き換え可。
  【名】occurrence 出来事, 発生 ▶ -ence 名尾
- **prejudice** [prédʒədəs] 【名】偏見；先入観
  【動】[prejudice 人 against ～] ～に対して人に偏見を持たせる
  ▶ pre- 前もって・jud 裁く(=judge)。bias(偏見, えこひいき)はよい意味にも使用可。
- **pursue** [pərsú:] 【動】～を(はっきりした目的で執拗に)追いかける → ～を追求する
  ▶ follow は単に「跡に続く；後から追いかける」の意で、後に続く目的は特に問題にしない。
  【名】pursuit 追跡
- **brief** [brí:f] 【形】短い；簡潔な ▶「始めと終わりの距離が短い」イメージ。
  【名】brevity (時の)短さ；簡潔さ ▶ -ity 名尾(状態)
- **plenty** [plénti] 【名】豊富；たくさん ▶ ple- 満たす・-ty 名尾 ⟷ lack 不足
  《連語》plenty of ～ たくさんの～ ▶「～」には可算／不可算名詞共に使用可。
  【形】plentiful 豊富な ▶ -ful 形尾(満ちている)
- **emerge** [ɪmə́:dʒ] 【動】(突然)現れる ▶「(水中に浸っている状態から急に外に出てくる)→ 物事が突発的に現れる」イメージ。
  【名】emergence 出現 ▶ -ence 名尾 【名】emergency 緊急事態 ▶ -ency 名尾
- **solid** [sɑ́:ləd] 【形】固体の → しっかりした 【名】固体
  ▶「液体」は liquid、「流体」は fluid、「気体」は gas。

EXERCISE A

各文の下線部分に入る適切な語を左ページの見出し語から選びましょう。

1. For the _____ of his health, he decided to stop smoking.
2. There is no need to _____ for the car accident. It was not your fault.
3. Japan started to _____ with Portugal in the 16th century, and many things were brought into Japan.
4. I'm glad that the evil man is now in prison. He did some very _____ things.
5. The man had never borrowed any money, so he had never been in _____ .
6. Since I don't have much time, I will have to make my speech _____ .
7. I keep my hamster in a _____ .
8. You don't have to write the essay tonight. There's _____ of time before we have to hand it in.
9. My grandmother died last year. I try to visit her _____ at least once a month.
10. I saw a man _____ from the darkness.

EXERCISE B

次の各文の空所に入る適切な語を (a) ~ (d) から選び、○をしましょう。

1. If you are deep in _____ now, you may have problems getting a credit card in the future.
   a. grave
   b. cage
   c. debt
   d. slide

2. Is his hair naturally blond or is it _____ ?
   a. occurred
   b. pursued
   c. bleached
   d. emerged

3. This is to _____ you that your electricity bill is past due.
   a. inform
   b. occur
   c. trade
   d. disturb

4. My father always told me to be a _____ of the truth so as not to be fooled by others.
   a. pursuing
   b. pursuer
   c. pursuit
   d. pursue

5. By law, all manufacturers must _____ a list of the ingredients on all products.
   a. flow
   b. trade
   c. advertise
   d. provide

6. Today, many details _____ about the scandal.
   a. emerged
   b. traded
   c. informed
   d. disturbed

Unit 27

- **ash** [ǽʃ] 【名】灰 ▶「灰皿」は ash tray。
- **committee** [kəmíti] 【名】委員会 ▶-ee 名尾（〜された人）
  - 【動】commit 〜を委ねる‐[罪に自身を委ねる] → [commit a crime] 罪を犯す
  - ▶com- 共に・-mit 送る。commit suicide で「自殺する」。由来は commit (a crime of) suicide（自殺という罪を犯す）で，神に与えられた命に手を加えることが神への大罪と考えられた。commit の派生語については commitment の項参照。
- **flash** [flǽʃ] 【名】きらめき → 閃光（せんこう）；フラッシュ → （考えなどの）ひらめき
  - ▶flush（どっと流れる；顔を赤らめる）との違いに注意。
- **loan** [lóʊn] 【名】貸付金【動】（有料で）貸す，[英]（銀行などが）金を貸し付ける
- **mercy** [mɜ́ːsi] 【名】慈悲 ▶ mercy killing で「安楽死」の意。
  - 《連語》at the mercy of 〜 〜のなすがままに
  - 【形】merciful 慈悲深い ▶-ful 形尾（満ちている）⟷ merciless 無慈悲な
- **relieve** [rilíːv] 【動】[relieve (人) of 〜]（人を）（苦痛など）から解放する ▶ of は「分離」。
  - 【名】relief（苦痛などからの）解放 → 安心
- **scent** [sént] 【名】（獲物の）においの跡 →（かすかな）芳香 ▶ sense（感覚）と同源。
- **fierce** [fíərs] 【形】獰猛（どうもう）な →（嵐などが）激しい ▶ fierce animal で「猛獣」の意。
  - 【副】fiercely 獰猛に；激しく ▶ -ly 副尾
  - 【名】fierceness 獰猛さ，激しさ ▶ -ness 名尾
- **temper** [témpər] 【名】（性質の適度な釣り合い）‐[人の心が調和した状態]
  - → 心の落ち着き ‐[一時的な精神状態] → 機嫌 ‐[意味の悪化] → 短気
  - 【形】temperate 控えめな ▶ -ate 形尾
  - 【名】temperament 気質 ▶ -ment 名尾
  - 【名】temperance 節制 → 禁酒 ▶ -ance 名尾
- **creep** [kríːp] 【動】這う →（赤ちゃんが）ハイハイする，肌がむずむずする
  - 【名】這うこと [the creeps] ぞっとする感じ
  - 【形】creepy ぞっとする；身の毛がよだつ ▶ -y 形尾
- **dine** [dáin] 【動】夕食をとる；1日のうちの主たる食事をする ▶ dinner の動詞形。
- **disappear** [dìsəpíər] 【動】姿を消す；（視界から消えて）見えなくなる ⟷ appear 現れる
  - ▶ dis- 逆。vanish は「突然消えていなくなる」，fade は「徐々に見えなくなる」。
  - 【名】disappearance 見えなくなること ▶ -ance 名尾
- **generate** [dʒénərèit] 【動】〜を発生させる ▶ gene- 生まれ・-ate 動尾。「同じものを生み出す」イメージ。
  - 【名】generation 発生，世代 ▶ -ation 名尾【名】generator 発電機 ▶ -or 名尾（もの）
  - 【形】generative 発生の → 生殖・生成力のある ▶ -ative 形尾
- **murder** [mɜ́ːdər] 【動】（人を）殺害する【名】殺人 ▶ kill は，殺す対象は人以外でも可。
  - 【名】murderer 殺人者 ▶ -er 名尾（〜する人）
- **rescue** [réskjuː] 【動】〜を救助する【名】救助
  - ▶「救出行為」に重点。save は救出結果の「安全」に重点。
- **whisper** [wíspər] 【動】〜を囁（ささや）く【名】囁き；囁き声
- **fond** [fáːnd] 【形】[be fond of 〜] 〜が好きである ▶ 強意の副詞 very は fond の前に置く。
- **temple** [témpəl] 【名】（古代ギリシア，ローマ，エジプトの）神殿；（仏教，ヒンドゥー教の）寺院
  - ▶日本の「寺」には temple，「神社」には shrine が用いられる。
- **responsible** [rispɑ́nsəbl] 【形】[be responsible for 〜] 〜に責任がある
  - ▶ re- 元の場所へ・-spons 約束・-ible =able 形尾（可能）
  - 【名】responsibility 責任；義務 ▶ -ity 名尾
- **altogether** [ɔ̀ːltəgéðər] 【副】全体に → 完全に → 全く
  - ▶ 否定語を伴うと部分否定（「〜というわけではない」と訳される）。

EXERCISE A

各文の下線部分に入る適切な語を左ページの見出し語から選びましょう。

1. The fact that nobody was injured in the car accident will _____ her.
2. What did you _____ in his ear?
3. The child was in a bad _____ . He cried and screamed all morning.
4. The firemen will try to _____ the man from the burning building.
5. The driver is _____ for the safety of his passengers.
6. At a power station, they _____ electricity.
7. For my birthday, we sometimes _____ at a French restaurant in the city center.
8. I'm very _____ of music. I enjoy listening to music all the time.
9. To buy a house, we had to take a big _____ from the bank.
10. I love the _____ of lavender. It's my favorite smell.

EXERCISE B

次の各文の空所に入る適切な語を (a) ~ (d) から選び、○をしましょう。

1. It is said that Michael had a great _____ for children.
    a. fondle
    b. fondly
    c. fond
    d. fondness

2. Wash your hands _____ with soap and water before you handle any food.
    a. altogether
    b. thoroughly
    c. frequently
    d. meanwhile

3. The purpose of _____ is to teach children how to behave properly.
    a. discipline
    b. mercy
    c. responsibility
    d. relief

4. Most cities _____ large amounts of garbage.
    a. disappear
    b. rescue
    c. generate
    d. creep

5. Little did they know that while they were watching the movie, a man was being _____ just outside with a knife.
    a. crept
    b. generated
    c. disappeared
    d. murdered

6. I'd like to get some work done, but I have a _____ meeting until 8 p.m. tonight.
    a. committee
    b. companion
    c. reflection
    d. mercy

Unit 28

- ☐ **blade** [bléɪd] 【名】(柳など細長い)葉 − [形の類似] → 刃 ▶「木の葉」は leaf。
- ☐ **century** [séntʃəri] 【名】100 年間；1 世紀
  ▶ cent- 100・-y 名尾。「10 年間」は decade,「1000 年間」は millennium。
- ☐ **organ** [ɔ́ɚgən] 【名】(管) − [消化器官] ⇒ 器官；臓器 − [全体を構成するもの] → (体の)組織
  ⇒ [姿・形の類似] − [パイプオルガン] → オルガン
  【形】organic 組織的な ▶ -ic 形尾 【名】organism 有機体 ▶ -ism 名尾
  【動】organize 〜を組織化する ▶ -ize 動尾 【名】organization 組織 ▶ -ation 名尾
- ☐ **dust** [dʌ́st] 【名】塵(ちり)；埃(ほこり)
- ☐ **fright** [fráɪt] 【名】(一時的な,突然でどきっとするような)恐怖
  ▶ fear は「危険に対する恐怖心」, horror は「身の毛をよだつような恐怖；嫌悪」。
  【動】frighten 〜を怖がらせる ▶ -en 動尾
  【形】frightened 怯(おび)えて ▶ -ed 形尾(〜された)
- ☐ **instant** [ínstənt] 【名】瞬間 【形】瞬間の ▶ in- 接触(＝on)・st- 立つ(＝stand) → 生じる・-ant 形尾
  【副】instantly 即座に ▶ -ly 副尾
  【形】instantaneous 即座の ▶ -aneous 形尾 【名】instance 事例 ▶ -ance 名尾
- ☐ **lump** [lʌ́mp] 【名】こぶ → しこり；固まり 【動】〜をひとかたまりにする
- ☐ **remedy** [rémədi] 【名】治療；治療薬 → 救済策 【動】〜を治療する → 〜を改善する
  ▶ re- 元の場所へ → 元の状態へ・med- 治療する・-y 名尾
- ☐ **sympathy** [símpəθi] 【名】同情 ▶ sym- 共に・-pathy 苦しみ。詳しくは pity の項参照。
  【動】sympathize with 人 〜に同情する ▶ -ize 動尾
  【形】sympathetic 同情的な ▶ -ic 形尾
- ☐ **beware** [bɪwéɚ] 【動】〜に用心する ▶ Be ware!(気づけ！)という命令文に由来。
- ☐ **cultivate** [kʌ́ltəveɪt] 【動】〜を耕作する；栽培する − [心の育成] → (能力や才能を)育てる
  ▶ cult- 耕す・-ate 動尾。culture(教養,文化)と同源。詳しくは culture の項参照。
  【形】cultivated 耕作された,栽培された,教養のある ▶ -ed 形尾(〜された)
  【名】cultivation 耕作,栽培,(能力や才能などの)育成 ▶ -ation 名尾
- ☐ **drag** [drǽg] 【動】(重いものなどを)引きずる 【名】ひっぱること ▶ drug は「麻薬」。
- ☐ **grind** [gráɪnd] 【動】〜を(穀物などを)挽(ひ)く ⇒ こする → 〜を磨く；刃物を砥ぐ
  ⇒ [身を粉にして教える] → (教えや知識を)たたきこむ
- ☐ **hug** [hʌ́g] 【動】(愛情を持って両手でしっかりと)抱きしめる
- ☐ **regret** [rɪgrét] 【動】[regret to do](未来の行為に)残念に思う
  [regret 〜 ing](過去の行為を)残念に思う；後悔する 【名】遺憾；後悔
- ☐ **satisfy** [sǽtəsfaɪ] 【動】〜を満足させる ▶ sati- 必要に足る(＝enough)・-fy 動尾
  ⟷ dissatisfy 〜を不満足にさせる ▶ dis- 逆
  《連語》be satisfied with 〜 〜に満足している
  【形】satisfactory 満足できる ▶ -ory 形尾 【名】satisfaction 満足 ▶ -tion 名尾
- ☐ **horrible** [hɔ́rəbl] 【形】ぞっとするほどおそろしい
  ▶ horr- 恐怖(＝horror)・-ible ＝-able 形尾(可能)。terrorism の項参照。
- ☐ **tender** [téndɚ] 【形】柔らかい → か弱い；もろい − [心の繊細さ] → 優しい
  【名】tenderness 柔らかさ,か弱さ；もろさ,優しさ ▶ -ness 名尾
- ☐ **ahead** [əhéd] 【副】(場所的に)前方に →(時間的に)先に；先立って
  ▶ a＝ad- 方向・head 頭 → 前方。「進行方向の前方」のイメージ。in front of は「(静止したものの)前方に／で」。
- ☐ **submit** [səbmít] 【動】[submit (A) to B](A を)B に提出する [submit to 〜] 〜に服従する
  ▶ sub- 下・-mit 送る。「相手の影響下に置く → その権限下に置く」イメージ。
  【形】submissive 服従的な ▶ -ive 形尾 【名】submission 提出,服従 ▶ -sion 名尾

EXERCISE A

各文の下線部分に入る適切な語を左ページの見出し語から選びましょう。

1. There is a popular _____ for stomachache.
2. Don't forget to _____ your homework to your teacher by Friday.
3. The old car in the garage had lots of _____ on it.
4. I had a terrible cold and could hardly work, but my boss didn't show any _____ .
5. I _____ telling Jane my secret because she told it to all her friends.
6. _____ the seeds into a powder.
7. Farmers _____ the land so that they can grow vegetables.
8. The heart is a very important _____ of the body.
9. Beethoven died in the early nineteenth _____ .
10. _____ of the dog! It might bite you.

EXERCISE B

次の各文の空所に入る適切な語を (a) ~ (d) から選び、○をしましょう。

1. The emergency landing was very _____ for all the passengers.
    a. frightening
    b. frighten
    c. frightened
    d. fright

2. The locals here _____ many kinds of vegetables.
    a. beware
    b. cultivate
    c. inform
    d. frighten

3. Even though he was using a microphone, I could _____ hear his voice.
    a. barely
    b. instantly
    c. rapidly
    d. tenderly

4. I must tell you how much I _____ with your problem.
    a. sympathizer
    b. sympathy
    c. sympathetic
    d. sympathize

5. Despite the _____ in the economy, George's business is doing quite well.
    a. dip
    b. drag
    c. horror
    d. remedy

6. _____ of jellyfish when swimming in the ocean.
    a. sympathize
    b. cultivate
    c. beware
    d. frighten

Unit 29

- **individual** [ɪndəvídʒuəl]
  - 【形】個々の；個人の 【名】個々；個人 ▶ in- 否定・-divid 分割する・-al 形尾
  - 【名】individuality 個性 ▶ -ity 名尾 【名】individualism 個人主義 ▶ -ism 名尾(主義)
  - 【名】individualist 個人主義者 ▶ -ist 名尾(主義者)

- **border** [bɔ́ːdɚ]
  - 【名】国境；国境線, 境界；境界線 【動】〜に接する
  - ▶「異なる領域の仕切り」を表す。boundary は「同一領域内での仕切り」のイメージ。

- **crime** [kráɪm]
  - 【名】罪 ▶ commit a crime(罪を犯す)については committee の項参照。
  - 【形/名】criminal 犯罪の, 犯罪者 ▶ -al 形尾(〜に関する)

- **republic** [rɪpʌ́blɪk]
  - 【名】共和国 ⟷ monarchy 君主国
  - 【形】republican 共和国の, [Republican] [米] 共和党の, 共和党員 ▶ -an 形尾
  - ⟷ Democratic 民主党の ▶ demo- 人々(= people)・-crat 政治・-ic 形尾

- **tame** [téɪm]
  - 【形】飼い慣らされた；従順な → 単調な；つまらない
  - ⟷ wild 野生の 「野良犬」は stray dog。
  - 【動】〜を飼いならす

- **bless** [blés]
  - 【動】〜に(十字を切って)神の加護を祈る ⟷ curse 〜を呪う
  - ▶ blood(血)と同源。「(いけにえの血で清める)→ 神が恵みを与える」イメージ。bliss は「至福」。"Bless you!"((くしゃみをした人に対して)神のご加護を!)と言うのは, くしゃみをすると神の息吹で与えられた魂が抜けてしまうという聖書に由来。
  - 【名】blessing 恵み；ありがたいもの ▶ -ing 名尾(〜されるもの)

- **cape** [kéɪp]
  - 【名】岬 ▶ cap- 頭。「頭のように海や湖に突き出した陸地」のイメージ。

- **ornament** [ɔ́ːnəmənt]
  - 【名】(外観を美しくするために加える)装飾；装飾品 【動】〜を飾る
  - 【形】ornamental 装飾用の；装飾的な ▶ -al 形尾

- **bundle** [bʌ́ndl]
  - 【名】(運んだり蓄えたりしやすいようにした)束；包み 【動】〜を束ねる
  - ▶ bunch の項参照。

- **achieve** [ətʃíːv]
  - 【動】(努力して困難を克服して)〜を成し遂げる；達成する
  - ▶ accomplish(〜を達成する)は「計画や使命などを遂行する点」に重点。
  - 【名】achievement 達成 ▶ -ment 名尾

- **concentrate** [kɑ́nsəntreɪt]
  - 【動】〜を一点に集める, [concentrate A on / upon B] A を B に集中する
  - ▶ con- 共に・center 中心・-ate 動尾
  - 【名】concentration 集中 ▶ -ation 名尾

- **foster** [fɔ́ːstɚ]
  - 【動】(子供を)養育する - [物事の成長を助ける] → 〜を促進する；助長する
  - ▶「親のいない子を愛情と努力をもって育てること」を含意。foster parent は「里親」。

- **imply** [ɪmpláɪ]
  - 【動】〜を含意する ▶ im- 中に・-ply 包む
  - 【名】implication 含意 ▶ -ation 名尾

- **obtain** [əbtéɪn]
  - 【動】〜を(努力して)得る
  - ▶ get は「努力や意思の有無に関係なく入手する」, gain は「利になるものを努力して得る」, receive は「いやおうなく手に入る」, acquire は「長い時間をかけて得る」。

- **scratch** [skrǽtʃ]
  - 【動】〜をひっかく；(痒いところを)かく → 〜をこすり取る
  - 【名】ひっかき傷
  - ▶「すりむき傷」は scrape, 「切り傷」は cut, 「虫さされや動物にかまれた傷」は bite。

- **split** [splít]
  - 【動】〜を(縦向きに何らかの層に沿って)裂く → 〜を分ける；分裂させる
  - ▶ 接続部分からや縫い目などの線に沿って裂く場合は rip。

- **huge** [hjúːdʒ]
  - 【形】巨大な → 莫大な(⟷ tiny 小さい) ▶ 詳しくは immense の項参照。

- **splendid** [spléndəd]
  - 【形】壮麗(そうれい)な；素晴らしい
  - ▶「輝かしくきらびやかな」イメージ。

- **aside** [əsáɪd]
  - 【副】わきへ → 別にして；とっておいて ▶ a- = ad- 方向・side 側

- **seldom** [séldəm]
  - 【副】めったに〜ない

EXERCISE A

各文の下線部分に入る適切な語を左ページの見出し語から選びましょう。

1. I _____ go to the movie theater. It's too expensive.
2. You're a student, so you should _____ on your studies.
3. Standing on the _____ , she could feel the sea breeze.
4. San Diego is an American city that is close to the _____ with Mexico.
5. Russia is a _____ country. It extends from Northern Asia to Europe.
6. The birds in the park are really _____ . They will come really close to you.
7. Your cooking is absolutely _____ !
8. I went to the library to _____ a book that I had been looking for.
9. The man was involved in a very serious _____ .
10. I was in a car accident last week. Don't worry. I only got a small _____ .

EXERCISE B

次の各文の空所に入る適切な語を (a) ~ (d) から選び、○をしましょう。

1. I find it hard to _____ on my work when other people are talking.
    a. imply
    b. achieve
    c. concentrate
    d. foster

2. His garden is full of all types of _____ flowers and plants.
    a. ornamental
    b. ornamented
    c. ornamentation
    d. ornament

3. I'm not trying to _____ that you are lazy; however, you'll need to work harder on the project.
    a. foster
    b. obtain
    c. achieve
    d. imply

4. This liquid _____ a harmful substance, so please handle it with care.
    a. obtains
    b. contains
    c. maintains
    d. implies

5. If you intend on crossing the _____ between Spain and Morocco, you'll need a boat.
    a. root
    b. ditch
    c. border
    d. passage

6. Could you put that work _____ for a moment and give me a hand with this?
    a. aside
    b. ahead
    c. punctually
    d. exactly

Unit 30

- **steep** [stíːp] 【形】(坂などが)急な；険しい－[上昇／降下の激しさ] → 急激な
- **canal** [kənǽl] 【名】運河 ▶ can- 茎。「運河」と「茎」が持つ「管」状の姿・形が類似。
- **conversation** [kɑ̀ːnvɚséɪʃən] 【名】談話 ▶ con- 共に・verse 回す・-ation 名尾。「複数人で話を回し合う」イメージ。
  【動】converse 談話する ▶「逆の；正反対の」の意の converse は別語源。
- **loaf** [lóʊf] 【名】パン1個；一斤
  ▶ 焼いたパンで切っていないもの。切ったものは slice や piece で表す。
- **monitor** [mɑ́ːnətɚ] 【名】(ブラウン管などの)モニター 【動】～を監視する
  ▶「企業から依頼されて新商品の意見を述べる人」の意でのモニターは consumer reception tester。
- **vary** [véri] 【動】(断続的に／不規則に)変わる；変える → 様々である
  【形】various 様々な ▶ -ous 形尾 【名】variety 多様(性)；変化 ▶ -ty 名尾
  【形／名】variant 異なった(もの), 異なる発音／綴り ▶ -ant 形尾(～の性質の)
  【名】variation 変化, 差異 ▶ -ation 名尾
- **funeral** [fjúːnərəl] 【名】葬式；葬儀 ▶「埋葬」は burial。
- **razor** [réɪzɚ] 【名】剃刀(かみそり) ▶ shaver は「電気剃刀」のみを意味する。
- **straw** [strɔ́ː] 【名】麦わら, (飲み物を飲むための)ストロー
  ▶ 昔の「ストロー」は「麦わら」そのものが利用されていたことに由来。
- **ugly** [ʌ́gli] 【形】醜い ▶ an ugly duckling は「醜いアヒルの子」(アンデルセン童話より)。
- **affect** [əfékt] 【動】～に影響を与える ▶ af-=ad- 方向・-fect 作る。affect(～を気取る), affected(気取った), affectation(気取り)は別語源。
  【名】affection 影響－[心が動かされる] → 愛着 ▶ -tion 名尾
  【形】affectionate 影響のある, 愛着ある ▶ -ate 形尾
- **cease** [síːs] 【動】(続いていることを)終える, [cease to do] ～することを止める
  ▶ stop は「突然の停止」を表す。"Cease fire!" は号令で「撃ち方止め！」の意。
  【形】ceaseless 絶え間ない ▶ -less 形尾(～のない)
- **harvest** [hɑ́ɚvəst] 【名】収穫 →(成果としての)収穫 【動】～を収穫する
  ▶ crop は収穫前の「作物」の意にも用いられる。
- **respond** [rɪspɑ́ːnd] 【動】[respond to ～] ～に応答する ▶ re- 元の場所へ・-spons 約束
  【名】response 応答；答え ▶ その他の派生語については responsible の項参照。
- **resist** [rɪzíst] 【動】～に抵抗する →(誘惑などに)耐える
  ▶ re- 元の場所へ → 逆方向に；逆らって・-sist 立つ(=stand)。「踏みとどまる」イメージ。
  【形／名】resistant 抵抗する；抵抗力のある, 抵抗する人／物 ▶ -ant 形尾・名尾
  【名】resistance 抵抗；抵抗力, レジスタンス ▶ -ance 名尾
  【形】irresistible 抵抗できない → 非常に魅力的な
  ▶ ir-=in- 否定・-ible=-able 形尾(可能)
- **scold** [skóʊld] 【動】(親が子供などを怒って大声で)叱る
  ▶ 上司が部下を叱る場合には reprimand が用いられる。
- **trace** [tréɪs] 【動】(足跡・跡を)辿(たど)る →(起源を)辿る 【名】足跡；跡
  ▶ train(列車)と同源。「足を引きずったところ → 足跡」が原義。
- **definite** [défənɪt] 【形】限定された → 明確な ▶ -ite 形尾 ⟷ indefinite 際限のない；漠然とした
  【動】define ～を定める；定義する ▶「あるものの境界線を定める」イメージ。
  【名】definition 定義 ▶ -tion 名尾
- **gross** [gróʊs] 【形】総計の－[程度の大きさが悪い意味へ] → ひどい
  ▶ GDP とは Gross Domestic Product(国内総生産)のこと。
- **polish** [pɑ́ːlɪʃ] 【動】～を磨く 【名】磨くこと；艶(つや)
  ▶ 語源は古代ギリシャ都市 Polis。その人々の「洗練された」振る舞いに由来。

EXERCISE A

各文の下線部分に入る適切な語を左ページの見出し語から選びましょう。

1. I would like a bag of potatoes and a _____ of bread.
2. A lot of people went to the singer's _____ . They were very sad because he died so young.
3. Before you leave on vacation, could you _____ the wood floors? They look dull.
4. The horses on the farm usually eat _____ .
5. I had an interesting _____ with my grandfather about his childhood.
6. My dog is not _____ at all! She's beautiful!
7. Rice farmers are busy in autumn because it is _____ time.
8. The mountain path was very _____ . It was very hard work to climb to the top.
9. It was decided that the fighting would _____ at midnight.
10. What was the _____ profit before tax?

EXERCISE B

次の各文の空所に入る適切な語を (a) ~ (d) から選び、○をしましょう。

1. I just can't _____ eating any kind of chocolate.
    a. affect
    b. respond
    c. resist
    d. trace

2. Ticket prices to New York _____ , depending on the time of year.
    a. polish
    b. respond
    c. trace
    d. vary

3. Due to the poor _____ , many people will go without enough food this season.
    a. loaf
    b. canal
    c. harvest
    d. straw

4. His _____ nature made him the perfect choice for the position as kindergarten teacher.
    a. affection
    b. affecting
    c. affected
    d. affectionate

5. Although they were unsure of the _____ cause of the problem, they knew something had to be done.
    a. pure
    b. definite
    c. strict
    d. gross

6. Anne _____ shopping at that store when she found out that they underpaid their staff.
    a. ceased
    b. responded
    c. affected
    d. traced

Section C

Unit 1

- **gender** [dʒéndɚ] 【名】(文化的・社会的役割としての)性；性別 ▶gene(種)と同源。
- **consequence** [kɑ́:nsəkwɛns] 【名】(必然の)結果
  ▶con- 共に・sequence 連続。result と consequence を対比した場合, 前者は「良い結果」, 後者は「良くない結果」を表す場合が多い。
- **isolation** [aɪsəléɪʃən] 【名】孤立；隔離 ▶-ation 名尾
  【動】isolate 〜を孤立させる；隔離する ▶-ate 動尾。island(孤島)と同源。
- **residence** [rézədəns] 【名】住宅；家
  【形】resident 住んでいる【名】住民；滞在者 ▶-ent 形尾・名尾
  【形】residential 住宅の；居住用の ▶-al 形尾
  【動】[reside in 〜] 〜に住む ▶re- 元の場所へ・-side 座る(＝sit)
- **role** [róʊl] 【名】(劇の)役 → 役割 ▶roll と同源。原義は「役者のせりふを書いた巻物」。
- **structure** [strʌ́ktʃɚ] 【名】構造 ▶struct- 建てる・-ure 名尾【動】〜を構造化する；構築する
  【動】restructure 〜を再構築する ▶re- 元の場所へ → 再び
- **conform** [kənfɔ́ɚm] 【動】[conform to 〜](規則・慣習に)従う；合わせる ▶con- 共に・form 形
  【名】conformity 服従；一致 ▶-ity 名尾
- **evolve** [ɪvɑ́:lv] 【動】展開する → 進化する
  【名】evolution 展開, 進化 ▶-tion 名尾
- **cooperate** [koʊɑ́:pəreɪt] 【動】[cooperate with 〜] 〜と協力する ▶co- 共に・operate 働く
  【形】cooperative 協力的な ▶-ative 形尾【名】cooperation 協力 ▶-ation 名尾
- **decline** [dɪkláɪn] 【動】〜を傾ける, 〜を辞退する
  ▶de- 分離・-cline 傾く。拒否の強さは refuse の項参照。
- **inhabit** [ɪnhǽbət] 【動】〜に居住している ▶in- 中に・-habit 住む
  【名】inhabitant 住民(≒resident) ▶-ant 名尾(〜する人)
- **interact** [ìntɚǽkt] 【動】相互に作用する；交流する ▶inter- 二者間(＝between)・act 作用する
- **rely** [rɪláɪ] 【動】[rely on/upon A [for B]] [B を求めて] A に頼る
  (≒depend on/upon A [for B])
  【形】reliable 信頼できる ▶-able 形尾(可能)
  ⟷ unreliable 信頼できない ▶un- 否定【名】reliance 依存 ▶-ance 名尾
- **retain** [rɪtéɪn] 【動】〜を保つ ▶re- 元の場所へ・-tain 張る → 保つ
- **transform** [trænsfɔ́ɚm] 【動】〜を変形させる；変質させる ▶trans- 越えて・-form 形作る
  【名】transformation 変形 ▶-ation 名尾
- **diverse** [daɪvɚ́s] 【形】多様な；種々の
  ▶di- 二つの・-verse 回る → 向きを変える。「2つ以上の向きがある」イメージ。divert (わきへそらす；方向転換する)と同源。
  【名】diversity 多様性 ▶-ity 名尾
  【動】diversify 〜を多様化する；変化を与える ▶-ify 動尾
- **domestic** [dəméstɪk] 【形】家庭の ー [共に生活をする者の場所内] → 国内の ▶domes- 家庭・-ic 形尾
  ▶domestic violence は「家庭内暴力」(＝DV), domestic animal は「家畜」。
- **nuclear** [nú:kliɚ] 【形】核の；原子力の ▶nucle 原子核(≒nucleus)・-ar 形尾
  ▶nuclear weapon は「核兵器」, nuclear family は「核家族」。
- **furthermore** [fɚ́ðɚmɔ̀ɚ] 【副】おまけに；さらに
  ▶further さらなる程度(far の比較級)・more より多く
- **eventually** [ɪvéntʃuəli:] 【副】結果的に
  ▶event 結果・-ly 副尾。派生語は event の項参照。

次の文章を読んで以下の質問に答えましょう。

Modern Society

 Our contemporary society differs dramatically from the society of just two or three generations earlier. Naturally, the most significant development is that more and more people inhabit the cities. Yet the transformations that this shift in population has made not only affect the way we live our everyday lives, but they also affect the various types of interactions that we have with others.

 Most notable is the ethnic variety that characterizes the modern city. Due to increasing globalization and the general decline in immigration barriers between modernized nations, we can literally walk down any city street and meet people who themselves came from other nations or are the descendants of those who left their countries of birth to look for new lives in a foreign country.

 Furthermore, in large part to urbanization, differences in our attitudes toward gender and the family have evolved as well. When people live in rural areas or small towns, the bonds of family and community are much stronger. Because of the relative isolation of the city, there has been a weakening of the connections between people, which has caused numerous social and psychological problems. On the other hand, the diversity of people living together in the city has forced a breakdown of gender stereotypes and prejudices. The nuclear family, as well, has been transformed. No longer are women enforced by traditional family structures to stay at home and to take care of their husbands and children. As a result, the number of women who are working outside of the home increases annually, and they are now doing jobs that only men did in the past.

1. What does this passage explain?
    a. How cities are not popular for immigrants.
    b. How urbanization has strengthened the traditional family.
    c. What changes are taking place in modern cities.
    d. What immigrants are missing in foreign countries.

2. What is the main reason why there is more crime in the city than in the country?
    a. People are living more isolated lives.
    b. People living in the city are more violent.
    c. People of different cultures cannot live together peacefully.
    d. People no longer live in nuclear families.

3. Why do women now have more opportunities?
    a. Society has changed its view of women.
    b. Technology has given them free time.
    c. They are not having children.
    d. Women are refusing to get married.

4. Which of the following can be inferred about life in the modern city?
    a. Equality among men and women in the workplace is the law.
    b. More and more families have a mother who works outside the home.
    c. The number of immigrants that come to the city increases every year.
    d. There are more immigrants than people who were born there.

Unit 2

- ☐ **attitude** [ǽtətuːd] 【名】姿勢 →（物事に対する）態度
- ☐ **belief** [bəlíːf] 【名】信じること；信念，信仰
  - 【動】believe 〜を信じている
  - 《連語》believe in 〜 〜の存在を信じている；信仰する，〜の人格を信じている
  - ▶ believe him は「彼の言葉を信じている」，believe in him は「彼の中身まで信じている」。
- ☐ **ethics** [éθɪks] 【名】倫理学 ▶ eth- 倫理・-ics 学問
  - 【名】ethic 倫理，価値観 ▶ the work ethic は「労働を善とする価値観」。
  - 【形】ethical 倫理的な ▶ -al 形尾
- ☐ **philosophy** [fəlɑ́ːsəfi] 【名】哲学 ▶ philo- = -phile 好む・-sophy 知識。bibliophile（< biblio- 本 + -phile）で「愛書家」。
- ☐ **harmony** [hɑ́ːrməni] 【名】調和（⟷ discord 不調和），バランス（⟷ disharmony 不一致）
  - 《連語》in harmony with 〜 〜と調和して
- ☐ **hymn** [hím] 【名】賛歌；賛美歌
- ☐ **notion** [nóʊʃən] 【名】観念 ▶ not- 知る（= know）・-tion 名尾
- ☐ **ritual** [rítʃuəl] 【名】（宗教的）儀式 【形】儀式の
  - ▶ rite 儀式・-al 形尾。ritual は rite よりも堅苦しい儀式。
- ☐ **sect** [sékt] 【名】宗派；教派 −[思想，利害関係で結びついた小集団] → 党派；派閥
- ☐ **symbol** [símbəl] 【名】象徴 −[ある意味内容を示す印] → 記号
  - ▶「シンボル・マーク」は和製英語。正しくは symbol もしくは mark。
- ☐ **obligation** [ɑbləɡéɪʃən] 【名】義務 −[報いるべき義務] → 恩義 ▶ -ation 名尾
  - 【動】obligate 〜を義務づける ▶ -ate 動尾。原義は「縛る」。
  - 【動】[be obliged to do] 〜せざるを得ない
- ☐ **conduct** [（動）kəndʌ́kt] [（名）kɑ́ːndʌkt] 【動】〜を導く → 〜を案内する，〜を指揮する，（熱・電気などを）伝導する
  - ▶ con- 共に・-duct 引く。つまり，「引いていく；引率する」イメージ。
  - 【名】（道徳上の）行い ▶「道徳と共に引き出されるもの」のイメージ。
  - 【名】conductor 車掌；添乗員，指揮者，伝導体 ▶ -or = -er 名尾（〜する人）
- ☐ **contribute** [kəntríbjuːt] 【動】[contribute (A) to B] (A を) B に寄付する；貢献する
  - ▶ con- 共に・tribute 貢献
  - 【名】contribution 寄付；貢献 ▶ -tion 名尾
- ☐ **meditate** [médɪteɪt] 【動】〜を黙想する；熟考する → 〜をもくろむ
  - ▶ medit- 計る・-ate 動尾。「物事の大きさを計る」イメージ。mediate（仲介する；調停する）との違いに注意。なお，mediate の medi- は middle（中間）に由来。
  - 【名】meditation 黙想；熟考 ▶ -ation 名尾
- ☐ **reinforce** [riːɪnfɔ́ːrs] 【動】〜を補強する；強化する
  - ▶ re- 元の場所へ → 再び・-inforce 強化する（= enforce）
- ☐ **seek** [síːk] 【動】〜を得ようと求める [seek to do] 〜しようと努める
- ☐ **divine** [dəváɪn] 【形】神の；神聖な
  - ▶ To err is human, to forgive divine.（過ちは人の常，許すのは神のわざ）
- ☐ **fundamental** [fʌndəméntl] 【形】基本的な；根本的な 【名】[fundamentals] 基本事項；原則
  - ▶ funda- 基礎を築く（= found）・-ment 名尾（〜すること）・-al 形尾
  - ▶ fundamental human rights は「基本的人権」。
- ☐ **rigid** [rídʒəd] 【形】（物が）かたい −[考え方がかたい] → 融通性のきかない，厳格な
- ☐ **traditional** [trədíʃənl] 【形】伝統的な；慣習的な ▶ -al 形尾
  - 【名】tradition 伝統；慣習 ▶ trad-（手で）渡す・-tion 名尾

次の文章を読んで以下の質問に答えましょう。

Religion and Society

The American Benjamin Franklin once stated, "Religion will be a powerful regulator of our actions, gives us peace and tranquility* within our minds, and renders* us benevolent,* useful and beneficial to others." Although many people do not believe in the existence of God today, religion continues to play an important role in modern society.

No matter what your attitudes are toward religion, it would be impossible for you to deny that religion has greatly contributed to the foundation of morals and ethics in society. Our religious beliefs mediate the ways in which we interact with other people. In Japan, for example, the Shinto religion encourages people to live in harmony with nature. Thus, it is commonly said that the Japanese make extreme efforts to preserve purity and harmony in all aspects of life. Even today, we can say that the religious beliefs that have developed over centuries continue to represent the basic value system of a particular society. A common religion can give the people in a culture a common identity and feeling of social membership by making individuals part of society through shared rituals and ceremonies that mark life. In this way, a shared religion creates stability within society.

Religion also has made important contributions to culture. Name any of the cultural sites on the list of World Heritage properties, and you will soon discover that the majority of these are religious sites, or are closely connected to religion. In fact, all but one of the properties among the Historic Monuments of Ancient Kyoto, are Buddhist temples or Shinto shrines that have played an important role in the religious, cultural, and political development of Japan. In addition to these physical objects, religious belief has also impacted other aspects of culture as well, including literature, music and even the language we use every day.

* **tranquility** 静穏
* **render** (〜に)する
* **benevolent** 善意の

Read the following statements and mark them T (true) or F (false).
1. _____ No one in the world today still believes in God.
2. _____ The way we behave with people is based originally upon laws.
3. _____ Japanese people try to avoid conflict partly because of the beliefs of Shinto.
4. _____ A country with many religious beliefs may be more likely to have more social problems.
5. _____ A shared religion helps people feel that they are a part of society.
6. _____ In order to be listed as World Heritage Site, a place must be connected to a religion.
7. _____ Culture is defined in this passage as a building or physical organization.

Unit 3

- **aisle** [áɪl] 【名】(商品陳列棚間・座席間などの)狭い通路
  ▶ [英] では，教会に aisle，劇場に aisle / corridor，列車に corridor を用いる。
- **bar code** [báɚ kóʊd] 【名】バーコード
  ▶ bar 棒・code コード
- **category** [kǽtəgɔri] 【名】範疇(はんちゅう)；カテゴリー
  【動】categorize 〜を範疇化する；分類する ▶ -ize 動尾
- **brand** [brǽnd] 【名】焼印 − [区別する印] → 銘柄；商標 ▶ 「ブランド品」は brand name item。
  ▶ 以下のカタカナ語と英単語との意味の違いに注意しよう。
  - コンセント：outlet　　　　　※ consent 同意している
  - カンニング：cheating　　　　※ cunning ずる賢い
  - トランプ：cards　　　　　　 ※ trump 切り札
  - ハンドル：steering wheel 　※ handle ドアなどの取っ手
  - メリット：利点：advantage 　※ merit 長所
  - マンション：apartment house ※ mansion 大邸宅
  - リタイアする：drop out 　　 ※ retire 〜を辞職する
- **budget** [bʌ́dʒət] 【名】予算；予算案 【動】予算を立てる →(金／時を)割り振る
  ▶ budg- 皮袋・-et 名尾(小さいもの)。「小さな皮袋；財布 → その中身；予算」。
- **cash** [kǽʃ] 【名】現金；即金 【動】(手形などを)現金に換える；換金する
  ▶ 「現金で」は by / in cash。「クレジット・カードで」は by (credit) card。
- **clerk** [klɚ́k] 【名】事務員；[米] 店員
- **counter** [káʊntɚ] 【名】勘定台；カウンター ▶ 「反対の；逆の」の意の counter とは同音異義語。
- **display** [dɪspléɪ] 【名】表示,展示 【動】(感情・考えを)〜をはっきりと示す → 〜を展示する
- **impulse** [ímpʌls] 【名】衝動 【形】衝動的な ▶ im-=in- 中に・-pulse 押しやられる
- **item** [áɪtəm] 【名】個々の項目；品目 → 記事項目
- **label** [léɪbəl] 【名】はり札；ラベル −[人物の内容] →(好ましくない)通り名；レッテル
  【動】〜にラベルを貼る，〜にレッテルを貼る
- **mode** [móʊd] 【名】仕様 ▶ model(模型；ひな型)と同源。「型」のイメージ。
- **purse** [pɚ́s] 【名】(女性がハンドバッグに入れて携帯する)財布；小銭入れ，
  [米] (肩ひものない)ハンドバッグ
- **refund** [(名)rífʌnd] 【名】払い戻し；返済(金)
  [(動)rɪfʌ́nd] 【動】〜を払い戻す ▶ re- 元の場所へ・-fund 注ぐ
- **retail** [ríːteɪl] 【名】小売り 【動】〜を小売りする
  ▶ re- 元の場所へ → 再び・-tail 切る。原義は「切り売りする」。retailer で「小売商」。
- **wallet** [wɑ́ːlət] 【名】(男性用の革製／ビニール製の)札入れ；財布
- **acquire** [əkwáɪɚ] 【動】〜を獲得する；習得する ▶ ac-=ad- 方向・-quire 捜し求める(question と同源)
  【名】acquisition 獲得；習得
  ▶ -tion 名尾。language acquisition は「言語習得」。M&A は merger and acquisition の略で「(企業などの)合併吸収；合併と買収」。
  【形】acquired 獲得された；後天的な ▶ -ed 形尾(〜された)
  ⟷ hereditary 先天的な ▶ heredity 遺伝・-ary 形尾
  ▶ AIDS は Acquired Immune Deficiency Syndrome(後天性免疫不全症候群)の略。
- **adjust** [ədʒʌ́st] 【動】〜に適合させる ▶ ad- 方向・-just 近くに。「〜の近くに置く」イメージ。
  《連語》adjust oneself to 〜(〜に自身を適合させる)→ 〜に順応する
  【名】adjustment 順応 ▶ -ment 名尾
- **purchase** [pɚ́ːtʃəs] 【動】〜を購入する 【名】購入；購入品 ▶ pur- 求めて・chase 追跡する

次の文章を読んで以下の質問に答えましょう。

Black Friday

Walk into any shopping mall in America in the weeks before or after Christmas, and you will find the aisles filled with shoppers with their wallets and purses ready to make a purchase. The Christmas season is the most important month for retailers in the United States. In fact, this one month can account for more than 80% of sales, and thus it is easy to understand the importance that is placed on having stores filled with customers, and more importantly, customers at the counter.

Typically, the beginning of the Christmas shopping season begins on the day after Thanksgiving, or the last Friday of November. Most people, except for those working in retail, have this day off. Stores and shopping malls open early, some as early as 5 or 6 a.m., and advertize a number of bargains in the newspaper on the previous day. This day is called "Black Friday" mainly because it is the day when most retailers begin making a profit. That is, it marks the point at which they begin operating "in the black" rather than "in the red."* In recent years, more and more people are deciding to avoid the crowds and traffic and instead, are choosing to purchase items online. The busiest day for Internet shopping during the Christmas season is the Monday following Black Friday, a day that has now come to be known as "Cyber Monday."

Yet, data shows that these two days are not the busiest for retailers. In fact, most people wait to buy their Christmas presents until the Saturday before Christmas and this is usually the day that most people do their shopping. Moreover, the days following Christmas are also very busy. Many people return gifts that they have received and either exchange them or get a refund. Retailers also try to get rid of items that they were not able to sell before Christmas by selling them at greatly reduced prices.

* **in the black** 黒字，**in the red** 赤字

1. Why is the last Friday of November called "Black Friday"?
    a. It is an important day for retailers since it is the day that they start making a profit.
    b. Many people wake up early to go shopping.
    c. Most shoppers would rather not go to the stores.
    d. Most retail workers have the day off.

2. When do most people shop during the Christmas season?
    a. on Christmas Day
    b. on Black Friday
    c. on the Saturday before Christmas
    d. on Cyber Monday

3. Why are shopping malls busy after Christmas?
    a. Many people do not have to work.
    b. People are returning presents.
    c. Many retailers have gone out of business.
    d. Shoppers are buying Christmas gifts.

Unit 4

- **audit** [ɑ́:dət] 【名】会計検査；監査 ▶ 原義は「証言を聞くこと」。audience(聴衆)と同源。
- **bond** [bɑ́:nd] 【名】絆(きずな)；結束 − [縛るもの] → (債務)証書, 公債；社債；債権
- **bonus** [bóʊnəs] 【名】特別手当；賞与, 特別配当金；特典 ▶ 原義は「良いもの」。
- **credit** [krédɪt] 【名】信用 − [信用貸し] → クレジット
- **currency** [kə́:rənsi] 【名】通貨 ▶ -ency 名尾。「金の流れ＝水の流れ」で認識。例：資金の流れを凍結した。
  - 【形／名】current 流通している, 現在の, (川／時の)流れ, 風潮
  - ▶ cur- 走る − [直線の連続性] → 流れる・-ent 形尾・名尾。「電流」は electric current,「時事問題」は current events。
- **deficit** [défəsət] 【名】不足；不足額 → 赤字 ▶ de- 分離・-fect 行う。defect(欠点)と同源。
- **deposit** [dɪpɑ́:zət] 【名】預金；頭金 ▶ de- 下・-posit 置かれたもの。「銀行の業務下に置かれたもの」。
  - 【動】〜を置く, 〜を預ける
- **equity** [ékwəti] 【名】(平等)→ 公正；公平 − [会社に対する平等な発言権に至るもの]
  - → 株；株式
  - ▶ equ- 等しい(＝equal)・-ity 名尾。equal(等しい)と同源。
- **finance** [fáɪnæns] 【名】財政 ▶ fina- 終える(＝finish)・-ance 名尾。「収支を終えたもの」。
  - 【形】financial 財政的な ▶ -ial 形尾
- **inflation** [ɪnfléɪʃən] 【名】(物価の)暴騰；インフレ ▶ -ation 名尾
  - ⟷ deflation 通貨収縮；デフレ
  - 【動】inflate 〜を膨(ふく)らませる ▶ in- 中に・-flate 吹く
- **fund** [fʌ́nd] 【名】基金；資金 【動】〜に資金を提供する
  - ▶ found(基礎を築く → 設立する), fundamental(基礎となる)と同源。
- **asset** [ǽset] 【名】財産 → 有用なもの；貴重なもの
  - ▶ as-＝ad- 方向・-set 十分な。原義は「所有物」。
- **principal** [prínsəpəl] 【名】元金, 社長；会長；校長 【形】元金の, 主要な
  - ▶「最初のもの → 主要なもの」のイメージ。同音の principle(原則)との違いに注意。
- **recession** [rɪséʃən] 【名】(後退)→ 不景気；不況 ▶ -sion 名尾
  - 【動】recede (徐々に)退く；後退する ▶ re- 元の場所へ・-cede 行く(＝go)
- **recovery** [rɪkʌ́vəri] 【名】取り戻すこと；回復 ▶ -y 名尾
  - 【動】recover 〜を取り戻す, [recover from 〜] 〜から回復する
  - ▶ re- 元の場所へ → 元の状態へ・cover(欠けたところを)覆う
- **remittance** [rɪmítəns] 【名】送金；送金額 ▶ -ance 名尾
  - 【動】remit 〜を送金する ▶ re- 元の場所へ・-mit 送る
  - ▶ -mit(送る)で捉えられる他の英単語に以下が挙げられる。
  - 1. submit to 〜 〜に服従する, 〜に提出する
  - ・sub- は「下」。submit は「相手の影響下(sub-)に送る(-mit)→ その権限下に置く」。
  - 2. intermit 一時的に中断する
  - ・inter- は「二者間」。intermit は「間に(sub-)送る(-mit)→ 間を置いて不連続にする」。
- **statistic** [stətístɪk] 【名】統計値 [statistics] 統計学 ▶ state(状態)と同源。「分布状態を調べるもの」。
  - 【形】statistical 統計の；統計上の, 統計学の ▶ -ical 形尾
- **surplus** [sə́:pləs] 【名】余剰；過剰 ▶ sur- 越えて・-plus 加えた。「貿易黒字」は trade surplus。
- **withdraw** [wɪðdrɑ́:] 【動】〜を引っ込める；引きこもる, 〜を撤退させる, 〜を撤回する, (預金を)引き出す ▶ with 対抗(＝against)→ 出ている方向と逆向きに・draw 引く
  - 【名】withdrawal 引っ込めること, 撤退, 撤回, 預金の引き出し
- **fiscal** [fískəl] 【形】国庫の；国庫収入の → 財政上の；会計の 【名】収入印紙
  - ▶ fisc- 国庫・-al 形尾

次の文章を読んで以下の質問に答えましょう。

Make Your University Education Pay

The majority of students choose to attend a four-year university because they believe that, with a diploma, they will be able to get a better paying job than if they had gone immediately into the job market after high school. However, recent research in Great Britain seriously questions whether most students can get jobs that justify paying increasingly high tuition and living expenses that are necessary for a university education. According to researchers at the University of Warwick, statistics show that many students would be financially better off* if they chose to begin work rather than go to university, especially students in the humanities or students with poor grades and students with degrees from lower-ranking universities.

So, how can you make the most of your university experience and become more financially sound during your university years? First of all, make the most of the educational opportunities at your university. Do not merely try to pass your classes; rather try to get excellent grades, too. By doing so, not only will you be able to impress people at interviews, but you will also learn more.

Also, try to learn to build good money habits. Deposit your pay from your part-time job into a bank account. Never spend the money you get immediately. First make a budget and decide how much money you have to spend on necessities and how much you want to save. You can spend the remainder on things that you want but do not necessarily need. If you build up your savings, think about withdrawing the money and investing it in the stock market. Although there is always the risk that you will lose money when you buy stocks, if you manage your portfolio* wisely, you will likely find that your money will grow and be a protection against inflation in the future.

Your time at university is an important step between living at home and living in the real world. Make sure that you use this time to become educationally and financially sound.

* **better off** 〔〜した方が〕もっとよい状態になる、(ここでは)より裕福になる
* **portfolio** 有価証券の一覧表

Read the following statements and mark them T (true) or F (false).

1. _____ Most students expect that their university education will be a good investment.
2. _____ It always makes financial sense for people to attend university.
3. _____ Studying humanities subjects can be a disadvantage in the job market.
4. _____ Getting good grades will help you get work.
5. _____ It is important to carefully manage how you use your income.
6. _____ If you buy stocks with your savings, you will always make your money grow.
7. _____ This passage encourages all readers to find a job immediately after high school.

Unit 5

- **commodity** [kəmάːdəti] 【名】産物；商品 ▶com- = con- 強意・mod 便利な・-ity 名尾。「日常品」は (daily) commodities,「物価」は commodity prices。

- **dividend** [dívədend] 【名】株の配当；配当金
  ▶ divide（分ける；分割する）・-end 名尾

- **economy** [ikάːnəmi] 【名】経済 ▶eco- 家・-nomy 学問。原義は「家政管理学」。
  【形】economic 経済の ▶-ic 形尾【形】economical 倹約的な ▶-ical 形尾

- **expenditure** [ikspéndɪtʃɚ] 【名】出費，歳出 ▶-ure 名尾 ⟷ revenue 歳入
  【動】expend（金／労力／時を）費やす ▶ex- 外へ・-pend 吊るす。「天秤」に由来。
  【名】expense 支出；必要経費
  【形】expensive 費用のかかる；高価な ▶-sive 形尾 ⟷ inexpensive 安価な

- **franchise** [frǽntʃaɪz] 【名】公民権，[米]（官庁が与える）特権；（チェーン店の）営業権
  ▶ franch- 自由な・-ise 動尾

- **globalization** [gloubəlɪzéɪʃən] 【名】国際化（＝各国の多様性を認め合うこと）▶-ation 名尾
  【形】global 地球規模の；世界的な ▶-al 形尾
  【名】globalize 〜を世界規模にする；国際化する ▶-ize 動尾

- **percentage** [pɚséntɪdʒ] 【名】百分率；パーセンテージ，割合；利率
  ▶ per- 〜につき・-cent 100・-age 割合・「〜％」は〜 percent。

- **revenue** [révənuː] 【名】歳入；収入源 ▶re- 元の場所へ・-venue 来る ⟷ expenditure 歳出

- **transaction** [trænzǽkʃən] 【名】（業務上の）処理 → 取引 ▶-tion 名尾
  【動】transact（業務・取引を）行なう ▶trans- 越えて・-act 行う

- **authorize** [άːθəraɪz] 【動】〜に権限を与える → 〜を認定する；認可する ▶-ize 動尾
  【名】authorization 権限，認可 ▶-ation 名尾
  【名】authority 権限，権威 ▶author- 生み出す人・-ity 名尾。author（著者）と同源。

- **export** [（動）ɛkspóɚt] [（名）ékspoɚt] 【動】〜を輸出する 【名】輸出；輸出品 ▶ex- 外へ・-port 港へ運ぶ
  【名】exportation 輸出 ▶-ation 名尾

- **import** [（動）ɪmpóɚt] [（名）ímpoɚt] 【動】〜を輸入する 【名】輸入；輸入品 ▶in- 中へ・-port 港へ運ぶ
  【名】importation 輸入 ▶-ation 名尾

- **integrate** [íntəgreɪt] 【動】〜を統合する ▶integ- 完全な・-ate 動尾
  【名】integration 統合 ▶-ation 名尾

- **negotiate** [nɪɡóʊʃieɪt] 【動】交渉する → 〜を取り決める ▶neg- 否定・-oti 暇（ひま）・-ate 動尾
  【名】negotiation 交渉，話し合い ▶-ation 名尾

- **regulate** [réɡjəleɪt] 【動】〜を規制する；調整する ▶regul- 規則正しい（＝regular）・-ate 動尾
  【名】regulation 規制；規則 ▶-ation 名尾

- **undertake** [ʌndɚtéɪk] 【動】（仕事などを）引き受ける；〜に取りかかる
  ▶ under 下に → 手もとに・take 取る

- **liable** [láɪəbl] 【形】[be liable to do]（習慣・傾向から悪いことを）しがちである
  ▶ lie- 縛る・-able 形尾（可能）
  【名】liability 傾向があること,（法的）責任；債務 ▶-ity 名尾

- **subsequent** [sʌ́bsəkwənt] 【形】次に起こる；（時間的に）後の
  ▶ sub- 下に → 服従して・-sequent 続いている

- **subsidiary** [səbsídieri] 【形】補助的な 【名】系列子会社 ▶-ary 形尾
  【名】subsidy 補助金 ▶sub- 下に → 副次的に・-sidi 座る → 位置する・-y 名尾

- **worldwide** [wɚ́ːldwáɪd] 【形】世界的な；世界中に広まった
  ▶ world 世界・wide 広い → 広範囲の

次の文章の空所に枠内の適切な語を入れて文章を完成させましょう。

It's a Small World

Where was your watch made? How about your shoes? For most people in the world, the answer is probably not their own country. The (1)_____ of the world economy began hundreds of years ago, and has continued until this day. However, although the world is becoming more and more (2)_____ , people are increasingly asking, "Is globalization really a good thing?"

On the one hand, globalization has certainly made the world richer. For instance, a Korean company can cheaply buy copper from Africa. After (3)_____ the copper into China, the company could have Chinese labor use the (4)_____ to help make televisions. Next, the televisions could be (5)_____ to Germany for a large profit. The Korean company would receive a lot of (6)_____ from selling the televisions and could make large (7)_____ payments to its international shareholders.

On the other hand, it is argued that globalization does not benefit the weak. For example, the Korean company mentioned above could (8)_____ a very cheap price for the copper. And most of the money may go directly to the African leaders, and only a small (9)_____ to the African people. Next, the Chinese workers might be paid very little and work in very dangerous conditions. Finally, because the Korean televisions are very cheap, the German people may no longer want to buy expensive German televisions. Therefore, German workers could lose their jobs.

There are a lot of disagreements about globalization; however, it is agreed that it is becoming an increasingly important (10)_____ issue. What do you think should be the future of the world economy?

> a) commodity   b) dividend   c) exported   d) globalization   e) importing
> f) integrated   g) negotiate   h) percentage   i) revenue   j) worldwide

Unit 6

- **arson** [ɑ́ɚsn]
  - 【名】放火；放火罪 ▶ ardor(燃えるような)情熱；熱心，ardent(情熱的な)と同源。
  - 【名】arsonist 放火犯 ▶ -ist 名尾(〜する人)
- **evidence** [évədəns]
  - 【名】証拠 ▶ -ence 名尾
  - 【形】evident 明白な
  - ▶ e- = ex- 外へ・-vid 見る・-ent 形尾。「はっきり見ている」イメージ。
- **felony** [féləni]
  - 【名】重罪 ▶ felon 重罪犯人・-y 名尾。関連語として criminal(犯人)，perpetrator((犯罪や悪事の)犯人)，offender(違反者)，convict((有罪宣告を受けた)囚人)。
- **jury** [dʒʊ́əri]
  - 【名】陪審員 ▶ just(公正な；公平な)と同源。「陪審員制度」は jury system。
- **misdemeanor** [mɪsdɪmíːnɚ]
  - 【名】軽罪
  - ▶ mis- 悪い・demeanor 態度
- **offense** [əféns]
  - 【名】攻撃, 立腹；無礼, 違反；罪 [give offense to 〜] 〜を怒らせる
  - 【形】offensive 攻撃の, 不快な；嫌な ▶ -ive 形尾
  - 【動】offend(刃を向ける) → 〜を怒らせる；感情を害する ー [反逆する] ─ (法律・規則を)犯す ▶ of- = ad- 方向・-fend 先の尖った武器で)刺す
- **penalty** [pénəlti]
  - 【名】刑罰 ▶ -ty 名尾
  - 【形】penal 刑罰の ▶ pen- 尖ったもの・-al 形尾
- **testimony** [téstəmoʊni]
  - 【名】証言；証拠 ▶ proof(証拠)よりかたい語。
  - 【動】testify 〜を証言する ▶ test- 証言・-ify 動尾
- **theft** [θéft]
  - 【名】盗み；窃盗(せっとう) ▶ thef- 泥棒する(= thief)・-ft 名尾(抽象名詞)
  - 【名】thief 泥棒 ▶ 「強盗」は robber,「空き巣」は stealer,「押し込み夜盗」は burglar。
- **verdict** [vɚ́dɪkt]
  - 【名】(陪審員の)評決
  - ▶ verdict に基づく裁判官の判決は judgment, 刑の判決は sentence。
- **victim** [víktəm]
  - 【名】犠牲者；被害者
  - 《連語》fall victim to 〜 〜の犠牲となる
- **capture** [kǽptʃɚ]
  - 【動】〜を(力ずくで)捕らえる → (人の心・注意などを)引きつける
  - 【名】捕獲 ▶ cap- 捕らえる(= catch)・-ure 名尾
  - 【形/名】captive 捕虜になった, 心を奪われた, 捕虜, とりこ ▶ -ive 形尾
  - 【動】captivate 〜を魅惑する ▶ -ate 動尾
- **convict** [kənvíkt]
  - 【動】〜に有罪判決を下す [be convicted of 〜] 〜の有罪判決を受ける
  - ▶ con- 強意・-vict 征服する ⟷ be acquitted of 〜 〜の無罪判決を受ける
- **enact** [ɪnǽkt]
  - 【動】(法律を)制定する；(法案を)成立させる ▶ en- 中に・act 法令
- **enforce** [ɪnfɔ́ɚs]
  - 【動】〜を強制する ー [守らせる] → (法律などを)施行する
  - ▶ en- 与える・force 力
- **investigate** [ɪnvéstəgeɪt]
  - 【動】〜を詳細に調べる(≒ look into) ▶ in- 中に・-vestig 足跡をたどる・-ate 動尾
  - 【名】investigation (詳細な)調査 ▶ -ation 名尾
- **plead** [plíːd]
  - 【動】嘆願(たんがん)する；弁護する → (裁判で)申し立てる
  - 【名】plea 嘆願；弁解, 申し立て
- **prosecute** [prɑ́ːsɪkjuːt]
  - 【動】〜を遂行する ー [追い詰める] → 〜を起訴する
  - 【名】prosecution 遂行, 起訴 ▶ -tion 名尾
- **sentence** [séntəns]
  - 【動】〜に判決を与える 【名】判決
  - ▶ sent- 感じる・-ence 名尾。原義は「感じたことを文字で表現する → 文」。
- **innocent** [ínəsənt]
  - 【形】無罪の ー [罪の無い] → 無邪気な
  - ▶ in- 否定・-noc 傷つける・-ent 形尾 ⟷ guilty 有罪の
  - 【名】innocence 無罪, 無邪気 ▶ -ence 名尾

次の文章を読んで以下の質問に答えましょう。

The Jury System

The jury has a long and complicated legal history. The word "jury" originally meant "to swear an oath"; and although the term came from French, its exact origins are unknown. In England during the early middle ages, jurors were composed of people from the neighborhood. These juries judged a case based upon what they themselves knew of it. Later, the jury was only employed in determining the facts of a case, and it was the king's court that would render a verdict. The jury trial as it exists today appeared in the 15th century. Although the jury system is used in a number of countries, its real home is the United States, where more than 90 percent of all jury trials in the world are held for both criminal (felonies and misdemeanors) and civil cases.

In the U.S. jury system, potential jurors are selected from a list of citizens who are living within the jurisdiction* of the court that will hear a case. When jurors receive a summons they must appear in court on a specific day and can only be excused due to illness or if they would suffer hardship by serving on the jury. For each trial, a number of jurors are chosen at random. They are questioned by both sides of the case. Both the prosecution and the defense can eliminate jurors that they do not wish to have hear the case. When nine jurors are left, these nine make up the jury for the trial.

After the trial is completed, the nine jurors talk in private and determine the verdict. Originally, all members of the jury had to agree upon a verdict, however, in recent years many states allow verdicts when only a majority of the jurors agree. Sentencing then follows, but that also varies by state. In a civil case, the jury decides both the verdict and the sentence. In criminal cases, however, in most states the sentence is decided by the judge, especially in states that retain the death penalty.

* **jurisdiction** 管轄区

Match the sentence beginnings (1-7) and endings (a-g) to make true statements.

1. _____ Less than 1/10 of all jury trials...   a. is given after the verdict.
2. _____ Juries in the U.S....   b. have nine members.
3. _____ When called for jury duty...   c. have the right to eliminate jurors.
4. _____ The word "jury"...   d. occur outside the United States.
5. _____ When convicted of murder...   e. one must appear in court on a certain day.
6. _____ Both sides of a case...   f. originally is from French.
7. _____ In a trial, sentencing...   g. sentencing is usually done by a judge.

Unit 7

- **annuity** [ənúːəti] 【名】年金（≒ pension）；年金制度 ▶ annu- 毎年の（= annual）・-ity 名尾
- **benefit** [bénəfɪt] 【名】利益；有益【動】〜を益する → 〜のためになる
  【形】beneficial 有益な ▶ -al 形尾
- **casualty** [kǽʒuəlti] 【名】（事故・災害などの）死傷者；被害者
  ▶ casual- 機会 → 事件（= case）・-ty 名尾（状態）
- **compensation** [kɑmpənséɪʃən] 【名】埋め合わせ；（損失などの）補償，[米] 報酬 ▶ -ation 名尾
  【動】compensate 埋め合わせる；補償する，報酬を支払う
  ▶ com- = con- 共に・-pensate 重さを量る
  《連語》compensate for 〜 〜を埋め合わせる（≒ make up for）
- **injury** [índʒəri] 【名】負傷 ▶ in- 否定・-jury 正しいこと。jury（陪審員）と同源。
  【動】injure 〜を傷つける；怪我させる [be injured in 〜] 〜で怪我をする
- **co-payment** [kóʊpeɪmənt] 【名】共同支払い；（医療費などの）自己負担（金）
  ▶ co- = con- 共に・pay 支払う・-ment 名尾
- **co-signer** [kóʊsaɪnɚ] 【名】連帯保証人
  ▶ co- = con- 共に・sign サインをする・-er 名尾（〜する人）
- **deductible** [dɪdʌ́ktəbl] 【名】控除免責金額；控除免責条項，（税などの）控除【形】控除可能な
  ▶ -ible = -able 形尾（可能）
  【動】deduct（一定の金額を全体額から）差し引く；控除する
- **homeowner** [hóʊmoʊnɚ] 【名】自宅所有者
  ▶ home 家；家庭・own 所有する・-er 名尾（〜する人）
- **loss** [lɑ́ːs] 【名】損失 ▶ be at a loss は「途方にくれて」。
  【動】lose 〜を失う，見失う
- **liability** [laɪəbíləti] 【名】傾向があること，（法的）責任；債務 ▶ -ity 名尾。liable の項参照。
- **lien** [líːn] 【名】先取特権；担保権 ▶ 原義は「縛（しば）る」。liable と同源。
- **mortgage** [mɔ́ːrgɪdʒ] 【名】抵当（権）；抵当で借りたローン
  ▶ mort- 死んでいる → 実効力のない・-gage 誓約。「抵当設定によりいずれかが抵当への効力を失う」ことに由来。mortal（死ぬ運命にある）と同源。
- **policy** [pɑ́ːləsi] 【名】政策 → 方針，保険証書
  ▶ 原義は「統治」。police（警察）と同源。「保険証書」の意はイタリア語 polizza の英訳に由来。
- **premium** [príːmiəm] 【名】賞金；報奨金 → 保険料
  ▶ pre- 前に・-mium 買う。「買う前に意欲をそそるもの」に由来。なお，「保険料」の意は「病気や怪我をする前に買うもの」に由来。
- **survivor** [sɚváɪvɚ] 【名】生存者 − [他の人の死後に残された者] → 遺族 ▶ -or = -er 名尾（〜する人）
  【動】survive 困難を乗り越えて生き残る → 〜より長生きする
  【名】survival 生き残ること ▶ -al 名尾
- **underwriter** [ʌ́ndɚraɪtɚ] 【名】（証券の）引受人（= 保険契約引き受けの全権を与えられている人）
  ▶ 保険引き受けをした際に，保険証券の「下（under）の欄に署名をする（write）人（-er）」のイメージ。
- **widow** [wídoʊ] 【名】未亡人 ▶ 男性形，すなわち「男やもめ」は widower。
- **lapse** [lǽps] 【動/名】（つるっと滑る）→ ちょっとした誤り；過失
  [あっという間に時が過ぎ去ること] → 時の経過；一時期 − [時効による消滅] → 無効になる；失効する
- **terminate** [tɚ́məneɪt] 【動】〜を終わらせる
  ▶ -ate 動尾。terminal の項参照。

次の文章を読んで以下の質問に答えましょう。

Insurance

  Broadly speaking, insurance is a means for individuals to recover more easily from financial or other loss by cooperating with other individuals. The insurer, usually an insurance company, receives monetary contributions from many individuals, invests that money, then pays out money as compensation to people who have policies with that company when they suffer injury or loss. There are many types of insurance which reflects the complexity of modern life. Property insurance covers homeowners in the case that damage is caused to their homes. It can also include other kinds of property, such as automobiles, personal and business property. Life insurance pays out money in the case of the death of a family member. Health insurance covers medical expenses when you are sick or hospitalized. Premiums for health insurance depend upon your age and physical condition at the time you purchase your policy, as well as the amount of money that you must pay out of your own wallet which is not covered by insurance.

  Naturally there are many individuals who hope to benefit illegally. For example, in the U.S. state of North Carolina, a man bought a box of expensive cigars* and insured them against fire. After he had smoked all of the cigars, he filed a claim against the insurance company even before he had paid the first premium on his policy. The man claimed that the cigars were lost in a series of small fires, but the insurance company refused to pay because it was obvious that the man had consumed the cigars in the normal fashion. The judge in the court case decided in favor of the man, saying that the insurance company failed to define "fire" in its insurance policy. After the man received compensation from the insurance company, he was arrested and charged with 24 counts of arson*. He was convicted of intentionally burning his insured property and sentenced to 24 months in jail and fined $24,000. As funny as this story is, attempting to collect money by making fraudulent claims costs the insurance industry billions of dollars every year.

* **cigars** 葉巻
* **arson** 放火（罪）

Read the following statements and mark them T (true) or F (false).

1. _____ Without insurance, it would be more difficult for people to recover from a loss.
2. _____ Even with health insurance, you may still have to pay some of the costs yourself.
3. _____ Health insurance premiums are partly based on how old you are.
4. _____ A North Carolina man insured 24 cigars.
5. _____ A North Carolina man was not able to collect money for the loss of his cigars.
6. _____ The smoker who received compensation from the insurance company was charged with arson.
7. _____ Because of insurance fraud, many insurance companies make profits.

Unit 8

- **analogue** [ǽnəlɑːg] 【名】類似 − [構造が類似したもの] → アナログ
  ▶ analogous(類似した)と同源。「アナログ」は [米] analog とも。
- **antenna** [ænténə] 【名】触覚 − [探知し受信するもの] → アンテナ
- **circulation** [sɚːkjəléɪʃən] 【名】循環 − [情報の流れ；流通] → 印刷物の発行部数 ▶ -ation 名尾
  【動】circulate 循環する；流通する
  ▶ circul- 輪；円(＝circle)・-ate 動尾。circuit(円周，回路)，circus(円形広場 − [そこで実施された競技] → サーカス)も同源。
- **cable** [kéɪbl] 【名】太綱(ふとづな) → ケーブル線 ▶「ケーブルテレビ」は cable TV。
- **column** [kɑ́ːləm] 【名】円柱 − [姿・形の類似] →（新聞・雑誌の）縦の欄 − [寄稿欄] → コラム
- **correspondent** [kɔːrəspɑ́ːndənt] 【名】通信員；記者 【形】合致している ▶ -ant 形尾
  【動】correspond（共に応じる）
    → [correspond with〜] 〜と文通する；通信する
    → [correspond with/to〜] 〜に合致する → [correspond to〜] 〜に相当する
  ▶ cor- ＝ con- 共に・respond 応じる
  【名】correspondence 文通；通信，合致すること，相当すること ▶ -ence 名尾
- **documentary** [dɑːkjəméntəri] 【名】(記録証拠となる)文書の；書類の 【名】記録作品 ▶ -ary 形尾
  【名】document(記録証拠となる)文書；書類 ▶ docu- 教え示す・-ment 名尾
- **headline** [hédlaɪn] 【名】大見出し → 主なニュース項目 ▶ head 頭 → 上部・line 線 → 行
- **highlight** [háɪlaɪt] 【名】最も明るい部分 → 呼び物；目玉商品
  【動】〜に明るい光を当てる → 〜を目立たせる ▶ high 高い → 並でない・light 光
- **journal** [dʒɚ́ːnl] 【名】日誌 − [定期的な実行記録] →（専門誌・紀要などの）定期刊行物
- **magazine** [mǽgəziːn] 【名】雑誌, 定期刊行物
  ▶「日刊以外の定期刊行物」は periodical とも。
- **media** [míːdɪə] 【名】媒介物，マスコミ機関；メディア ▶ medium の複数形。data の項参照。
- **satellite** [sǽtəlaɪt] 【名】衛星 → 人工衛星 ▶「人工衛星」の意は artificial satellite の略。
- **series** [síriːz] 【名】一続き → シリーズもの ▶ sequence(連続)と同源。
- **broadcast** [brɔ́ːdkæst] 【動】〜を放送する 【名】放送 → 番組
  ▶ broad 広い；広範囲の・-cast 投げられた
- **communicate** [kəmjúːnəkeɪt] 【動】(意志・情報を)伝達する
  ▶ com- ＝ con- 共に・-muni 交換する・-ate 動尾
  【形】communicative 意志・情報交換の → 話し好きの ▶ -ative 形尾
  【名】communication 意志・情報伝達；コミュニケーション ▶ -ation 名尾
- **edit** [édət] 【動】〜を編集する
  【名】editor 編集者，編集長
  ▶ -or ＝ -er 名尾(〜する人)。「編集長」の意は editor in chief の略。
  【名】edition(編集したもの；改版したもの) →（出版物の）版 ▶ -tion 名尾
  【形/名】editorial 編集の − [編集者が論じたもの] → 社説；論説 ▶ -ial 形尾
- **subscribe** [səbskráɪb] 【動】〜に署名する − [書類に意思決定のサインをする] → 〜に参加申し込みをする, 予約購読する ▶ sub- 下に・-scribe 書く
- **transmit** [trænsmít] 【動】〜を送る → 〜を(電波・ケーブルで)伝える ▶ trans- 越えて・-mit 送る
  【名】transmission 伝達, 通信 ▶ -sion 名尾
- **digital** [dídʒətl] 【形】指の；指状の − [数量を数字で表現する] → デジタルの ▶ -al 形尾
  【名】digit 指 − [指で数えたことから] → アラビア数字
  ▶「手の指」は finger,「足の指」は toe。

次の文章を読んで以下の質問に答えましょう。

Censorship

Daily we are showered by information coming from more traditional sources such as radio, TV and newspapers to more recent media such as the Internet and cell phones. It seems these days that any information that we want is out there if we know how to get it. And anyone with an opinion to share, no matter how crazy, is able to get his or her message out.

Yet as long as there has been mass media, governments and other organizations have tried to limit or even stop information that they consider to be harmful in some way. The reasons for censorship, as this is called, are various, but the most common forms are moral censorship, military censorship, political censorship and religious censorship. Moral censorship includes the removal of material that could be harmful to the morals of society. Most often this involves pornography, but it could include works of art as well. Military censorship is especially important during war and is the attempt by the government and military to hide military secrets from the enemy. When governments are afraid of losing power, political censorship of information and the restriction of free speech in the media are often the ways in which they maintain control over a country. Finally, religious groups may try to limit access to information that is not in accord with their beliefs.

In modern democratic societies, censorship still exists. For example, in the United States and other countries, many types of pornography are censored in the media. While information may not be completely censored in a country, information that is considered harmful in some way may still be censored in some types of media. Schools are still places where there is less freedom of information than in society at large. In the United States, many schools have banned books from their libraries that parents and teachers feel are not suitable for children. Censorship of historical information in textbooks can also have political and international importance as in the case of the treatment of World War II by Japanese history textbooks.

Match the sentence beginnings (1-7) and endings (a-g) to make true statements.

1. _____ TV and newspapers are...
2. _____ Military censorship is...
3. _____ Moral censorship is one of...
4. _____ In democratic countries...
5. _____ Freedom of information is...
6. _____ Textbook censorship is...
7. _____ Parent's opinions are important in the banning of...

a. also important for relations between countries.
b. censorship is still common.
c. common in time of war.
d. books in schools.
e. still uncommon in schools.
f. the most common types of restriction of information.
g. traditional forms of mass media.

Unit 9

- **territory** [térətɔri] 【名】領土；なわばり → (興味・活動の)領域
- **region** [ríːdʒən] 【名】(広大な)地域 → (境界線が不明確な)領域
  - 《連語》be in the region of ～ ～のあたりで
  - 【形】regional 地域の；地方の ▶-al 形尾
- **tariff** [térəf] 【名】関税；関税率
- **terrorism** [térərɪzm] 【名】テロリズム ▶-ism 名尾(行動；特性)
  - 【名】terror 恐怖(≒horror)；テロ
  - ▶terr- ぎょっとさせる・-or＝-er 名尾(～するもの)
  - 【動】terrify ～を恐れさせる(≒horrify) ▶-ify 動尾
  - 【形】terrible 恐ろしい；ひどい(≒horrible) ▶-ible＝-able 形尾(可能)
- **invasion** [ɪnvéɪʒən] 【名】侵入；侵略 ▶-sion 名尾
  - 【動】invade ～に侵入する；～を侵略する ▶in- 中に・-vade 行く
- **sphere** [sfíɚ] 【名】球；球体 → (三次元空間で捉える)領域
- **province** [prɑ́ːvəns] 【名】(カナダなどの)州 [the provinces](首都・大都会に対する)地方
  - ▶「米・豪などの州」は state,「英の州」は county,「日本・仏などの県」は prefecture。
  - 【形】provincial 州の, 地方の ▶-al 形尾
- **area** [ériə] 【名】地域；地方 ▶region より小さい区域を指す。
- **aid** [éɪd] 【名】援助 【動】～を援助する
  - ▶assist とは異なり, 援助側が被援助側よりも優位にある。「溺れている人を助ける」は rescue。
- **military** [mílətèri] 【名】軍人, 軍隊 【形】軍人の, 軍隊の ▶milti- 兵士・-ary 形尾(～に関する)
- **regime** [reɪʒíːm] 【名】政治制度, 政体；政権 ▶語源は「統治」。
- **resource** [ríːsɔɚs] 【名】資源 → 財源 ▶re- 元の場所へ → 再び・-source 湧き出る → 源
- **smuggle** [smʌ́gl] 【動】～を密輸する, 密航する
- **assist** [əsíst] 【動】～を(補助的に)助ける ▶「困難・危険から助ける」場合は assist は不可。
  - 【名】assistant 助手 【形】補助の ▶-ant 名尾(～に関係する人)・形尾
  - 【名】assistance 補助 ▶-ance 名尾
- **eliminate** [ɪlímənèɪt] 【動】(不要なものを)除去する ▶e-＝ex- 外へ・-limin 敷居・-ate 動尾
  - 【名】elimination 除去 ▶-ation 名尾
- **exploit** [ɪksplɔ́ɪt] 【動】(鉱山・天然資源を)開発する；掘る ┐
  - └→ 労働資源を労働者から取り出す] → ～を搾取(さくしゅ)する
  - ▶ex- 外へ・-ploit 折りたたんだ。「折りたたんだものを広げる → 埋もれているものを外に出す」イメージ。
  - 【名】exploitation 開発, 搾取 ▶-ation 名尾
- **overseas** [òʊvɚsíːz] 【形】海外の；海外への
  - 【副】海外へ ▶over- 越えて・sea 海・-s 副尾
- **remote** [rɪmóʊt] 【形】遠い → 辺ぴな
  - ▶remove(別の場所へ移す)と同源。「別の場所へ移された－[距離が離れた] → 遠い－[都会から離れた] → 辺ぴな」。「リモコン」は remote control(遠隔操作)の略。
- **external** [ɪkstɚ́ːnl] 【形】外部の → 国外の ▶extern- 外側・-al 形尾
  - ⟷ internal 内部の ▶inter- 内側
- **legal** [líːgl] 【形】法律の；法律に関する → 合法の, 法定の ▶leg- 法律(＝law)・-al 形尾
  - ⟷ illegal 非合法の(≒unlawful), 違法の ▶il-＝in- 否定
  - ▶legislate(～を法律で定める)なども同源。詳しくは legislature の項を参照。

次の文章の空所に枠内の適切な語を入れて文章を完成させましょう。

Illegal Immigration

The United States is a country built on immigration. People from all parts of the world have traveled to the States in the hope of becoming Americans. Nevertheless, the U.S. is becoming increasingly worried about the invasion of an estimated one million people that secretly cross the border into American (1)_____ from Mexico each year. Due to the number of new arrivals, there are a lot of people asking, "Are the illegal immigrants a problem or a benefit?"

On the one hand, the U.S. needs cheap labor and the (2)_____ need work, a perfect match. In addition, immigrants are often prepared to do jobs that Americans do not want to do, such as food service or hotel cleaning. However, it must be noted that there are many employers who (3)_____ immigrants by giving them very low wages or dangerous work. A further benefit of immigration is that it gives people from (4)_____ , who may never have had political or religious freedom, a better life for themselves. Lastly, the immigrants can send some of the money that they earn in the States to (5)_____ their poor friends and relatives back home.

On the other hand, although immigrants use a lot of government (6)_____ , such as healthcare and education, they pay little in taxes. Also, more importantly, illegal immigrants from Mexico often (7)_____ drugs into the country. Furthermore, since the attacks of 9/11, the U.S. has become even more concerned that (8)_____ might be able to secretly make their way into America across the Mexican border.

In recent years, the American border patrol and (9)_____ have been trying to reduce the number of "illegals". However, the border between the United States and Mexico not only passes through many (10)_____ areas, it is also 3,140 kilometers long! And since the arrivals are coming by sea, land and air, the illegal immigration battle looks like it will be a very hard fight to win.

| a) assist | b) exploit | c) immigrants | d) military | e) overseas |
| f) remote | g) resources | h) smuggle | i) territory | j) terrorists |

Unit 10

- **apartment** [əpάːrtmənt]
  - 【名】[米] アパートの貸室
  - ▶ apart 分離された・-ment 名尾。「アパートやマンションの建物全体」は apartment house, apartments。[英] では flat と呼び, 全室が同一階にあるものを言う。「ワンルームマンション」は studio apartment,「(個人の)大邸宅」は mansion,「(高級な)分譲マンション」は condominium,「長屋式住宅」は townhouse。なお, house は「一戸建て住宅」, home は「一戸建て住宅, アパート, マンション」等どのような住まいでも構わない。

- **attic** [ǽtɪk]
  - 【名】屋根裏 → 屋根裏部屋
  - ▶ アッティカ様式の柱を用いたことから。garret(汚くて小さな屋根裏部屋)とは異なり, 小奇麗な感じ。

- **backyard** [bǽkjάːrd]
  - 【名】裏庭 ▶ back 背中 → 背後・-yard 庭。[米] では, 一家だんらんができるような芝生の場所。[英] では物を置くための舗装された場所。

- **balcony** [bǽlkəni]
  - 【名】バルコニー ▶ ヨーロッパ南部に多い。網戸はつけない。

- **basement** [béɪsmənt]
  - 【名】地階；地下室
  - ▶ base 基座・-ment 名尾(場所)

- **ceiling** [síːlɪŋ]
  - 【名】天井 ▶ hit the ceiling で「頭打ちになる」。天井窓は hatch, 屋根裏部屋は attic。

- **chimney** [tʃímni]
  - 【名】煙突 ▶ 原義は「暖炉を伴った所」。

- **closet** [klάːzət]
  - 【名】小部屋 → 物置；収納室 - [小物を置く空間] → 戸棚

- **couch** [káʊtʃ]
  - 【名】長いす；寝いす
  - ▶ [米] couch potato は「(長いすに寝そべりジャガイモのようにごろごろして)テレビにかじりついている人；カウチ・ポテト族」。

- **driveway** [dráɪvweɪ]
  - 【名】(道路から家・車庫などに通じる)私設車道
  - ▶ drive 追う・way 道のり。本来は「家畜を追う道のり」の意で用いられた。

- **hallway** [hɔ́ːlweɪ]
  - 【名】玄関の広間；玄関, [米] 廊下 ▶ hall 屋根のあるところ・way 道のり

- **laundry** [lɔ́ːndri]
  - 【名】洗濯場；洗濯室 → 洗濯屋；クリーニング店 → 洗濯物 ▶ laund- 洗濯する・-ry 名尾(場所)
  - 《連語》do the laundry 洗濯をする(≒ do the washing)

- **lawn** [lɔ́ːn]
  - 【名】芝生；芝地
  - ▶ land(土地)と同源。「隣の芝生は青い」は The grass is always greener on the other side (of the fence / hill)。

- **microwave** [máɪkroʊweɪv]
  - 【名】マイクロ波
  - ▶ microwave oven は「電子レンジ」。

- **patio** [pǽtioʊ]
  - 【名】(スペイン式家屋に見られる)中庭・パティオ ▶ 食事；憩い用のテラス。

- **refrigerator** [rɪfrídʒəreɪtər]
  - 【名】冷蔵庫 ▶ -or = -er 名尾(〜するもの)。省略形は fridge。
  - 【動】refrigerate 〜を冷やす
  - ▶ re- 元の場所へ → 元の状態へ・-friger 冷やす・-ate 動尾

- **sofa** [sóʊfə]
  - 【名】(背もたれ・ひじ付きの)長いす；ソファ

- **stairs** [stéərz]
  - 【名】階段 ▶ stair (1段) の複数形。

- **storage** [stɔ́ːrɪdʒ]
  - 【名】収納庫；物置, 貯蔵；保管 ▶ -age 名尾(〜すること)
  - 【動】store 〜を蓄える；貯蔵する 【名】(様々な品を扱う)商店
  - ▶ shop は特定の商品を扱う専門店。[英] では store は大型店を指すことが多い。

- **vacuum** [vǽkjuːm]
  - 【名】真空の ▶「空(から)の」のイメージ。vacation(仕事活動が空 → 休暇)と同源。live in a social vacuum は「社会的に孤立して暮らす」。

次の文章の空所に枠内の適切な語を入れて文章を完成させましょう。

Cat Burns Down House

Most people consider cats to be kind, lovable animals. After all, many people keep cats as pets. However, a cat recently burned down his owner's house. How did this happen?

Late one Sunday afternoon, Oscar the cat was upstairs playing in the bathroom. While Oscar was playing, he accidentally turned on the (1) _____ faucets and water started pouring out. Meanwhile, his owners, John and Christine Smith, were in the living room on the first floor doing some housework. While John was (2) _____ some shirts, Christine was slowly (3) _____ the carpet. After a while, Christine left the room and was surprised to see a river of water running down the (4) _____ from the second floor, across the (5) _____ , and down a second set of stairs into the (6) _____ . The Smiths used the basement as a storage room and a (7) _____ . So after Christine had turned the tap off, the couple ran downstairs to try and save their papers, old books and clothes. Water was everywhere! It was even dripping into the basement through the (8) _____ . Unfortunately, in the excitement, John left the iron on one of his shirts! While the Smiths were busy downstairs, a fire started in the living room. When the Smiths smelled the smoke, they ran back up the stairs and tried to put the fire out. However, it was too late and they had to run out of the house to safety, closing the back door behind them. But where was Oscar? He had also smelled the smoke and was standing outside on the second floor (9) _____ . When John noticed his pet, he ran back into the house and saved the scared cat.

Luckily, no one was injured in the fire. The Smiths no longer have a house, but they still have a cat. Oscar has been forgiven and they all now sleep in the (10) _____ next to where their old house was.

a) balcony	b) basement	c) ceiling	d) garage	e) hallway
f) ironing	g) laundry	h) sink	i) stairs	j) vacuuming

Index

A

- [ ] abroad 60
- [ ] absence 66
- [ ] absolutely 68
- [ ] accept 8
- [ ] accord 36
- [ ] account 24
- [ ] accuse 64
- [ ] accustom 80
- [ ] ache 94
- [ ] achieve 120
- [ ] acquire 130
- [ ] act 12
- [ ] actual 32
- [ ] add 14
- [ ] address 10
- [ ] adequate 76
- [ ] adjust 130
- [ ] admire 92
- [ ] admit 2
- [ ] adopt 40
- [ ] advance 6
- [ ] advantage 16
- [ ] advertise 98
- [ ] advice 90
- [ ] affair 42
- [ ] affect 122
- [ ] afford 24
- [ ] afraid 58
- [ ] agent 86
- [ ] agree 10
- [ ] agriculture 74
- [ ] ahead 118
- [ ] aid 142
- [ ] aim 70
- [ ] aisle 130
- [ ] alike 84
- [ ] allow 28
- [ ] almost 14
- [ ] alone 2
- [ ] aloud 82
- [ ] already 8
- [ ] altogether 116

- [ ] always 18
- [ ] ambition 82
- [ ] amount 4
- [ ] amuse 74
- [ ] analogue 140
- [ ] ancient 16
- [ ] anger 112
- [ ] angle 100
- [ ] animation 40
- [ ] annoy 68
- [ ] annuity 138
- [ ] another 46
- [ ] answer 18
- [ ] antenna 140
- [ ] anxiety 98
- [ ] apartment 144
- [ ] apologize 114
- [ ] appear 34
- [ ] applaud 78
- [ ] apply 42
- [ ] appoint 36
- [ ] approach 92
- [ ] appropriate 98
- [ ] approve 88
- [ ] area 142
- [ ] argue 70
- [ ] arise 38
- [ ] army 38
- [ ] arrange 56
- [ ] arrest 94
- [ ] arrive 46
- [ ] arrow 80
- [ ] arson 136
- [ ] art 4
- [ ] article 50
- [ ] artificial 80
- [ ] ash 116
- [ ] ashamed 86
- [ ] aside 120
- [ ] asleep 88
- [ ] assess 102
- [ ] asset 132
- [ ] assist 142

- [ ] association 22
- [ ] astonish 104
- [ ] attack 44
- [ ] attempt 46
- [ ] attend 58
- [ ] attic 144
- [ ] attitude 128
- [ ] attract 108
- [ ] audience 110
- [ ] audit 132
- [ ] authorize 134
- [ ] available 82
- [ ] average 6
- [ ] avoid 112
- [ ] awake 86
- [ ] awkward 94

B

- [ ] backyard 144
- [ ] baggage 64
- [ ] balcony 144
- [ ] bank 12
- [ ] bar 48
- [ ] bar code 130
- [ ] bare 104
- [ ] bargain 104
- [ ] barrel 106
- [ ] base 14
- [ ] basement 144
- [ ] basin 78
- [ ] battle 22
- [ ] bay 94
- [ ] bear 16
- [ ] beard 74
- [ ] beast 60
- [ ] beat 82
- [ ] beauty 26
- [ ] become 18
- [ ] beg 70
- [ ] begin 10
- [ ] behave 90
- [ ] belief 128
- [ ] believe 20

☐ belong	24	
☐ bend	78	
☐ beneath	12	
☐ benefit	138	
☐ beverage	92	
☐ beware	118	
☐ bill	32	
☐ bind	80	
☐ bit	52	
☐ bite	88	
☐ bitter	78	
☐ blade	118	
☐ blame	72	
☐ bleach	114	
☐ bless	120	
☐ blood	32	
☐ blow	34	
☐ board	44	
☐ boast	58	
☐ boil	60	
☐ bold	90	
☐ bond	132	
☐ bonus	132	
☐ border	120	
☐ boundary	78	
☐ bow	96	
☐ branch	30	
☐ brand	130	
☐ brave	106	
☐ breadth	34	
☐ break	26	
☐ breath	54	
☐ bribe	68	
☐ bridge	28	
☐ brief	114	
☐ bright	32	
☐ bring	6	
☐ broad	102	
☐ broadcast	140	
☐ brunch	106	
☐ budget	130	
☐ build	12	
☐ bunch	88	
☐ bundle	120	
☐ burn	48	
☐ burst	76	
☐ bury	66	
☐ bush	102	
☐ business	8	
☐ busy	12	
☐ butter	58	

C

☐ cable	140	
☐ cage	114	
☐ calculate	78	
☐ calm	102	
☐ campaign	64	
☐ canal	122	
☐ cape	120	
☐ capital	20	
☐ capture	136	
☐ care	48	
☐ carriage	84	
☐ carry	26	
☐ case	24	
☐ cash	130	
☐ casualty	138	
☐ catch	16	
☐ category	130	
☐ cause	22	
☐ caution	112	
☐ cease	122	
☐ ceiling	144	
☐ center	36	
☐ century	118	
☐ certain	20	
☐ chance	4	
☐ change	14	
☐ character	10	
☐ charge	50	
☐ charm	88	
☐ cheap	18	
☐ cheat	68	
☐ cheer	100	
☐ chief	16	
☐ chimney	144	
☐ choose	12	
☐ church	40	
☐ circle	6	
☐ circulation	140	
☐ circumstance	108	
☐ civilize	104	
☐ claim	46	
☐ class	2	
☐ clean	4	
☐ clear	22	
☐ clerk	130	
☐ clever	58	
☐ climb	56	
☐ clock	30	
☐ close	28	
☐ closet	144	
☐ cloth	104	
☐ clothing	98	
☐ club	50	
☐ coarse	86	
☐ coast	26	
☐ collar	70	
☐ colleague	74	
☐ collect	66	
☐ college	12	
☐ colony	110	
☐ column	140	
☐ combine	88	
☐ comfort	72	
☐ command	32	
☐ committee	116	
☐ commodity	134	
☐ common	16	
☐ communicate	140	
☐ companion	98	
☐ company	6	
☐ compare	30	
☐ compensation	138	
☐ compete	90	
☐ complain	76	
☐ complete	24	
☐ complicated	92	

☐ compose	72	☐ court	56	☐ defeat	108
☐ concentrate	120	☐ cover	52	☐ defend	60
☐ concept	66	☐ crack	112	☐ deficit	132
☐ concern	58	☐ crash	94	☐ define	94
☐ condition	38	☐ creature	42	☐ definite	122
☐ conduct	128	☐ credit	132	☐ degree	32
☐ confess	82	☐ creep	116	☐ delay	104
☐ confidence	94	☐ crime	120	☐ delight	100
☐ conflict	80	☐ crop	84	☐ deliver	36
☐ conform	126	☐ cross	60	☐ demand	4
☐ confuse	92	☐ crowd	28	☐ department	96
☐ congratulate	84	☐ cruel	108	☐ depend	56
☐ connect	32	☐ crush	110	☐ deposit	132
☐ conquer	106	☐ cry	2	☐ descend	70
☐ conscience	68	☐ cultivate	118	☐ describe	12
☐ consequence	126	☐ cupboard	80	☐ desert	50
☐ consider	44	☐ cure	68	☐ deserve	66
☐ consist	100	☐ curious	76	☐ desire	26
☐ constant	68	☐ currency	132	☐ despair	84
☐ contain	26	☐ current	14	☐ destroy	6
☐ content	46	☐ curse	90	☐ detail	20
☐ continue	34	☐ curve	98	☐ determine	18
☐ contrast	102	☐ custom	46	☐ develop	40
☐ contribute	128			☐ devil	72
☐ control	4	**D**		☐ die	10
☐ convenience	74	☐ damp	70	☐ difference	24
☐ conversation	122	☐ danger	18	☐ difficult	30
☐ convict	136	☐ dare	34	☐ dig	76
☐ cook	56	☐ dark	16	☐ digital	140
☐ cooperate	126	☐ date	60	☐ dine	116
☐ co-payment	138	☐ dawn	76	☐ dip	80
☐ corner	18	☐ deaf	72	☐ direct	46
☐ correct	80	☐ deal	44	☐ disappear	116
☐ correspondent	140	☐ debt	114	☐ disappoint	104
☐ co-signer	138	☐ decay	86	☐ discipline	76
☐ cost	58	☐ deceive	96	☐ discover	38
☐ couch	144	☐ decide	30	☐ disease	38
☐ cough	108	☐ declare	28	☐ disgust	98
☐ council	14	☐ decline	126	☐ dismiss	102
☐ count	50	☐ decrease	68	☐ display	130
☐ counter	130	☐ deductible	138	☐ distance	46
☐ country	36	☐ deed	94	☐ distinguish	106
☐ courage	104	☐ deep	40	☐ district	48

☐ disturb	114	
☐ ditch	104	
☐ dive	106	
☐ diverse	126	
☐ divide	50	
☐ dividend	134	
☐ divine	128	
☐ documentary	140	
☐ dollar	56	
☐ domestic	126	
☐ double	36	
☐ doubt	6	
☐ dozen	110	
☐ drag	118	
☐ draw	54	
☐ drawer	64	
☐ driveway	144	
☐ drown	88	
☐ due	34	
☐ dull	70	
☐ dust	118	
☐ duty	108	

E

☐ eager	90
☐ early	10
☐ earn	94
☐ earnest	74
☐ earth	30
☐ ease	110
☐ economy	134
☐ edge	12
☐ edit	140
☐ educate	66
☐ effect	48
☐ efficient	66
☐ effort	42
☐ elastic	106
☐ elect	68
☐ electricity	104
☐ eliminate	142
☐ emerge	114
☐ empire	78

☐ employ	30
☐ enact	136
☐ enclose	92
☐ encounter	72
☐ encourage	76
☐ enemy	14
☐ enforce	136
☐ enjoy	32
☐ enough	24
☐ enter	44
☐ entertain	84
☐ entire	36
☐ envelope	98
☐ envy	80
☐ equal	8
☐ equity	132
☐ escape	20
☐ essence	96
☐ establish	96
☐ estimate	82
☐ ethics	128
☐ evaluate	72
☐ evening	16
☐ event	2
☐ eventually	126
☐ everywhere	14
☐ evidence	136
☐ evil	40
☐ evolve	126
☐ exact	100
☐ examination	80
☐ example	28
☐ excellent	4
☐ excess	88
☐ exchange	6
☐ excite	90
☐ excuse	108
☐ exercise	10
☐ exhaust	88
☐ exist	2
☐ expect	8
☐ expenditure	134
☐ expense	20

☐ experience	26
☐ experiment	36
☐ explain	54
☐ explode	102
☐ exploit	142
☐ explore	112
☐ export	134
☐ expose	110
☐ express	42
☐ extend	64
☐ external	142
☐ extraordinary	72
☐ extreme	106

F

☐ fact	16
☐ factory	12
☐ fade	68
☐ fail	22
☐ faint	78
☐ fair	36
☐ faith	34
☐ false	102
☐ familiar	26
☐ famous	8
☐ fancy	60
☐ farm	6
☐ fashion	26
☐ fate	78
☐ fault	72
☐ favorite	10
☐ fear	50
☐ feast	108
☐ feather	96
☐ feed	6
☐ feel	18
☐ fellow	24
☐ felony	136
☐ female	96
☐ few	14
☐ field	28
☐ fierce	116
☐ figure	22

☐ fill	4
☐ final	28
☐ finance	132
☐ fine	6
☐ finish	42
☐ firm	92
☐ fiscal	132
☐ fit	54
☐ fix	10
☐ flame	106
☐ flash	116
☐ flavor	78
☐ flesh	112
☐ flexible	44
☐ float	74
☐ flood	70
☐ flour	78
☐ flow	114
☐ fold	90
☐ follow	48
☐ fond	116
☐ fool	86
☐ forbid	58
☐ force	56
☐ forecast	64
☐ foreign	12
☐ forget	28
☐ forgive	60
☐ form	52
☐ former	40
☐ fortune	46
☐ forward	16
☐ foster	120
☐ frame	64
☐ franchise	134
☐ freeze	98
☐ frequent	76
☐ fresh	58
☐ fright	118
☐ fruitful	102
☐ fund	132
☐ fundamental	128
☐ funeral	122

☐ furnish	76
☐ furniture	76
☐ further	22
☐ furthermore	126
☐ future	40

G

☐ gain	26
☐ gallon	74
☐ garden	28
☐ gate	44
☐ gather	16
☐ gender	126
☐ general	42
☐ generate	116
☐ generous	82
☐ gentle	4
☐ glad	14
☐ glass	2
☐ globalization	134
☐ glory	74
☐ god	38
☐ govern	70
☐ grace	108
☐ gradual	84
☐ graduate	86
☐ grain	110
☐ grand	94
☐ grateful	104
☐ grave	114
☐ grind	118
☐ gross	122
☐ ground	10
☐ group	4
☐ grow	36
☐ guard	24
☐ guess	98
☐ guilty	112

H

☐ habit	48
☐ hall	18
☐ hallway	144

☐ hammer	60
☐ handkerchief	102
☐ handle	40
☐ hang	8
☐ happen	2
☐ hard	36
☐ hardly	16
☐ harm	70
☐ harmony	128
☐ harvest	122
☐ haste	96
☐ hate	82
☐ headline	140
☐ heal	80
☐ health	14
☐ heap	88
☐ hear	10
☐ heat	44
☐ heaven	34
☐ heavy	18
☐ height	82
☐ hesitate	82
☐ hide	2
☐ high	28
☐ highlight	140
☐ hill	54
☐ hinder	94
☐ hire	68
☐ history	30
☐ hollow	64
☐ holy	72
☐ homeowner	138
☐ honest	86
☐ honor	10
☐ hope	6
☐ horizon	92
☐ horrible	118
☐ hospital	2
☐ host	108
☐ hug	118
☐ huge	120
☐ human	24
☐ humble	70

☐ hunger	112	
☐ hunt	66	
☐ hurt	108	
☐ hut	76	
☐ hymn	128	

I

☐ idea	46
☐ ideal	80
☐ idle	84
☐ ill	84
☐ imagine	74
☐ imitate	64
☐ immediate	70
☐ immense	110
☐ imply	120
☐ import	134
☐ improve	90
☐ impulse	130
☐ inch	26
☐ include	12
☐ increase	14
☐ indeed	2
☐ individual	120
☐ industry	84
☐ inferior	94
☐ inflation	132
☐ influence	6
☐ inform	114
☐ ingredient	96
☐ inhabit	126
☐ injury	138
☐ innocent	136
☐ inquire	100
☐ insect	112
☐ insist	72
☐ instant	118
☐ instead	8
☐ instrument	110
☐ insult	98
☐ insure	112
☐ integrate	134
☐ intend	4

☐ intense	90
☐ interact	126
☐ interest	42
☐ interfere	110
☐ interrupt	72
☐ introduce	50
☐ invasion	142
☐ invent	78
☐ investigate	136
☐ invite	80
☐ involve	34
☐ inward	88
☐ iron	38
☐ isolation	126
☐ item	130

J

☐ jealous	80
☐ job	42
☐ join	36
☐ journal	140
☐ joyful	66
☐ judge	48
☐ jury	136
☐ justify	66

K

☐ keep	46
☐ kill	40
☐ knee	100
☐ kneel	98
☐ knot	106

L

☐ label	130
☐ lack	44
☐ ladder	72
☐ land	4
☐ language	8
☐ lapse	138
☐ last	2
☐ late	22
☐ latter	88

☐ laundry	144
☐ law	6
☐ lawn	144
☐ lay	40
☐ lazy	78
☐ lead	46
☐ leaf	60
☐ lean	66
☐ learn	42
☐ leather	126
☐ leave	4
☐ left	52
☐ legal	142
☐ lend	76
☐ length	44
☐ less	40
☐ letter	48
☐ level	24
☐ liability	138
☐ liable	134
☐ liberty	112
☐ library	50
☐ lid	98
☐ lie	52
☐ lien	138
☐ life	8
☐ lift	32
☐ light	54
☐ likely	10
☐ limb	66
☐ limit	12
☐ liquid	90
☐ listen	26
☐ literature	112
☐ live	48
☐ load	96
☐ loaf	122
☐ loan	116
☐ local	8
☐ locate	92
☐ lodging	114
☐ loose	92
☐ lose	54

☐ loss	138	☐ military	142	☐ noun	98
☐ lot	58	☐ mind	58	☐ nowhere	20
☐ low	20	☐ minute	34	☐ nuclear	126
☐ loyal	82	☐ misdemeanor	136	☐ nuisance	80
☐ lump	118	☐ miserable	72	☐ number	16
☐ lung	110	☐ miss	44	☐ nut	102

M

		☐ mistake	96		
		☐ mode	130	**O**	
☐ machine	2	☐ moderate	92	☐ oar	106
☐ mad	94	☐ modern	30	☐ obey	84
☐ magazine	140	☐ modest	68	☐ object	42
☐ main	2	☐ modify	110	☐ obligation	128
☐ male	86	☐ moment	14	☐ observe	22
☐ manage	86	☐ money	38	☐ obtain	120
☐ manner	30	☐ monitor	122	☐ occasion	36
☐ manufacture	104	☐ month	6	☐ occupy	36
☐ many	38	☐ moral	80	☐ occur	114
☐ march	22	☐ moreover	12	☐ offend	88
☐ mark	56	☐ morning	60	☐ offense	136
☐ market	28	☐ mortgage	138	☐ offer	8
☐ mass	52	☐ motor	16	☐ office	56
☐ material	4	☐ mouth	50	☐ oil	20
☐ matter	54	☐ mud	90	☐ omit	102
☐ mean	30	☐ multiply	74	☐ operation	28
☐ meanwhile	82	☐ murder	116	☐ opinion	14
☐ measure	30			☐ opportunity	10
☐ mechanic	92			☐ opposite	96
☐ media	140	**N**		☐ order	26
☐ meditate	128	☐ narrow	18	☐ ordinary	30
☐ melt	58	☐ nasal	92	☐ organ	118
☐ member	48	☐ nation	24	☐ organize	38
☐ memory	54	☐ native	28	☐ origin	110
☐ mend	78	☐ nature	54	☐ ornament	120
☐ mention	24	☐ neat	78	☐ otherwise	22
☐ merchant	92	☐ necessary	10	☐ ounce	70
☐ mercy	116	☐ neglect	84	☐ overcome	104
☐ mere	48	☐ negotiate	134	☐ overseas	142
☐ merry	110	☐ neighbor	40	☐ owe	38
☐ metal	46	☐ nevertheless	68	☐ own	18
☐ microwave	144	☐ noble	84		
☐ mighty	70	☐ normal	18	**P**	
☐ mild	60	☐ note	22		
☐ mile	52	☐ notice	20	☐ pack	84
		☐ notion	128	☐ page	38

154

☐ pain	4
☐ paint	14
☐ pale	100
☐ pardon	64
☐ part	54
☐ participate	94
☐ particular	64
☐ party	12
☐ pass	28
☐ passage	86
☐ paste	102
☐ patient	82
☐ patio	144
☐ patriotic	108
☐ pause	82
☐ pay	16
☐ peace	32
☐ peculiar	82
☐ penalty	136
☐ perceive	102
☐ percentage	134
☐ perfect	34
☐ perhaps	8
☐ permanent	50
☐ permit	20
☐ philosophy	128
☐ picture	46
☐ piece	60
☐ pile	96
☐ pinch	86
☐ pity	112
☐ plain	56
☐ plant	46
☐ plead	136
☐ plenty	114
☐ policy	138
☐ polish	122
☐ polite	102
☐ political	30
☐ poor	32
☐ popular	22
☐ population	24
☐ position	54

☐ possess	26
☐ possible	10
☐ postpone	108
☐ pound	6
☐ pour	76
☐ poverty	52
☐ power	34
☐ practical	42
☐ practice	106
☐ praise	110
☐ pray	100
☐ preach	112
☐ precious	110
☐ prefer	66
☐ prejudice	114
☐ premium	138
☐ prepare	32
☐ present	52
☐ preserve	50
☐ press	40
☐ pretend	96
☐ pretty	24
☐ prevent	10
☐ price	58
☐ principal	132
☐ principle	70
☐ print	22
☐ prison	104
☐ private	6
☐ prize	60
☐ probable	60
☐ problem	56
☐ process	66
☐ produce	26
☐ program	36
☐ progress	52
☐ prohibit	72
☐ project	48
☐ promise	42
☐ promote	88
☐ prompt	90
☐ pronounce	64
☐ proper	52

☐ property	84
☐ propose	14
☐ prosecute	136
☐ protect	38
☐ proud	88
☐ prove	44
☐ provide	24
☐ province	142
☐ public	46
☐ punctual	106
☐ punish	106
☐ purchase	130
☐ purpose	50
☐ purse	130
☐ pursue	114

Q

☐ qualify	92
☐ quality	42
☐ quantity	66
☐ quarrel	76
☐ quarter	30
☐ questionnaire	90
☐ quiet	16
☐ quite	12

R

☐ race	26
☐ raise	30
☐ rake	94
☐ range	76
☐ rank	24
☐ rapid	94
☐ rare	110
☐ rate	48
☐ rather	40
☐ raw	102
☐ ray	104
☐ razor	122
☐ reach	2
☐ ready	36
☐ real	52
☐ reason	40

☐ receive	34	☐ require	92	☐ rule	38
☐ recent	68	☐ rescue	116	☐ rush	32
☐ recession	132	☐ resemble	82	☐ rust	72
☐ recognize	24	☐ reserve	108		
☐ recommend	72	☐ residence	126	**S**	
☐ record	82	☐ resign	96	☐ sacred	102
☐ recovery	132	☐ resist	122	☐ sacrifice	100
☐ reduce	16	☐ resource	142	☐ safe	48
☐ refer	98	☐ respect	4	☐ sail	12
☐ reflect	104	☐ respond	122	☐ sake	114
☐ refrigerator	144	☐ responsible	116	☐ salary	64
☐ refund	130	☐ result	6	☐ satellite	140
☐ refuse	18	☐ retail	130	☐ satisfy	118
☐ regard	28	☐ retain	126	☐ save	54
☐ regime	142	☐ retire	78	☐ scale	30
☐ region	142	☐ return	52	☐ scarce	38
☐ regret	118	☐ reveal	74	☐ scatter	100
☐ regular	14	☐ revenge	64	☐ scene	2
☐ regulate	134	☐ revenue	134	☐ scent	116
☐ reinforce	128	☐ review	98	☐ science	24
☐ rejoice	94	☐ revise	100	☐ scissors	58
☐ relation	50	☐ reward	44	☐ scold	122
☐ relieve	116	☐ rid	106	☐ scorn	96
☐ religion	74	☐ rigid	128	☐ scratch	120
☐ rely	126	☐ ring	8	☐ scream	38
☐ remain	48	☐ ripe	84	☐ season	32
☐ remark	22	☐ rise	48	☐ seat	4
☐ remedy	118	☐ risk	74	☐ secret	28
☐ remember	20	☐ ritual	128	☐ secretary	20
☐ remind	112	☐ rival	104	☐ sect	128
☐ remittance	132	☐ river	44	☐ seek	128
☐ remote	142	☐ road	52	☐ seize	22
☐ remove	66	☐ roar	76	☐ seldom	120
☐ rent	108	☐ rob	88	☐ sell	2
☐ repair	84	☐ role	126	☐ send	40
☐ repeat	54	☐ roll	36	☐ sense	88
☐ replace	72	☐ rot	92	☐ sentence	136
☐ reply	50	☐ rough	44	☐ separate	32
☐ report	50	☐ round	54	☐ series	140
☐ represent	78	☐ row	86	☐ serious	6
☐ republic	120	☐ rub	56	☐ serve	28
☐ reputation	112	☐ rude	70	☐ settle	16
☐ request	90	☐ ruin	90	☐ several	2

☐ severe	112	☐ sound	20	☐ straight	12
☐ sew	58	☐ source	80	☐ strange	26
☐ shadow	36	☐ space	56	☐ straw	122
☐ shake	8	☐ speak	52	☐ stream	22
☐ shallow	76	☐ special	42	☐ strength	66
☐ shame	102	☐ spell	60	☐ stress	80
☐ shape	48	☐ spend	18	☐ stretch	36
☐ share	24	☐ sphere	142	☐ strict	96
☐ sharp	34	☐ spill	106	☐ strike	46
☐ shave	44	☐ spirit	52	☐ strip	74
☐ shelf	106	☐ spit	90	☐ structure	126
☐ shield	60	☐ spite	70	☐ struggle	6
☐ shine	34	☐ splendid	120	☐ stuff	94
☐ shore	92	☐ split	120	☐ stupid	56
☐ shoulder	16	☐ spoil	42	☐ subject	68
☐ show	46	☐ spot	54	☐ submit	118
☐ shut	56	☐ spread	4	☐ subscribe	140
☐ sight	34	☐ spring	8	☐ subsequent	134
☐ sign	60	☐ square	58	☐ subsidiary	134
☐ significant	98	☐ stain	44	☐ substance	32
☐ silence	36	☐ stairs	144	☐ succeed	70
☐ simple	32	☐ stand	10	☐ suck	100
☐ sincere	112	☐ standard	58	☐ sudden	54
☐ sink	108	☐ state	80	☐ suffer	12
☐ situation	52	☐ station	60	☐ suggest	42
☐ skill	86	☐ statistic	132	☐ summer	50
☐ skyscraper	70	☐ status	64	☐ support	44
☐ slave	78	☐ stay	20	☐ suppose	38
☐ slight	66	☐ steady	90	☐ sure	50
☐ slip	40	☐ steal	4	☐ surface	82
☐ smell	64	☐ steel	26	☐ surplus	132
☐ smooth	56	☐ steep	122	☐ surround	48
☐ smuggle	142	☐ steer	86	☐ survive	68
☐ society	34	☐ step	10	☐ survivor	138
☐ sofa	144	☐ stick	74	☐ suspect	84
☐ soft	54	☐ stiff	88	☐ swallow	72
☐ soil	84	☐ still	52	☐ swear	98
☐ solar	100	☐ stir	82	☐ sweat	110
☐ soldier	86	☐ stock	78	☐ sweep	66
☐ solemn	100	☐ stomach	94	☐ sweet	20
☐ solid	114	☐ stone	42	☐ swift	108
☐ solve	104	☐ storage	144	☐ sword	68
☐ sort	14	☐ story	38	☐ symbol	128

- [ ] sympathy 118
- [ ] system 28

T

- [ ] table 52
- [ ] tame 120
- [ ] tap 94
- [ ] tariff 142
- [ ] taste 8
- [ ] tax 108
- [ ] tear 46
- [ ] temper 116
- [ ] temple 116
- [ ] tempt 100
- [ ] tend 64
- [ ] tender 118
- [ ] terminate 138
- [ ] terrible 54
- [ ] territory 142
- [ ] terrorism 142
- [ ] test 12
- [ ] testimony 136
- [ ] text 102
- [ ] theft 136
- [ ] theory 100
- [ ] therefore 18
- [ ] thin 108
- [ ] think 18
- [ ] thirst 102
- [ ] thorough 72
- [ ] thought 30
- [ ] thread 42
- [ ] threaten 114
- [ ] throat 96
- [ ] through 20
- [ ] throw 30
- [ ] thunder 90
- [ ] tie 110
- [ ] tiny 64
- [ ] toe 100
- [ ] together 20
- [ ] tongue 80
- [ ] tool 58
- [ ] total 50
- [ ] touch 40
- [ ] tough 66
- [ ] town 8
- [ ] trace 122
- [ ] track 68
- [ ] trade 114
- [ ] traditional 128
- [ ] tragedy 78
- [ ] train 58
- [ ] transaction 134
- [ ] transfer 108
- [ ] transform 126
- [ ] translate 86
- [ ] transmit 140
- [ ] transportation 90
- [ ] trap 74
- [ ] travel 28
- [ ] treasure 106
- [ ] tremble 100
- [ ] trial 76
- [ ] trick 86
- [ ] trouble 22
- [ ] true 64
- [ ] trust 76
- [ ] try 26
- [ ] tuition 88
- [ ] turn 2
- [ ] twilight 112
- [ ] type 32

U

- [ ] ugly 122
- [ ] uncle 22
- [ ] understand 8
- [ ] undertake 134
- [ ] underwriter 138
- [ ] union 52
- [ ] unite 34
- [ ] university 40
- [ ] upright 112
- [ ] upset 96
- [ ] urge 88
- [ ] usual 10

V

- [ ] vacuum 144
- [ ] vague 74
- [ ] vain 38
- [ ] valley 20
- [ ] value 70
- [ ] various 38
- [ ] vary 122
- [ ] verdict 136
- [ ] vessel 100
- [ ] victim 136
- [ ] victory 98
- [ ] view 56
- [ ] village 18
- [ ] violent 56
- [ ] virtue 92
- [ ] visit 32
- [ ] voice 8
- [ ] vote 16
- [ ] voyage 104

W

- [ ] wake 56
- [ ] wallet 130
- [ ] wander 64
- [ ] war 2
- [ ] warm 32
- [ ] warn 44
- [ ] waste 44
- [ ] watch 30
- [ ] water 34
- [ ] wave 22
- [ ] wealth 68
- [ ] weapon 86
- [ ] weave 68
- [ ] week 34
- [ ] weigh 84
- [ ] welcome 60
- [ ] wheel 110
- [ ] whip 74
- [ ] whisper 116

☐ whistle	20	
☐ whole	76	
☐ wicked	114	
☐ wide	48	
☐ widow	138	
☐ wild	58	
☐ wind	56	
☐ window	18	
☐ winter	4	
☐ wipe	86	
☐ wise	50	
☐ wish	42	
☐ withdraw	132	
☐ witness	106	
☐ wonder	46	
☐ world	18	
☐ worldwide	134	
☐ worship	98	
☐ worth	26	
☐ wound	92	
☐ wrap	82	
☐ wreck	106	
☐ wrist	74	
☐ write	14	
☐ wrong	54	

Y

☐ yard	104	
☐ yet	14	
☐ yield	96	

Essential English Vocabulary 1400

| 検印省略 | © 2019 年 1 月 31 日　第 1 版 発行
2025 年 1 月 31 日　第 4 刷 発行 |

編著者　　　　語彙力向上研究会
　　　　　　　　　森　節子
　　　　　　　　　田邉義隆
　　　　　　　　　森山智浩
　　　　　　　　　Paul Joyce
　　　　　　　　　Torrin Shimono

発行者　　　　小川　洋一郎

発行所　　　　株式会社　朝 日 出 版 社
　　　　　101-0065　東京都千代田区西神田 3-3-5
　　　　　　　電話　東京 (03) 3239-0271/72
　　　　　　　FAX　東京 (03) 3239-0479
　　　　　　　e-mail　text-e@asahipress.com
　　　　　　　振替口座　00140-2-46008
　　　　　　組版／ファースト　製版／錦明印刷

乱丁・落丁はお取り替えいたします。
ISBN978-4-255-15631-6　C 1082